国家林业和草原局普通高等教育"十三五"规划教材

林业国际公约导读

李 芝 娄瑞娟 主 编

中国林业出版社
China Forestry Publishing House

图书在版编目(CIP)数据

林业国际公约导读 / 李芝，娄瑞娟主编 . —北京：中国林业出版社，2019.12
国家林业和草原局普通高等教育"十三五"规划教材
ISBN 978-7-5219-0406-2

Ⅰ. ①林… Ⅱ. ①国… Ⅲ. ①林业-国际公约-英语-高等学校-教材 Ⅳ. ①F316.2

中国版本图书馆 CIP 数据核字(2019)第 276877 号

国家林业和草原局普通高等教育"十三五"规划教材

中国林业出版社·教育分社

策划、责任编辑：许 玮 曹鑫茹
电　　话：(010)83143576

出版发行	中国林业出版社(100009　北京市西城区德内大街刘海胡同7号)
	http://www.forestry.gov.cn/lycb.html　电话：(010)83143576
经　　销	新华书店
印　　刷	北京中科印刷有限公司
版　　次	2019年12月第1版
印　　次	2019年12月第1次印刷
开　　本	787mm×1092mm　1/16
印　　张	14.25
字　　数	416千字
定　　价	40.00元

未经许可，不得以任何方式复制或抄袭本书之部分或全部内容。

版权所有　侵权必究

编写人员名单

主　编 李　芝　娄瑞娟

参　编（按姓氏笔画排序）

　　　　王雪梅　朱红梅　靳丽莹

前 言

2018年教育部、农业农村部、国家林业和草原局发布了《关于加强农科教结合实施卓越农林人才教育培养计划2.0的意见》，意见中提出要创新农林人才培养模式，加快推进拔尖创新型农林人才培养，加强研究性教学，注重个性化培养，拓宽国际化视野，着力提升学生的创新意识、创新能力和科研素养，培养一批引领农林业创新发展的高层次、高水平、复合型高素质农林人才。教育部高等教育司司长吴岩表示，中国高等教育已经从规模扩张转到内涵发展的轨道上来，面对新科技革命和产业革命的时代浪潮，我们应该超前识变、积极应变、主动求变。新农科建设是高等农林教育战线对新时代高等农林教育改革发展的新认识和新思考，农林类高校在国家培养卓越农林人才教育培养计划中肩负着重要时代责任。

卓越农林人才的培养离不开农林学科领域专业国际化知识，在目前双一流高校建设背景下，培养一流的国际化人才，使他们在各自的学科领域内具有国际竞争力和国际话语权是农林类高校新的历史使命。国际化人才必须具备的关键素质包括宽广的国际化视野、扎实的本专业国际化知识、熟悉和掌握国际惯例、较强的跨文化沟通能力和独立的国际活动能力。在经济全球化和高等教育国际化的新时代，英语已成为世界上各学科成果交流和科技经济发展的国际通用语。国际化人才应该具备的素质离不开高水平的外语能力，尤其是专业领域内的英语交流能力，《林业国际公约导读》的编写是在这样的时代大背景下诞生的。

我们处在一个全球化日益加深的国际社会大环境中。国际公约是涉及政治、经济、文化、技术等方面的多边条约，是国际交往的重要工具和国际政治关系的法律原则基础。面对当前依然严峻的全球环境保护和森林退化的形势，包括中国在内的世界各国政府为推动全球环境合作进程，一起携手共同应对全球环境挑战，签署了多项国际林业公约。林业国际条约对于树立我国负责任大国的地位意义重大。本教材是为高校非英语专业本科生所开设的一门通识类课程教材，内容以涉林国际公约为基础，针对农林类高校学科特点和学生未来职业需求，将知识性内容学习和语言技能学习相融合，使学生了解相关的专业背景，提高国际交流能力、为确保我国现代林业目标的实现奠定人力基础。

《林业国际公约导读》共包括八章，涉及的林业国际公约包括《联合国气候变化框架公约》《京都议定书》《联合国防治荒漠化公约》《联合国湿地公约》《生物多样性公约》《濒危野生动植物国际贸易公约》《国际植物新品种保护公约》和《国际森林文书》。本教材概述各公约产生的背景和现实意义，学习公约的主要内容和相关英语表达，从而培养高校学生从国际化视角思考问题的视野和能力。本教材除了农林院校师生可以使用外，也可供政府部门、科研人员和对林业国际交流感兴趣的人士参阅。

本教材中国际公约文本选自联合国或相关公约的官网，北京林业大学学生张辛欣、金钊、张海洋、闫少宁、王晞月、朱镜霓，北京理工大学学生娄健参与了文稿的前期整理工作。本教材是中央高校基本科研业务费专项基金项目"本硕博英语一条龙教育体系研究"（2015ZCQ-WY-01）的部分研究成果。由于时间紧张和编写水平有限，不足之处还请广大读者不吝赐教，在此表示诚挚的感谢。

作　者
2019 年 12 月

目 录

前　言

第一章　联合国气候变化框架公约 …………………………………… 1

第二章　京都议定书 …………………………………………………… 33

第三章　联合国防治荒漠化公约 ……………………………………… 66

第四章　国际湿地公约 ………………………………………………… 102

第五章　生物多样性公约 ……………………………………………… 117

第六章　濒危野生动植物国际贸易公约 ……………………………… 150

第七章　国际植物新品种保护公约 …………………………………… 175

第八章　国际森林文书 ………………………………………………… 202

Contents

Preface

Unit 1　United Nations Framework Convention on Climate Change ········· 1

Unit 2　Kyoto Protocol to the United Nations Framework
　　　　Convention on Climate Change ·· 33

Unit 3　United Nations Convention to Combat Desertification in
　　　　Countries Experiencing Serious Drought and/or
　　　　Desertification, Particularly in Africa ·· 66

Unit 4　Convention on Wetlands of International Importance
　　　　especially as Waterfowl Habitat ·· 102

Unit 5　Convention on Biological Diversity ··· 117

Unit 6　Convention on International Trade in Endangered
　　　　Species of Wild Fauna and Flora ·· 150

Unit 7　International Convention for the Protection of
　　　　New Varieties of Plants ·· 175

Unit 8　Non-legally Binding Instrument on All Types of Forests ········· 202

第一章

联合国气候变化框架公约

United Nations Framework Convention on Climate Change

一、背景知识(Background)

早在1896年,瑞典科学家斯万特·阿累尼乌斯(Svante Arrhenius)提出了人为造成的大气中二氧化碳含量的升高会影响气候变化这一论断。直到20世纪70年代,世界才开始真正关注气候变化和全球变暖的趋势和影响,学术界和各国政府为此做了大量研究和会谈。1988年,联合国环境规划署(United Nations Environment Programme, UNEP)和世界气象组织(World Meteorological Organization, WMO)成立了政府间气候变化专门委员会(Intergovernmental Panel on Climate Change, IPCC)。1990年,经过数百名顶尖科学家和专家的评议,IPCC发布了第一份评估报告,确定了气候变化的科学依据。

1990年,第二次世界气候大会呼吁建立一个气候变化框架条约,经过两年艰苦的谈判和沟通,1992年5月9日,联合国大会正式通过了《联合国气候变化框架公约》(United Nations Framework Convention on Climate Change, UNFCCC或FCCC)。同年6月,联合国环境与发展会议在巴西里约热内卢召开,参会的世界多国政府首脑参与签署了这一公约。该公约由序言及26条正文组成,确立了发达国家和发展中国家"共同但有区别的责任"原则,最终目的是将大气中的温室气体含量稳定在一定水平,防止人为活动对气候系统造成危险的干扰。1994年3月21日,该公约正式生效。

该公约是世界上第一个为全面控制二氧化碳等温室气体排放、应对全球气候变暖给人类经济和社会带来不利影响的国际公约,也是国际社会在应对全球气候变化问题上进行国际合作的一个基本框架。为加强公约的实施,缔约国于1997年签订了《京都议定书》、2015年达成《巴黎气候变化协定》等一系列协定,对2020年后应对气候变化国际机制做出安排。目前,已有197个国家成为该公约的缔约国。

> 我国于1992年11月7日经全国人大批准加入《联合国气候变化框架公约》，2016年9月3日加入《巴黎气候变化协定》，成为第23个完成批准协定的缔约方。

二、公约原文（The Text of the Convention）

United Nations Framework Convention on Climate Change

The Parties to this Convention,

Acknowledging that change in the Earth's climate and its adverse effects are a common concern of humankind,

Concerned that human activities have been substantially increasing the atmospheric concentrations of greenhouse gases, that these increases enhance the natural greenhouse effect, and that this will result on average in an additional warming of the Earth's surface and atmosphere and may adversely affect natural ecosystems and humankind,

Noting that the largest share of historical and current global emissions of greenhouse gases has originated in developed countries, that per capita emissions in developing countries are still relatively low and that the share of global emissions originating in developing countries will grow to meet their social and development needs,

Aware of the role and importance in terrestrial and marine ecosystems of sinks and reservoirs of greenhouse gases,

Noting that there are many uncertainties in predictions of climate change, particularly with regard to the timing, magnitude and regional patterns thereof,

Acknowledging that the global nature of climate change calls for the widest possible cooperation by all countries and their participation in an effective and appropriate international response, in accordance with their common but differentiated responsibilities and respective capabilities and their social and economic conditions,

Recalling the pertinent provisions of the Declaration of the United Nations conference on the Human Environment, adopted at Stockholm on 16 June 1972,

Recalling also that States have, in accordance with the charter of the United Nations and the principles of international law, the sovereign right to exploit their own resources pursuant to their own environmental and developmental policies, and the responsibility to ensure that activities within their jurisdiction or control do not cause damage to the environment of other States or of areas beyond the limits of national jurisdiction,

Reaffirming the principle of sovereignty of States in international cooperation to address climate change,

Recognizing that States should enact effective environmental legislation, that environmental standards, management objectives and priorities should reflect the environmental and developmental context to which they apply, and that standards applied by some countries may be inappropriate and of unwarranted economic and social cost to other countries in particular developing countries,

Recalling the provisions of General Assembly resolution 44/228 of 22 December 1989 on the United Nations Conference on Environment and Development, and resolutions 43/53 of 6 December 1988, 44/207 of 22 December 1989, 45/212 of 21 December 1990 and 46/169 of 19 December 1991 on protection of global climate for present and future generations of mankind,

Recalling also the provisions of General Assembly resolution 44/206 of 22 December 1989 on the possible adverse effects of sea-level rise on islands and coastal areas, particularly low-lying coastal areas and the pertinent provisions of General Assembly resolution 44/172 of 19 December 1989 on the implementation of the Plan of Action to Combat Desertification,

Recalling further the Vienna Convention for the Protection of the Ozone Layer, 1985, and the Montreal Protocol on Substances that Deplete the Ozone Layer, 1987, as adjusted and amended on 29 June 1990,

Noting the Ministerial Declaration of the Second World Climate Conference adopted on 7 November 1990,

Conscious of the valuable analytical work being conducted by many States on climate change and of the important contributions of the World Meteorological Organization, the United Nations Environment Programme and other organs, organizations and bodies of the United Nations system, as well as other international and intergovernmental bodies, to the exchange of results of scientific research and the coordination of research,

Recognizing that steps required to understand and address climate change will be environmentally, socially and economically most effective if they are based on relevant scientific technical and economic considerations and continually re-evaluated in the light of new findings in these areas,

Recognizing that various actions to address climate change can be justified economically in their own right and can also help in solving other environmental problems,

Recognizing also the need for developed countries to take immediate action in a flexible manner on the basis of clear priorities, as a first step towards comprehensive response strategies at the global, national and, where agreed, regional levels that take into account all greenhouse gases, with due consideration of their relative contributions to the enhancement of the greenhouse effect,

Recognizing further that low-lying and other small island countries, countries with low-lying coastal, arid and semi-arid areas or areas liable to floods, drought and desertification, and developing countries with fragile mountainous ecosystems are particularly vulnerable to the adverse effects of climate change,

Recognizing the special difficulties of those countries, especially developing countries, whose economies are particularly dependent on fossil fuel production, use and exportation, as a consequence of action taken on limiting greenhouse gas emissions,

Affirming that responses to climate change should be coordinated with social and economic development in an integrated manner with a view to avoiding adverse impacts on the latter, taking into full account the legitimate priority needs of developing countries for the achievement of sustained economic growth and the eradication of poverty,

Recognizing that all countries, especially developing countries, need access to resources required to achieve sustainable social and economic development and that, in order for developing countries to progress towards that goal, their energy consumption will need to grow taking into account the possibilities for achieving greater energy efficiency and for controlling greenhouse gas emissions in general, including through the application of new technologies on terms which make such an application economically and socially beneficial,

Determined to protect the climate system for present and future generations,

Have agreed as follows:

Article 1 Definitions

For the purposes of this Convention:

1. "Adverse effects of climate change" means changes in the physical environment or biota resulting from climate change which have significant deleterious effects on the composition, resilience or productivity of natural and managed ecosystems or on the operation of socio-economic systems or on human health and welfare.

2. "Climate change" means a change of climate which is attributed directly or indirectly to human activity that alters the composition of the global atmosphere and which is in addition to natural climate variability observed over comparable time periods.

3. "Climate system" means the totality of the atmosphere, hydrosphere, biosphere and geosphere and their interactions.

4. "Emissions" means the release of greenhouse gases and/or their precursors into the atmosphere over a specified area and period of time.

5. "Greenhouse gases" means those gaseous constituents of the atmosphere, both natural and anthropogenic, that absorb and re-emit infrared radiation.

6. "Regional economic integration organization" means an organization constituted by sovereign States of a given region which has competence in respect of matters governed by this Convention or its protocols and has been duly authorized, in accordance with its internal procedures, to sign, ratify, accept, approve or accede to the instruments concerned.

7. "Reservoir" means a component or components of the climate system where a

greenhouse gas or a precursor of a greenhouse gas is stored.

8. "Sink" means any process, activity or mechanism which removes a greenhouse gas, an aerosol or a precursor of a greenhouse gas from the atmosphere.

9. "Source" means any process or activity which releases a greenhouse gas, an aerosol or a precursor of a greenhouse gas into the atmosphere.

Article 2 Objective

The ultimate objective of this Convention and any related legal instruments that the Conference of the Parties may adopt is to achieve, in accordance with the relevant provisions of the Convention, stabilization of greenhouse gas concentrations in the atmosphere at a level that would prevent dangerous anthropogenic interference with the climate system. Such a level should be achieved within a time-frame sufficient to allow ecosystems to adapt naturally to climate change, to ensure that food production is not threatened and to enable economic development to proceed in a sustainable manner.

Article 3 Principles

In their actions to achieve the objective of the Convention and to implement its provisions, the Parties shall be guided, *inter alia*, by the following:

1. The Parties should protect the climate system for the benefit of present and future generations of humankind, on the basis of equity and in accordance with their common but differentiated responsibilities and respective capabilities. Accordingly, the developed country Parties should take the lead in combating climate change and the adverse effects thereof.

2. The specific needs and special circumstances of developing country Parties, especially those that are particularly vulnerable to the adverse effects of climate change, and of those Parties, especially developing country Parties, that would have to bear a disproportionate or abnormal burden under the Convention, should be given full consideration.

3. The Parties should take precautionary measures to anticipate, prevent or minimize the causes of climate change and mitigate its adverse effects. Where there are threats of serious or irreversible damage, lack of full scientific certainty should not be used as a reason for postponing such measures, taking into account that policies and measures to deal with climate change should be cost-effective so as to ensure global benefits at the lowest possible cost. To achieve this, such policies and measures should take into account different socio-economic contexts, be comprehensive, cover all relevant sources, sinks and reservoirs of greenhouse gases and adaptation, and comprise all economic sectors. Efforts to address climate change may be carried out cooperatively by interested Parties.

4. The Parties have a right to, and should, promote sustainable development.

Policies and measures to protect the climate system against human-induced change should be appropriate for the specific conditions of each party and should be integrated with national development programmes, taking into account that economic development is essential for adopting measures to address climate change.

5. The Parties should cooperate to promote a supportive and open international economic system that would lead to sustainable economic growth and development in all Parties, particularly developing country Parties, thus enabling them better to address the problems of climate change. Measures taken to combat climate change, including unilateral ones, should not constitute a means of arbitrary or unjustifiable discrimination or a disguised restriction on international trade.

Article 4 Commitments

1. All Parties, taking into account their common but differentiated responsibilities and their specific national and regional development priorities, objectives and circumstances, shall:

(a) Develop, periodically update, publish and make available to the Conference of the Parties, in accordance with Article 12, national inventories of anthropogenic emissions by sources and removals by sinks of all greenhouse gases not controlled by the Montreal Protocol, using comparable methodologies to be agreed upon by the Conference of the Parties;

(b) Formulate, implement, publish and regularly update national and, where appropriate, regional programmes containing measures to mitigate climate change by addressing anthropogenic emissions by sources and removals by sinks of all greenhouse gases not controlled by the Montreal Protocol, and measures to facilitate adequate adaptation to climate change;

(c) Promote and cooperate in the development, application and diffusion, including transfer, of technologies, practices and processes that control, reduce or prevent anthropogenic emissions of greenhouse gases not controlled by the Montreal Protocol in all relevant sectors, including the energy, transport, industry, agriculture, forestry and waste management sectors;

(d) Promote sustainable management, and promote and cooperate in the conservation and enhancement, as appropriate, of sinks and reservoirs of all greenhouse gases not controlled by the Montreal Protocol, including biomass, forests and oceans as well as other terrestrial, coastal and marine ecosystems;

(e) Cooperate in preparing for adaptation to the impacts of climate change; develop and elaborate appropriate and integrated plans for coastal zone management, water resources and agriculture, and for the protection and rehabilitation of areas, particularly in Africa, affected by drought and desertification, as well as floods;

(f) Take climate change considerations into account, to the extent feasible, in their relevant social, economic and environmental policies and actions, and employ appropriate methods, for example impact assessments, formulated and determined nationally, with a view to minimizing adverse effects on the economy, on public health and on the quality of the environment, of projects or measures undertaken by them to mitigate or adapt to climate change;

(g) Promote and cooperate in scientific, technological, technical, socio-economic and other research, systematic observation and development of data archives related to the climate system and intended to further the understanding and to reduce or eliminate the remaining uncertainties regarding the causes, effects, magnitude and timing of climate change and the economic and social consequences of various response strategies;

(h) Promote and cooperate in the full, open and prompt exchange of relevant scientific, technological, technical, socio-economic and legal information related to the climate system and climate change, and to the economic and social consequences of various response strategies;

(i) Promote and cooperate in education, training and public awareness related to climate change and encourage the widest participation in this process, including that of non-governmental organizations; and

(j) Communicate to the Conference of the Parties information related to implementation, in accordance with Article 12.

2. The developed country Parties and other Parties included in annex I commit themselves specifically as provided for in the following:

(a) Each of these Parties shall adopt national[①] policies and take corresponding measures on the mitigation of climate change, by limiting its anthropogenic emissions of greenhouse gases and protecting and enhancing its greenhouse gas sinks and reservoirs. These policies and measures will demonstrate that developed countries are taking the lead in modifying longer-term trends in anthropogenic emissions consistent with the objective of the Convention, recognizing that the return by the end of the present decade to earlier levels of anthropogenic emissions of carbon dioxide and other greenhouse gases not controlled by the *Montreal Protocol* would contribute to such modification, and taking into account the differences in these Parties' starting points and approaches, economic structures and resource bases, the need to maintain strong and sustainable economic growth, available technologies and other individual circumstances, as well as the need for equitable and appropriate contributions by each of these Parties to the global effort regarding that objective. These Parties may implement such policies and measures jointly with other Parties and may assist other Parties in contributing to the achievement of the objective of the Convention and, in particular, that of this subparagraph;

---

① This includes policies and measures adopted by regional economic integration organizations.

(b) In order to promote progress to this end, each of these Parties shall communicate, within six months of the entry into force of the Convention for it and periodically thereafter, and in accordance with Article 12, detailed information on its policies and measures referred to in subparagraph (a) above, as well as on its resulting projected anthropogenic emissions by sources and removals by sinks of greenhouse gases not controlled by the Montreal Protocol for the period referred to in subparagraph (a), with the aim of returning individually or jointly to their 1990 levels these anthropogenic emissions of carbon dioxide and other greenhouse gases not controlled by the *Montreal Protocol*. This information will be reviewed by the Conference of the Parties, at its first session and periodically thereafter, in accordance with Article 7;

(c) Calculations of emissions by sources and removals by sinks of greenhouse gases for the purposes of subparagraph;

(d) above should take into account the best available scientific knowledge, including of the effective capacity of sinks and the respective contributions of such gases to climate change. The Conference of the Parties shall consider and agree on methodologies for these calculations at its first session and review them regularly thereafter;

(e) The Conference of the Parties shall, at its first session, review the adequacy of subparagraphs (a) and (b) above. Such review shall be carried out in the light of the best available scientific information and assessment on climate change and its impacts, as well as relevant technical, social and economic information. Based on this review, the Conference of the Parties shall take appropriate action, which may include the adoption of amendments to the commitments in subparagraphs (a) and (b) above. The Conference of the Parties, at its first session, shall also take decisions regarding criteria for joint implementation as indicated in subparagraph (a) above. A second review of subparagraphs (a) and (b) shall take place not later than 31 December 1998, and thereafter at regular intervals determined by the Conference of the Parties, until the objective of the Convention is met;

(f) Each of these Parties shall:

(i) coordinate as appropriate with other such Parties, relevant economic and administrative instruments developed to achieve the objective of the Convention; and

(ii) identify and periodically review its own policies and practices which encourage activities that lead to greater levels of anthropogenic emissions of greenhouse gases not controlled by the Montreal Protocol than would otherwise occur;

(g) The Conference of the Parties shall review, not later than 31 December 1998, available information with a view to taking decisions regarding such amendments to the lists in Annexes I and II as may be appropriate, with the approval of the Party concerned;

(h) Any Party not included in annex I may, in its instrument of ratification, acceptance, approval or accession, or at any time thereafter, notify the Depositary that it intends to be bound by subparagraphs (a) and (b) above. The Depositary shall inform the other signatories and Parties of any such notification.

3. The developed country Parties and other developed Parties included in annex II shall provide new and additional financial resources to meet the agreed full costs incurred by developing country Parties in complying with their obligations under Article 12, paragraph 1. They shall also provide such financial resources, including for the transfer of technology, needed by the developing country Parties to meet the agreed full incremental costs of implementing measures that are covered by paragraph 1 of this Article and that are agreed between a developing country Party and the international entity or entities referred to in Article 11, in accordance with that Article. The implementation of these commitments shall take into account the need for adequacy and predictability in the flow of funds and the importance of appropriate burden sharing among the developed country Parties.

4. The developed country Parties and other developed Parties included in annex II shall also assist the developing country Parties that are particularly vulnerable to the adverse effects of climate change in meeting costs of adaptation to those adverse effects.

5. The developed country Parties and other developed Parties included in annex II shall take all practicable steps to promote, facilitate and finance, as appropriate, the transfer of, or access to, environmentally sound technologies and know-how to other Parties, particularly developing country Parties, to enable them to implement the provisions of the Convention, in this process, the developed country Parties shall support the development and enhancement of endogenous capacities and technologies of developing country Parties. Other Parties and organizations in a position to do so may also assist in facilitating the transfer of such technologies.

6. In the implementation of their commitments under paragraph 2 above, a certain degree of flexibility shall be allowed by the Conference of the Parties to the Parties included in annex I undergoing the process of transition to a market economy, in order to enhance the ability of these Parties to address climate change, including with regard to the historical level of anthropogenic emissions of greenhouse gases not controlled by the *Montreal Protocol* chosen as a reference.

7. The extent to which developing country Parties will effectively implement their commitments under the Convention will depend on the effective implementation by developed country Parties of their commitments under the Convention related to financial resources and transfer of technology and will take fully into account that economic and

social development and poverty eradication are the first and overriding priorities of the developing country Parties.

8. In the implementation of the commitments in this Article, the Parties shall give full consideration to what actions are necessary under the Convention, including actions related to funding, insurance and the transfer of technology, to meet the specific needs and concerns of developing country Parties arising from the adverse effects of climate change and/or the impact of the implementation of response measures, especially on:

(a) Small island countries;

(b) Countries with low-lying coastal areas;

(c) Countries with arid and semi-arid areas, forested areas and areas liable to forest decay;

(d) Countries with areas prone to natural disasters;

(e) Countries with areas liable to drought and desertification;

(f) Countries with areas of high urban atmospheric pollution;

(g) Countries with areas with fragile ecosystems, including mountainous ecosystems;

(h) Countries whose economies are highly dependent on income generated from the production, processing and export, and/or on consumption of fossil fuels and associated energy-intensive products; and

(i) Land-locked and transit countries.

Further, the Conference of the Parties may take actions, as appropriate, with respect to this paragraph.

9. The Parties shall take full account of the specific needs and special situations of the least developed countries in their actions with regard to funding and transfer of technology.

10. The Parties shall, in accordance with Article 10, take into consideration in the implementation of the commitments of the Convention the situation of Parties, particularly developing country Parties, with economies that are vulnerable to the adverse effects of the implementation of measures to respond to climate change. This applies notably to Parties with economies that are highly dependent on income generated from the production, processing and export, and/or consumption of fossil fuels and associated energy-intensive products and/or the use of fossil fuels for which such Parties have serious difficulties in switching to alternatives.

Article 5 Research and systematic observation

In carrying out their commitments under Article 4, paragraph 1 (g), the Parties shall:

(a) Support and further develop, as appropriate, international and intergovernmental programmes and networks or organizations aimed at defining, conducting, assessing and financing research, data collection and systematic observation, taking into account the need to minimize duplication of effort;

(b) Support international and intergovernmental efforts to strengthen systematic observation and national scientific and technical research capacities and capabilities, particularly in developing countries, and to promote access to, and the exchange of, data and analyses thereof obtained from areas beyond national jurisdiction; and

(c) Take into account the particular concerns and needs of developing countries and cooperate in improving their endogenous capacities and capabilities to participate in the efforts referred to in subparagraphs (a) and (b) above.

Article 6　Education, training and public awareness

In carrying out their commitments under Article 4, paragraph 1 (i), the Parties shall:

(a) Promote and facilitate at the national and, as appropriate, subregional and regional levels, and in accordance with national laws and regulations, and within their respective capacities:

(i) the development and implementation of educational and public awareness programmes on climate change and its effects;

(ii) public access to information on climate change and its effects;

(iii) public participation in addressing climate change and its effects and developing adequate responses; and

(iv) training of scientific, technical and managerial personnel.

(b) Cooperate in and promote, at the international level, and, where appropriate, using existing bodies:

(i) the development and exchange of educational and public awareness material on climate change and its effects; and

(ii) the development and implementation of education and training programmes, including the strengthening of national institutions and the exchange or secondment of personnel to train experts in this field, in particular for developing countries.

Article 7　Conference of the parties

1. A Conference of the Parties is hereby established.

2. The Conference of the Parties, as the supreme body of this Convention, shall keep under regular review the implementation of the Convention and any related legal instruments that the Conference of the Parties may adopt, and shall make, within its mandate, the decisions necessary to promote the effective implementation of the Convention. To this end, it shall:

(a) Periodically examine the obligations of the Parties and the institutional arrangements under the Convention, in the light of the objective of the convention, the experience gained in its implementation and the evolution of scientific and technological knowledge;

(b) Promote and facilitate the exchange of information on measures adopted by the Parties to address climate change and its effects, taking into account the differing circumstances, responsibilities and capabilities of the Parties and their respective commitments under the Convention;

(c) Facilitate, at the request of two or more Parties, the coordination of measures adopted by them to address climate change and its effects, taking into account the differing circumstances, responsibilities and capabilities of the Parties and their respective commitments under the Convention;

(d) Promote and guide, in accordance with the objective and provisions of the Convention, the development and periodic refinement of comparable methodologies, to be agreed on by the Conference of the Parties *inter alia*, for preparing inventories of greenhouse gas emissions by sources and removals by sinks, and for evaluating the effectiveness of measures to limit the emissions and enhance the removals of these gases;

(e) Assess, on the basis of all information made available to it in accordance with the provisions of the Convention, the implementation of the Convention by the Parties, the overall effects of the measures taken pursuant to the Convention, in particular environmental, economic and social effects as well as their cumulative impacts and the extent to which progress towards the objective of the Convention is being achieved;

(f) Consider and adopt regular reports on the implementation of the Convention and ensure their publication;

(g) Make recommendations on any matters necessary for the implementation of the Convention;

(h) Seek to mobilize financial resources in accordance with Article 4, paragraphs 3, 4 and 5, and Article 11;

(i) Establish such subsidiary bodies as are deemed necessary for the implementation of the Convention;

(j) Review reports submitted by its subsidiary bodies and provide guidance to them;

(k) Agree upon and adopt, by consensus, rules of procedure and financial rules for itself and for any subsidiary bodies;

(l) Seek and utilize, where appropriate, the services and cooperation of, and information provided by, competent international organizations and intergovernmental and non-governmental bodies; and

(m) Exercise such other functions as are required for the achievement of the objective of the Convention as well as all other functions assigned to it under the

Convention.

3. The Conference of the Parties shall, at its first session, adopt its own rules of procedure as well as those of the subsidiary bodies established by the Convention, which shall include decision-making procedures for matters not already covered by decision-making procedures stipulated in the Convention. Such procedures may include specified majorities required for the adoption of particular decisions.

4. The first session of the Conference of the Parties shall be convened by the interim secretariat referred to in Article 21 and shall take place not later than one year after the date of entry into force of the Convention. Thereafter, ordinary sessions of the Conference of the Parties shall be held every year unless otherwise decided by the Conference of the Parties.

5. Extraordinary sessions of the Conference of the Parties shall be held at such other times as may be deemed necessary by the conference, or at the written request of any Party, provided that, within six months of the request being communicated to the Parties by the secretariat, it is supported by at least one-third of the Parties.

6. The United Nations, its specialized agencies and the International Atomic Energy Agency, as well as any State member thereof or observers thereto not Party to the Convention, may be represented at sessions of the Conference of the Parties as observers. Any body or agency, whether national or international, governmental or non-governmental, which is qualified in matters covered by the Convention, and which has informed the secretariat of its wish to be represented at a session of the Conference of the Parties as an observer, may be so admitted unless at least one-third of the Parties present object. The admission and participation of observers shall be subject to the rules of procedure adopted by the Conference of the Parties.

Article 8 Secretareat

1. A secretariat is hereby established.

2. The functions of the secretariat shall be

(a) To make arrangements for sessions of the Conference of the Parties and its subsidiary bodies established under the Convention and to provide them with services as required;

(b) To compile and transmit reports submitted to it;

(c) To facilitate assistance to the Parties, particularly developing country Parties, on request, in the compilation and communication of information required in accordance with the provisions of the Convention;

(d) To prepare reports on its activities and present them to the Conference of the Parties;

(e) To ensure the necessary coordination with the secretariats of other relevant international bodies;

(f) To enter, under the overall guidance of the Conference of the Parties, into such administrative and contractual arrangements as may be required for the effective discharge of its functions; and

(g) To perform the other secretariat functions specified in the Convention and in any of its protocols and such other functions as may be determined by the Conference of the Parties.

3. The Conference of the Parties, at its first session, shall designate a permanent secretariat and make arrangements for its functioning.

Article 9　Subsidiary body for scientific and technolog-ical advice

1. A subsidiary body for scientific and technological advice is hereby established to provide the conference of the Parties and, as appropriate, its other subsidiary bodies with timely information and advice on scientific and technological matters relating to the Convention. This body shall be open to participation by all Parties and shall be multidisciplinary. It shall comprise government representatives competent in the relevant field of expertise. It shall report regularly to the Conference of the Parties on all aspects of its work.

2. Under the guidance of the Conference of the Parties, and drawing upon existing competent international bodies, this body shall:

(a) Provide assessments of the state of scientific knowledge relating to climate change and its effects;

(b) Prepare scientific assessments on the effects of measures taken in the implementation of the Convention;

(c) Identify innovative, efficient and state-of-the-art technologies and know-how and advise on the ways and means of promoting development and/or transferring such technologies;

(d) Provide advice on scientific programmes, international cooperation in research and development related to climate change, as well as on ways and means of supporting endogenous capacity-building in developing countries; and

(e) Respond to scientific, technological and methodological questions that the Conference of the Parties and its subsidiary bodies may put to the body.

3. The functions and terms of reference of this body may be further elaborated by the Conference of the Parties.

Article 10　Subsidiary body for implementation

1. A subsidiary body for implementation is hereby established to assist the Conference of the Parties in the assessment and review of the effective implementation of the Convention. This body shall be open to participation by all Parties and comprise government representatives who are experts on matters related to climate change. It shall

report regularly to the Conference of the Parties on all aspects of its work.

2. Under the guidance of the Conference of the Parties, this body shall:

(a) Consider the information communicated in accordance with Article 12, paragraph 1, to assess the overall aggregated effect of the steps taken by the Parties in the light of the latest scientific assessments concerning climate change;

(b) Consider the information communicated in accordance with Article 12, paragraph 2, in order to assist the Conference of the Parties in carrying out the reviews required by Article 4, paragraph 2 (d); and

(c) Assist the Conference of the Parties, as appropriate, in the preparation and implementation of its decisions.

Article 11 Financial mechanism

1. A mechanism for the provision of financial resources on a grant or concessional basis, including for the transfer of technology, is hereby defined. It shall function under the guidance of and be accountable to the Conference of the Parties, which shall decide on its policies, programme priorities and eligibility criteria related to this Convention, its operation shall be entrusted to one or more existing international entities.

2. The financial mechanism shall have an equitable and balanced representation of all Parties within a transparent system of governance,

3. The Conference of the Parties and the entity or entities entrusted with the operation of the financial mechanism shall agree upon arrangements to give effect to the above paragraphs, which shall include the following:

(a) Modalities to ensure that the funded projects to address climate change are in conformity with the policies, programme priorities and eligibility criteria established by the Conference of the Parties;

(b) Modalities by which a particular funding decision may be reconsidered in light of these policies, programme priorities and eligibility criteria;

(c) Provision by the entity or entities of regular reports to the Conference of the Parties on its funding operations, which is consistent with the requirement for accountability set out in paragraph 1 above; and

(d) Determination in a predictable and identifiable manner of the amount of funding necessary and available for the implementation of this Convention and the conditions under which that amount shall be periodically reviewed.

4. The Conference of the Parties shall make arrangements to implement the above-mentioned provisions at its first session, reviewing and taking into account the interim arrangements referred to in Article 21, paragraph 3, and shall decide whether these interim arrangements shall be maintained, within four years thereafter, the Conference of the Parties shall review the financial mechanism and take appropriate measures.

5. The developed country Parties may also provide and developing country Parties

avail themselves of, financial resources related to the implementation of the Convention through bilateral, regional and other multilateral channels.

Article 12 Communication of information related to implementation

1. In accordance with Article 4, paragraph 1, each Party shall communicate to the Conference of the Parties, through the secretariat, the following elements of information:

(a) A national inventory of anthropogenic emissions by sources and removals by sinks of all greenhouse gases not controlled by the Montreal Protocol, to the extent its capacities permit, using comparable methodologies to be promoted and agreed upon by the Conference of the Parties;

(b) A general description of steps taken or envisaged by the Party to implement the Convention; and

(c) Any other information that the Party considers relevant to the achievement of the objective of the Convention and suitable for inclusion in its communication, including, if feasible, material relevant for calculations of global emission trends.

2. Each developed country Party and each other Party included in annex I shall incorporate in its communication the following elements of information:

(a) A detailed description of the policies and measures that it has adopted to implement its commitment under Article 4, paragraphs 2 (a) and 2 (b); and

(b) A specific estimate of the effects that the policies and measures referred to in subparagraph (a) immediately above will have on anthropogenic emissions by its sources and removals by its sinks of greenhouse gases during the period referred to in Article 4, paragraph 2 (a).

3. In addition, each developed country Party and each other developed Party included in annex II shall incorporate details of measures taken in accordance with Article 4, paragraphs 3, 4 and 5.

4. Developing country Parties may, on a voluntary basis, propose projects for financing, including specific technologies, materials, equipment, techniques or practices that would be needed to implement such projects, along with, if possible, an estimate of all incremental costs, of the reductions of emissions and increments of removals of greenhouse gases, as well as an estimate of the consequent benefits.

5. Each developed country Party and each other Party included in annex I shall make its initial communication within six months of the entry into force of the Convention for that Party. Each Party not so listed shall make its initial communication within three years of the entry into force of the Convention for that Party, or of the availability of financial resources in accordance with Article 4, paragraph 3. Parties that are least developed countries may make their initial communication at their discretion. The frequency of subsequent communications by all Parties shall be determined by the Conference of the Parties, taking into account the differentiated timetable set by this

paragraph.

6. Information communicated by Parties under this Article shall be transmitted by the secretariat as soon as possible to the Conference of the Parties and to any subsidiary bodies concerned. If necessary, the procedures for the communication of information may be further considered by the Conference of the Parties.

7. From its first session, the Conference of the Parties shall arrange for the provision to developing country Parties of technical and financial support, on request, in compiling and communicating information under this Article, as well as in identifying the technical and financial needs associated with proposed projects and response measures under Article 4. Such support may be provided by other Parties, by competent international organizations and by the secretariat, as appropriate.

8. Any group of Parties may, subject to guidelines adopted by the Conference of the Parties, and to prior notification to the Conference of the Parties, make a joint communication in fulfilment of their obligations under this Article, provided that such a communication includes information on the fulfilment by each of these Parties of its individual obligations under the Convention.

9. Information received by the secretariat that is designated by a Party as confidential, in accordance with criteria to be established by the Conference of the Parties, shall be aggregated by the secretariat to protect its confidentiality before being made available to any of the bodies involved in the communication and review of information.

10. Subject to paragraph 9 above, and without prejudice to the ability of any Party to make public its communication at any time, the secretariat shall make communications by Parties under this Article publicly available at the time they are submitted to the Conference of the Parties.

Article 13 Resolution of questions regarding implementation

The Conference of the Parties shall, at its first session, consider the establishment of a multilateral consultative process, available to Parties on their request, for the resolution of questions regarding the implementation of the Convention.

Article 14 Settlement of disputes

1. In the event of a dispute between any two or more Parties concerning the interpretation or application of the Convention, the Parties concerned shall seek a settlement of the dispute through negotiation or any other peaceful means of their own choice.

2. When ratifying, accepting, approving or acceding to the Convention, or at any time thereafter, a Party which is not a regional economic integration organization may declare in a written instrument submitted to the Depositary that, in respect of any dispute concerning the interpretation or application of the Convention, it recognizes as

compulsory ipso facto and without special agreement, in relation to any Party accepting the same obligation:

(a) Submission of the dispute to the International Court of Justice, and/or

(b) Arbitration in accordance with procedures to be adopted by the Conference of the Parties as soon as practicable, in an annex on arbitration.

A Party which is a regional economic integration organization may make a declaration with like effect in relation to arbitration in accordance with the procedures referred to in subparagraph (b) above.

3. A declaration made under paragraph 2 above shall remain in force until it expires in accordance with its terms or until three months after written notice of its revocation has been deposited with the Depositary.

4. A new declaration, a notice of revocation or the expiry of a declaration shall not in any way affect proceedings pending before the International Court of Justice or the arbitral tribunal, unless the parties to the dispute otherwise agree.

5. Subject to the operation of paragraph 2 above, if after twelve months following notification by one Party to another that a dispute exists between them, the Parties concerned have not been able to settle their dispute through the means mentioned in paragraph 1 above, the dispute shall be submitted, at the request of any of the parties to the dispute, to conciliation.

6. A conciliation commission shall be created upon the request of one of the parties to the dispute. The commission shall be composed of an equal number of members appointed by each party concerned and a chairman chosen jointly by the members appointed by each party. The commission shall render a recommendatory award, which the parties shall consider in good faith.

7. Additional procedures relating to conciliation shall be adopted by the Conference of the Parties, as soon as practicable, in an annex on conciliation.

8. The provisions of this Article shall apply to any related legal instrument which the Conference of the Parties may adopt, unless the instrument provides otherwise.

Article 15　Amendments to the convention

1. Any Party may propose amendments to the Convention.

2. Amendments to the Convention shall be adopted at an ordinary session of the Conference of the Parties. The text of any proposed amendment to the Convention shall be communicated to the Parties by the secretariat at least six months before the meeting at which it is proposed for adoption. The secretariat shall also communicate proposed amendments to the signatories to the convention and, for information, to the Depositary.

3. The Parties shall make every effort to reach agreement on any proposed amendment to the Convention by consensus. If all efforts at consensus have been exhausted, and no agreement reached, the amendment shall as a last resort be adopted by a three-

fourths majority vote of the Parties present and voting at the meeting. The adopted amendment shall be communicated by the secretariat to the Depositary, who shall circulate it to all Parties for their acceptance.

4. Instruments of acceptance in respect of an amendment shall be deposited with the Depositary. An amendment adopted in accordance with paragraph 3 above shall enter into force for those Parties having accepted it on the ninetieth day after the date of receipt by the Depositary of an instrument of acceptance by at least three-fourths of the Parties to the Convention.

5. The amendment shall enter into force for any other Party on the ninetieth day after the date on which that Party deposits with the Depositary its instrument of acceptance of the said amendment.

6. For the purposes of this Article, "Parties present and voting" means Parties present and casting an affirmative or negative vote.

Article 16　Adoption and amendment of annexes to the convention

1. Annexes to the convention shall form an integral part thereof and, unless otherwise expressly provided, a reference to the Convention constitutes at the same time a reference to any annexes thereto. Without prejudice to the provisions of Article 14, paragraphs 2 (b) and 7, such annexes shall be restricted to lists, forms and any other material of a descriptive nature that is of a scientific, technical, procedural or administrative character.

2. Annexes to the Convention shall be proposed and adopted in accordance with the procedure set forth in Article 15, paragraphs 2, 3, and 4.

3. An annex that has been adopted in accordance with paragraph 2 above shall enter into force for all Parties to the Convention six months after the date of the communication by the Depositary to such Parties of the adoption of the annex, except for those Parties that have notified the Depositary, in writing, within that period of their non-acceptance of the annex. The annex shall enter into force for Parties which withdraw their notification of non-acceptance on the ninetieth day after the date on which withdrawal of such notification has been received by the Depositary.

4. The proposal, adoption and entry into force of amendments to annexes to the Convention shall be subject to the same procedure as that for the proposal, adoption and entry into force of annexes to the Convention in accordance with paragraphs 2 and 3 above.

5. If the adoption of an annex or an amendment to an annex involves an amendment to the convention, that annex or amendment to an annex shall not enter into force until such time as the amendment to the Convention enters into force.

Article 17　Protocols

1. The Conference of the Parties may, at any ordinary session, adopt protocols to

the Convention.

2. The text of any proposed protocol shall be communicated to the Parties by the secretariat at least six months before such a session.

3. The requirements for the entry into force of any protocol shall be established by that instrument.

4. Only Parties to the Convention may be Parties to a protocol.

5. Decisions under any protocol shall be taken only by the Parties to the protocol concerned.

Article 18　Right to vote

1. Each Party to the Convention shall have one vote, except as provided for in paragraph 2 below.

2. Regional economic integration organizations, in matters within their competence, shall exercise their right to vote with a number of votes equal to the number of their member States that are Parties to the Convention. Such an organization shall not exercise its right to vote if any of its member States exercises its right, and *vice versa*.

Article 19　Depositary

The Secretary-General of the United Nations shall be the Depositary of the Convention and of protocols adopted in accordance with Article 17.

Article 20　Signature

This Convention shall be open for signature by States Members of the United Nations or of any of its specialized agencies or that are Parties to the Statute of the International Court of Justice and by regional economic integration organizations at Rio de Janeiro, during the United Nations Conference on Environment and Development, and thereafter at United Nations Headquarters in New York from 20 June 1992 to 19 June 1993.

Article 21　Interim arrangements

1. The secretariat functions referred to in Article 8 will be carried out on an interim basis by the secretariat established by the General Assembly of the United Nations in its resolution 45/212 of 21 December 1990, until the completion of the first session of the Conference of the Parties.

2. The head of the interim secretariat referred to in paragraph 1 above will cooperate closely with the Intergovernmental Panel on Climate Change to ensure that the Panel can respond to the need for objective scientific and technical advice. Other relevant scientific bodies could also be consulted.

3. The Global Environment Facility of the United Nations Development Programme, the United Nations Environment Programme and the International Bank for Reconstruction and Development shall be the international entity entrusted with the operation of the

financial mechanism referred to in Article 11 on an interim basis. In this connection, the Global Environment Facility should be appropriately restructured and its membership made universal to enable it to fulfil the requirements of Article 11.

Article 22   Ratification, acceptance, approval or accession

1. The Convention shall be subject to ratification, acceptance, approval or accession by States and by regional economic integration organizations. It shall be open for accession from the day after the date on which the Convention is closed for signature. Instruments of ratification, acceptance, approval or accession shall be deposited with the Depositary.

2. Any regional economic integration organization which becomes a Party to the Convention without any of its member States being a Party shall be bound by all the obligations under the Convention. In the case of such organizations, one or more of whose member States is a Party to the Convention, the organization and its member States shall decide on their respective responsibilities for the performance of their obligations under the Convention, in such cases, the organization and the member States shall not be entitled to exercise rights under the Convention concurrently.

3. In their instruments of ratification, acceptance, approval or accession, regional economic integration organizations shall declare the extent of their competence with respect to the matters governed by the Convention. These organizations shall also inform the Depositary, who shall in turn inform the Parties, of any substantial modification in the extent of their competence.

Article 23   Entry Into force

1. The Convention shall enter into force on the ninetieth day after the date of deposit of the fiftieth instrument of ratification, acceptance, approval or accession.

2. For each State or regional economic integration organization that ratifies, accepts or approves the Convention or accedes thereto after the deposit of the fiftieth instrument of ratification, acceptance, approval or accession, the Convention shall enter into force on the ninetieth day after the date of deposit by such State or regional economic integration organization of its instrument of ratification, acceptance, approval or accession.

3. For the purposes of paragraphs 1 and 2 above, any instrument deposited by a regional economic integration organization shall not be counted as additional to those deposited by States members of the organization.

Article 24   Reservations

No reservations may be made to the Convention.

Article 25   Withdrawal

1. At any time after three years from the date on which the Convention has entered

into force for a Party, that Party may withdraw from the Convention by giving written notification to the Depositary.

2. Any such withdrawal shall take effect upon expiry of one year from the date of receipt by the Depositary of the notification of withdrawal or on such later date as may be specified in the notification of withdrawal.

3. Any Party that withdraws from the Convention shall be considered as also having withdrawn from any protocol to which it is a Party.

Article 26 Authentic texts

The original of this Convention, of which the Arabic, Chinese, English, French, Russian and Spanish texts are equally authentic, shall be deposited with the Secretary-General of the United Nations.

IN WITNESS WHEREOF the undersigned, being duly authorized to that effect, have signed this Convention.

DONE at New York this ninth day of May one thousand nine hundred and ninety-two.

ANNEX I

Australia	Latvia[a]
Austria	Lithuania[a]
Belarus[a]①	Luxembourg
Belgium	Netherlands
Bulgaria[a]	New Zealand
Canada	Norway
Czechoslovakia[a]	Poland[a]
Denmark	Portugal
European Community	Romania[a]
Estonia[a]	Russian Federation[a]
Finland	Spain
France	Sweden
Germany	Switzerland
Greece	Turkey
Hungary[a]	Ukraine[a]
Ireland	United Kingdom of Great Britain and Northern Ireland
Italy	
Japan	United States of America

---

① a: countries that are undergoing the process of transition to a market economy.

ANNEX II

Australia	Japan
Austria	Luxembourg
Belgium	Netherlands
Canada	New Zealand
Denmark	Norway
European Community	Portugal
Finland	Spain
France	Sweden
Germany	Switzerland
Greece	Turkey
Iceland	United Kingdom of Great Britain and Northern Ireland
Ireland	United States of America
Italy	

(Source：https：//treaties. un. org/doc/Treaties/1994/03/19940321％2004-56％20AM/Ch_XXVII_07p. pdf)

三、注解(Notes)

1. Reservoirs, sinks and sources of greenhouse gases

温室气体的"库""汇""源"。"库"(reservoir)指气候系统内存储温室气体或其前体的一个或多个组成部分；"汇"(sink)指从大气中清除温室气体、气溶胶或温室气体前体的任何过程、活动或机制；"源"(source)指向大气排放温室气体、气溶胶或温室气体前体的任何过程或活动。

2. The United Nations Conference on Environment and Development

联合国环境与发展大会，于1992年6月在巴西里约热内卢召开，首次把环境保护作为主要议题。180多个国家派代表团出席了会议，100多位国家或政府元首到会。会议讨论并通过了包括《气候变化框架公约》《里约环境与发展宣言》和《21世纪议程》在内的多项环境与发展问题的决议。

3. The *Montreal Protocol*

《蒙特利尔议定书》，全名为《蒙特利尔破坏臭氧层物质管制议定书》(*Montreal Protocol on Substances that Deplete the Ozone Layer*)，是联合国为了避免工业产品中的氟氯碳化物对地球臭氧层继续造成恶化及损害，承续1985年保护臭氧层维也纳公约的大原则，于1987年9月16日邀请所属26个会员国在加拿大蒙特利尔所签署的环境保护公约。该公约自1989年1月1日起生效。

4. The International Court of Justice or the Arbitral Tribunal

国际法庭或仲裁庭。联合国国际法庭位于荷兰海牙，于1945年6月成立，是联合国六大主要机构之一和最主要的司法机关,是主权国家政府间的民事司法裁判机构。仲裁庭是国际仲裁机构,是指由争端当事国共同选任的仲裁人审理有关争端并做出有拘束力的裁决,所作裁决对争端当事国具有拘束力。

5. The Global Environment Facility of the United Nations Development Programme 联合国开发计划署(UNDP)全球环境基金(GEF),是世界银行1990年创建的实验项目,目的是支持环境友好工程。目前已有183个国家和地区加入了这一国际合作机构,其宗旨是与国际机构、社会团体及私营部门合作,协力解决环境问题。在1994年里约峰会期间,全球环境基金进行了重组,与世界银行分离,成为一个独立的常设机构,受托成为《联合国生物多样性公约》和《联合国气候变化框架公约》等协议的资金机制。

四、相关词汇(Key Words and Phrases)

1.	accession	[ækˈseʃn]	n.	正式加入;新增
2.	aerosol	[ˈeərəsɒl]	n.	气溶胶(由固体或液体小质点分散并悬浮在气体介质中的胶体分散体系)
3.	aggregate	[ˈægrɪgeɪt]	n. & v.	总计,合计
4.	amendment	[əˈmendmənt]	n.	修正案;改正
5.	annex	[əˈneks]	n.	附件;附加物
6.	anthropogenic	[ˌænθrəpəˈdʒenɪk]	adj.	人为的,人类引起的
7.	biota	[baɪˈəʊtə]	n.	一个地区的动植物;生物区系
8.	conciliation	[kənˌsɪliˈeɪʃn]	n.	和解,调解
9.	confidentiality	[ˌkɒnfɪˌdenʃiˈæləti]	n.	保密性;机密性
10.	cost-effective	[ˌkɒst ɪˈfektɪv]	adj.	合算的;有成本效益的
11.	deleterious	[ˌdeləˈtɪəriəs]	adj.	有害的;造成损害的
12.	designate	[ˈdezɪgneɪt]	v.	委任;指派
13.	differentiate	[ˌdɪfəˈrenʃieɪt]	v.	区别,区分
14.	diffusion	[dɪˈfjuːʒən]	n.	扩散,传播
15.	depositary	[dɪˈpɒzɪtəri]	n.	受托人,受托方;保存人
16.	disproportionate	[ˌdɪsprəˈpɔːʃənət]	adj.	不成比例的,不相称的
17.	eligibility	[ˌelɪdʒəˈbɪlɪti]	n.	适当性,合格性
18.	endogenous	[enˈdɒdʒənəs]	adj.	内源性的;内生的
19.	envisage	[ɪnˈvɪzɪdʒ]	v.	展望;设想
20.	equitable	[ˈekwɪtəbl]	adj.	公平合理的;公正的
21.	eradication	[ɪˌrædɪˈkeɪʃn]	n.	根除;消灭
22.	incremental	[ˌɪnkrɪˈment(ə)l]	adj.	增加的;递增的
23.	*inter alia*	[ˈɪntərˈeiliə]	adv.	(拉丁语)尤其;在其他事物之外

24. *ipso facto*	[ˌɪpsəʊ ˈfæktəʊ]	adv.	(拉丁语)根据该事实;根据事实本身
25. jurisdiction	[ˌdʒʊərɪsˈdɪkʃn]	n.	司法权;审判权;管辖权;管辖范围
26. mandate	[ˈmændeɪt]	n.	(政府或组织等经选举而获得的)授权;任期;委托书
27. mitigate	[ˈmɪtɪgeɪt]	v.	减轻;缓和
28. modality	[məʊˈdæləti]	n.	形式,样式
29. precursor	[priˈkɜːsə(r)]	n.	前体;先期产物
30. ratification	[ˌrætɪfɪˈkeɪʃn]	n.	批准;认可
31. resilience	[rɪˈzɪliəns]	n.	适应力;还原能力
32. revocation	[ˌrevəˈkeɪʃn]	n.	(法律等的)撤销,废除
33. secretariat	[ˌsekrəˈteəriət]	n.	(大型国际组织、政治组织的)秘书处,书记处
34. stipulate	[ˈstɪpjuleɪt]	v.	规定,明确要求
35. unwarranted	[ʌnˈwɒrəntɪd]	adj.	不合理的;无正当理由的
36. fossil fuel			化石燃料(如煤或石油)
37. in good faith			真诚地,真心实意地
38. on a grant or concessional basis			在赠与或转让基础上
39. state-of-the-art technologies			最先进的技术
40. land-locked and transit countries			内陆国与中转国
41. infrared radiation			红外辐射

五、长难句(Difficult Sentences)

1. Take climate change considerations into account, to the extent feasible, in their relevant social, economic and environmental policies and actions, and employ appropriate methods, for example impact assessments, formulated and determined nationally, with a view to minimizing adverse effects on the economy, on public health and on the quality of the environment, of projects or measures undertaken by them to mitigate or adapt to climate change. (Article 4, 1)

解析:本句主句型是祈使句,由 take 和 employ 两个动词并列引导。其中 to the extent feasible 是表示程度的状语插入语;formulated and determined nationally 作为过去分词修饰 impact assessments;句尾的 of projects or measures undertaken by them to mitigate or adapt to climate change 是修饰 adverse effects 的,指的是这些项目或措施的负面影响。

译文:在它们(缔约方)有关的社会、经济和环境政策及行动中,在可行的范围内将气候变化考虑进去,并采用由本国拟订和确定的适当办法,例如进行影响评估,以期尽量减少它们为了减缓或适应气候变化而进行的项目或采取的措施对经济、公共健康和环境质量产生的不利影响。

2. Support and further develop, as appropriate, international and intergovernmental programmes and networks or organizations aimed at defining, conducting, assessing and financing research, data collection and systematic observation, taking into account the need to minimize duplication of effort. (Article 5, a)

解析：在这个祈使句中，Support and further develop 是谓语动词，as appropriate 是插入语；programmes and networks or organizations 是宾语，aimed at 引导的是修饰宾语的目的短语，taking into account 引导的短语是现在分词短语做伴随状语。

译文：支持并酌情进一步制订旨在确定、执行、评估和资助研究、数据收集和系统观测的国际和政府间计划和网站或组织，同时考虑到有必要尽量减少重复工作。

3. Any body or agency, whether national or international, governmental or non-governmental, which is qualified in matters covered by the convention, and which has informed the secretariat of its wish to be represented at a session of the Conference of the Parties as an observer, may be so admitted unless at least one-third of the Parties present object. (Article 7, 6)

解析：在这个主从复合句中，主句的主语是 Any body or agency，谓语是 may be so admitted，whether 引导的四个形容词，以及两个 which 引导的定语从句，都是修饰主语的；从句是 unless 引导的让步状语从句。

译文：任何在本公约所涉事项上具备资格的团体或机构，不管其为国家或国际的、政府或非政府的，经通知秘书处其愿意作为观察员出席缔约方会议的某届会议，均可予以接纳，除非出席的缔约方超过1/3反对。

4. An annex that has been adopted in accordance with paragraph 2 above shall enter into force for all Parties to the Convention six months after the date of the communication by the Depositary to such Parties of the adoption of the annex, except for those Parties that have notified the Depositary, in writing, within that period of their non-acceptance of the annex. (Article 16, 3)

解析：该句主干是 An annex... shall enter into force... six months after the date of...；主句之后伴随了一个 except for 引导的介词短语，其中的介词宾语 those Parties 带有一个 that 引导的定语从句。

译文：按照上述第2款通过的附件，应于保存人向公约的所有缔约方发出关于通过该附件的通知之日起6个月后对所有缔约方生效，但在此期间以书面形式通知保存人不接受该附件的缔约方除外。

5. For each State or regional economic integration organization that ratifies, accepts or approves the Convention or accedes thereto after the deposit of the fiftieth instrument of ratification, acceptance, approval or accession, the Convention shall enter into force on the ninetieth day after the date of deposit by such State or regional economic integration organization of its instrument of ratification, acceptance, approval or accession.

解析：该句主句是 the Convention shall enter into force on the ninetieth day after the date of deposit，句子开始是一个 for 引导的介词结构，介词宾语 each State or regional economic integration organization 带有 that 引导的定语从句，这个定语从句里还包含一个 after 引导的介词结构。主句后半部分是 by 引导的介词结构。

译文：对于在第 50 份批准、接受、核准或加入的文书交存之后批准、接受、核准或加入本公约的每一个国家或区域经济一体化组织，本公约应自该国或该区域经济一体化组织交存其批准、接受、核准或加入的文书之日后第 90 天起生效。

六、课后练习（Exercises）

1. Skimming and Scanning

Directions：Read the following passage excerpted from the United Nations Framework Convention on Climate Change. At the end of the passage, there are six statements. Each statement contains information given in one of the paragraphs of the passage. Identify the paragraph from which the information is derived. Each paragraph is marked with a letter. You may choose a paragraph more than once. Answer the questions by writing the corresponding letter in the bracket in front of each statement.

The Parties to this Convention,

A. Concerned that human activities have been substantially increasing the atmospheric concentrations of greenhouse gases, that these increases enhance the natural greenhouse effect, and that this will result on average in an additional warming of the Earth's surface and atmosphere and may adversely affect natural ecosystems and humankind,

B. Noting that the largest share of historical and current global emissions of greenhouse gases has originated in developed countries, that per capita emissions in developing countries are still relatively low and that the share of global emissions originating in developing countries will grow to meet their social and development needs,

C. Acknowledging that the global nature of climate change calls for the widest possible cooperation by all countries and their participation in an effective and appropriate international response, in accordance with their common but differentiated responsibilities and respective capabilities and their social and economic conditions,

D. Recalling also that States have, in accordance with the charter of the United Nations and the principles of international law, the sovereign right to exploit their own resources pursuant to their own environmental and developmental policies, and the responsibility to ensure that activities within their jurisdiction or control do not cause damage to the environment of other States or of areas beyond the limits of national jurisdiction,

E. Recognizing that States should enact effective environmental legislation, that environmental standards, management objectives and priorities should reflect the environmental and developmental context to which they apply, and that standards applied by some countries may be inappropriate and of unwarranted economic and social cost to other countries in particular developing countries,

F. Conscious of the valuable analytical work being conducted by many States on climate change and of the important contributions of the World Meteorological Organization, the United Nations Environment Programme and other organs, organizations and bodies of the United Nations system, as well as other international and intergovernmental bodies, to the exchange of results of scientific research and the coordination of research,

G. Recognizing also the need for developed countries to take immediate action in a flexible manner on the basis of clear priorities, as a first step towards comprehensive response strategies at the global, national and, where agreed, regional levels that take into account all greenhouse gases, with due consideration of their relative contributions to the enhancement of the greenhouse effect,

H. Recognizing further that low-lying and other small island countries, countries with low-lying coastal, arid and semi-arid areas or areas liable to floods, drought and desertification, and developing countries with fragile mountainous ecosystems are particularly vulnerable to the adverse effects of climate change,

I. Recognizing that all countries, especially developing countries, need access to resources required to achieve sustainable social and economic development and that, in order for developing countries to progress towards that goal, their energy consumption will need to grow taking into account the possibilities for achieving greater energy efficiency and for controlling greenhouse gas emissions in general, including through the application of new technologies on terms which make such an application economically and socially beneficial.

(_____) (1) Developed countries need to take immediate and flexible action to enhance the greenhouse effect.

(_____) (2) A State's developmental activities are not supposed to cause damage to the environment of other States.

(_____) (3) Developing countries contribute to relatively low emission of greenhouse gases per capita.

(_____) (4) Developing countries need to apply new technologies for achieving greater energy efficiency.

(_____) (5) Some countries may apply inappropriate standards of unwarranted economic and social cost to other countries in particular developing countries.

(_____) (6) The concentrations of greenhouse gases have been greatly increased as a result of human activities.

2. Reading Comprehension

Directions: Read **Article 3 Principles** and **Article 4 Commitments** from the United Nations Framework Convention on Climate Change, and decide whether the following statements are True or False. Write T for True or F for False in the bracket in front of each statement.

A. Questions 1 to 3 are based on **Article 3 Principles.**

(1)(_____) Both the developed and developing country Parties share equal responsibilities for combating climate change and the adverse effects thereof.

(2)(_____) Lack of full scientific certainty should not be used as a reason for postponing measures to address climate change when there are threats of serious or irreversible damage.

(3)(_____) Consideration of international trade should not be taken as prevention against regional or national measures for combating climate change.

B. Questions 4 to 6 are based on **Article 4 Commitments.**

(4)(_____) Non-governmental organizations are encouraged to participate in promoting and cooperating in education, training and public awareness related to climate change.

(5)(_____) The developed country Parties shall provide new and additional financial resources to meet the agreed full costs incurred by developing country Parties in complying with their obligations concerned with climate change.

(6)(_____) The first and overriding priority of the developing country shall be combating adverse effects of climate change rather than social development and poverty eradication.

3. Extensive Reading

Directions: In this section, there is a passage with ten blanks. You are required to select one word for each blank from a list of choices given in a word bank following the passage. Read the passage through carefully before making your choices. Each choice in the bank is identified by a letter. You may not use any of the words in the bank more than once.

Thousands of studies conducted by researchers around the world have documented increases in temperature at Earth's surface, as well as in the atmosphere and oceans. Many other (1)_____ of global climate are changing as well. High temperature extremes and heavy precipitation events are increasing, glaciers and snow cover are (2)_____, and sea ice is retreating. Seas are warming, rising, and becoming more acidic, and flooding is become more (3)_____ along the U.S. coastline. Growing seasons are longer, and large wildfires occur more frequently. Many species are moving to new locations, and changes in the seasonal timing of important biological events are occurring in (4)_____ to climate change.

These trends are all consistent with a warming world and are expected to continue.

Many lines of evidence demonstrate that human activities, especially emissions of heat-trapping greenhouse gases from fossil fuel combustion, deforestation, and land-use change, are (5) _____ responsible for the climate changes observed in the industrial era, especially over the last six decades. The atmospheric concentration of carbon dioxide, the largest contributor to human-caused warming, has increased by about 40% over the industrial era. This change has (6) _____ the natural greenhouse effect, driving an increase in global surface temperatures and other widespread changes in Earth's climate that are unprecedented in the history of modern civilization.

Greenhouse gas emissions from human activities will continue to affect Earth's climate for decades and even (7) _____. Humans are adding carbon dioxide to the atmosphere at a rate far greater than it is (8) _____ by natural processes, creating a long-lived reservoir of the gas in the atmosphere and oceans that is driving the climate to a warmer and warmer state.

Beyond the next few decades, how much the climate changes will (9) _____ primarily on the amount of greenhouse gases emitted into the atmosphere; how much of those greenhouse gases are absorbed by the ocean, the biosphere, and other sinks; and how (10) _____ Earth's climate is to those emissions. (329 words)

A. aspects	B. centuries	C. depend	D. exploding	E. extensive
F. frequent	G. intensified	H. observation	I. perspective	J. primarily
K. removed	L. response	M. sensitive	N. shrinking	O. yielded

4. Vocabulary Expanding

Directions: In this section, there are ten sentences from the United Nations Framework Convention on Climate Change. You are required to complete these sentences with the proper form of the words given in the brackets.

(1) The Parties should take _____ measures to anticipate, prevent or minimize the causes of climate change and mitigate its adverse effects. (precaution)

(2) Where there are threats of serious or _____ damage, lack of full scientific certainty should not be used as a reason for postponing such measures, taking into account that policies and measures to deal with climate change should be cost-effective so as to ensure global benefits at the lowest possible cost. (reverse)

(3) Measures taken to combat climate change, including unilateral ones, should not constitute a means of arbitrary or _____ discrimination or a disguised restriction on international trade. (justify)

(4) Each of these Parties shall coordinate as appropriate with other such Parties,

relevant economic and _____ instruments developed to achieve the objective of the Convention. (administer)

(5) Each of these Parties shall identify and _____ review its own policies and practices which encourage activities that lead to greater levels of anthropogenic emissions of greenhouse gases not controlled by the Montreal Protocol than would otherwise occur. (period)

(6) The Conference of the Parties shall make _____ on any matters necessary for the implementation of the Convention. (recommend)

(7) The functions of the secretariat shall be to facilitate assistance to the Parties, particularly developing country Parties, on request, in the _____ and communication of information required in accordance with the provisions of the Convention. (compile)

(8) Under the guidance of the Conference of the Parties, and drawing upon existing competent international bodies, this body shall provide _____ of the state of scientific knowledge relating to climate change and its effects. (assess)

(9) A mechanism for the provision of financial resources on a grant or _____ basis, including for the transfer of technology, is hereby defined. (concession)

(10) The Conference of the Parties shall, at its first session, consider the establishment of a multilateral _____ process, available to Parties on their request, for the resolution of questions regarding the implementation of the Convention. (consult)

七、思考题(Questions for Discussion)

Directions: Work in groups and answer the following questions.

1. What is the background of the creation of UNFCCC?

2. What are basic ideas about climate change according to the Convention? Give some examples.

3. What is the objective of the Convention?

4. What do "common but differentiated responsibilities and respective capabilities" mean for the Parties of the Convention?

八、拓展学习(Further Studies)

Directions: Surf the Internet and find more information about the following topics before or after class. Present to the class some successful projects to illustrate the application of these concepts to practice.

1. When and where was the Convention formally established and which persons and agencies are in charge?

2. What role has China played in international negotiations on climate change?

3. What can ordinary people do to help in the climate change issues?

九、模拟联合国大会(Model United Nations Practice)

Directions: Work in teams and simulate the institutions and committees of the United Nations, featuring delegates of the United Nations members and the six committees of the General Assembly, negotiating issues of climate change in the world and working out resolutions. Students are suggested to focus on the following topics:

1. How to reduce global greenhouse gas emissions over the next few decades?
2. How much should their country be responsible for these emission reductions?
3. How will their country achieve these goals?

第二章

京都议定书

Kyoto Protocol to the United Nations Framework Convention on Climate Change

一、背景知识(Background)

《京都议定书》,全称《联合国气候变化框架公约的京都议定书》,是《联合国气候变化框架公约》(United Nations Framework Convention on Climate Change, UNFCCC)的补充条款。1997年12月,条约在日本京都通过,并于1998年3月16日至1999年3月15日间开放签字,共有84国签署。条约于2005年2月16日正式生效,其目标是"将大气中的温室气体含量稳定在一个适当的水平,进而防止剧烈的气候改变对人类造成伤害"。中国于1998年5月签署并于2002年8月核准了该议定书。截止2005年8月,全球已有142个国家和地区签署了该议定书。2011年12月,加拿大宣布退出《京都议定书》,成为继美国之后第二个签署后但又退出的国家。

(Source: https://baike.baidu.com/item/京都议定书/761287? fr=aladdin)

二、公约原文(The Text of the Convention)

Kyoto Protocol to the United Nations Framework Convention on Climate Change

The Parties to this Protocol,

Being Parties to the United Nations Framework Convention on Climate Change, hereinafter referred to as "the Convention",

In pursuit of the ultimate objective of the Convention as stated in its Article 2,

Recalling the provisions of the Convention,

Being guided by Article 3 of the Convention,

Pursuant to the Berlin Mandate adopted by decision 1/cp. 1 of the Conference of the Parties to the Convention at its first session,

Have agreed as follows:

Article 1

For the purposes of this Protocol, the definitions contained in Article 1 of the Convention shall apply. In addition:

1. "Conference of the Parties" means the Conference of the Parties to the Convention.

2. "Convention" means the United Nations Framework Convention on Climate Change, adopted in New York on 9 May 1992.

3. "Intergovernmental Panel on Climate Change" means the Intergovernmental Panel on Climate Change established in 1988 jointly by the World Meteorological Organization and the United Nations Environment Programme.

4. "*Montreal Protocol*" means the *Montreal Protocol on Substances that Deplete the Ozone Layer*, adopted in Montreal on 16 September 1987 and as subsequently adjusted and amended.

5. "Parties present and voting" means Parties present and casting an affirmative or negative vote.

6. "Party" means, unless the context otherwise indicates, a Party to this Protocol.

7. "Party included in Annex I" means a Party included in Annex I to the Convention, as may be amended, or a Party which has made a notification under Article 4, paragraph 2(g), of the Convention.

Article 2

1. Each Party included in Annex I, in achieving its quantified emission limitation and reduction commitments under Article 3, in order to promote sustainable development, shall:

(a) Implement and/or further elaborate policies and measures in accordance with its national circumstances, such as:

i. Enhancement of energy efficiency in relevant sectors of the national eco-nomy;

ii. Protection and enhancement of sinks and reservoirs of greenhouse gases not controlled by the Montreal Protocol, taking into account its commitments under relevant international environmental agreements; promotion of sustainable forest management practices, afforestation and reforestation;

iii. Promotion of sustainable forms of agriculture in light of climate change considerations;

iv. Research on, and promotion, development and increased use of, new and renewable forms of energy, of carbon dioxide sequestration technologies and of advanced and innovative environmentally sound technologies;

v. Progressive reduction or phasing out of market imperfections, fiscal incentives, tax and duty exemptions and subsidies in all greenhouse gas emitting sectors that run counter to the objective of the Convention and application of market instruments;

vi. Encouragement of appropriate reforms in relevant sectors aimed at promoting policies and measures which limit or reduce emissions of greenhouse gases not controlled by the Montreal Protocol;

vii. Measures to limit and/or reduce emissions of greenhouse gases not controlled by the Montreal Protocol in the transport sector;

viii. Limitation and/or reduction of methane emissions through recovery and use in waste management, as well as in the production, transport and distribution of energy;

(b) Cooperate with other such Parties to enhance the individual and combined effectiveness of their policies and measures adopted under this Article, pursuant to Article 4, paragraph 2(e); (i), of the Convention. To this end, these Parties shall take steps to share their experience and exchange information on such policies and measures, including developing ways of improving their comparability, transparency and effectiveness. The Conference of the Parties serving as the meeting of the Parties to this Protocol shall, at its first session or as soon as practicable thereafter, consider ways to facilitate such cooperation, taking into account all relevant information.

2. The Parties included in Annex I shall pursue limitation or reduction of emissions of greenhouse gases not controlled by the *Montreal Protocol* from aviation and marine bunker fuels, working through the International Civil Aviation Organization and the International Maritime Organization, respectively.

3. The Parties included in Annex I shall strive to implement policies and measures under this Article in such a way as to minimize adverse effects, including the adverse effects of climate change, effects on international trade, and social, environmental and economic impacts on other Parties, especially developing country Parties and in particular those identified in Article 4, paragraphs 8 and 9, of the Convention, taking into account Article 3 of the Convention. The Conference of the Parties serving as the meeting of the Parties to this Protocol may take further action, as appropriate, to promote the implementation of the provisions of this paragraph.

4. The Conference of the Parties serving as the meeting of the Parties to this Protocol, if it decides that it would be beneficial to coordinate any of the policies and measures in paragraph 1(a) above, taking into account different national circumstances and potential effects, shall consider ways and means to elaborate the coordination of such policies and measures.

Article 3

1. The Parties included in Annex I shall, individually or jointly, ensure that their

aggregate anthropogenic carbon dioxide equivalent emissions of the greenhouse gases listed in Annex A do not exceed their assigned amounts, calculated pursuant to their quantified emission limitation and reduction commitments inscribed in Annex B and in accordance with the provisions of this Article, with a view to reducing their overall emissions of such gases by at least 5 per cent below 1990 levels in the commitment period 2008 to 2012.

2. Each Party included in Annex I shall, by 2005, have made demonstrable progress in achieving its commitments under this Protocol.

3. The net changes in greenhouse gas emissions by sources and removals by sinks resulting from direct human-induced land-use change and forestry activities, limited to afforestation, reforestation and deforestation since 1990, measured as verifiable changes in carbon stocks in each commitment period, shall be used to meet the commitments under this Article of each Party included in Annex I. The greenhouse gas emissions by sources and removals by sinks associated with those activities shall be reported in a transparent and verifiable manner and reviewed in accordance with Articles 7 and 8.

4. Prior to the first session of the Conference of the Parties serving as the meeting of the Parties to this Protocol, each Party included in Annex I shall provide, for consideration by the Subsidiary Body for Scientific and Technological Advice, data to establish its level of carbon stocks in 1990 and to enable an estimate to be made of its changes in carbon stocks in subsequent years. The Conference of the Parties serving as the meeting of the Parties to this Protocol shall, at its first session or as soon as practicable thereafter, decide upon modalities, rules and guidelines as to how, and which, additional human-induced activities related to changes in greenhouse gas emissions by sources and removals by sinks in the agricultural soils and the land-use change and forestry categories shall be added to, or subtracted from, the assigned amounts for Parties included in Annex I, taking into account uncertainties, transparency in reporting, verifiability, the methodological work of the Intergovernmental Panel on Climate Change, the advice provided by the Subsidiary Body for Scientific and Technological Advice in accordance with Article 5 and the decisions of the Conference of the Parties. Such a decision shall apply in the second and subsequent commitment periods. A Party may choose to apply such a decision on these additional human-induced activities for its first commitment period, provided that these activities have taken place since 1990.

5. The Parties included in Annex I undergoing the process of transition to a market economy whose base year or period was established pursuant to decision 9/ cp. 2 of the Conference of the Parties at its second session shall use that base year or period for the implementation of their commitments under this Article. Any other Party included in Annex I undergoing the process of transition to a market economy which has not yet

submitted its first national communication under Article 12 of the Convention may also notify the Conference of the Parties serving as the meeting of the Parties to this Protocol that it intends to use a historical base year or period other than 1990 for the implementation of its commitments under this Article. The Conference of the Parties serving as the meeting of the Parties to this Protocol shall decide on the acceptance of such notification.

6. Taking into account Article 4, paragraph 6, of the Convention, in the implementation of their commitments under this Protocol other than those under this Article, a certain degree of flexibility shall be allowed by the Conference of the Parties serving as the meeting of the Parties to this Protocol to the Parties included in Annex I undergoing the process of transition to a market economy.

7. In the first quantified emission limitation and reduction commitment period, from 2008 to 2012, the assigned amount for each Party included in Annex I shall be equal to the percentage inscribed for it in Annex B of its aggregate anthropogenic carbon dioxide equivalent emissions of the greenhouse gases listed in Annex A in 1990, or the base year or period determined in accordance with paragraph 5 above, multiplied by five. Those Parties included in Annex I for whom land-use change and forestry constituted a net source of greenhouse gas emissions in 1990 shall include in their 1990 emissions base year or period the aggregate anthropogenic carbon dioxide equivalent emissions by sources minus removals by sinks in 1990 from land-use change for the purposes of calculating their assigned amount.

8. Any Party included in Annex I may use 1995 as its base year for hydrofluorocarbons（氢氟碳化物）, perfluorocarbons（全氟碳化物）and sulphur hexafluoride（六氟化硫）, for the purposes of the calculation referred to in paragraph 7 above.

9. Commitments for subsequent periods for Parties included in Annex I shall be established in amendments to Annex B to this Protocol, which shall be adopted in accordance with the provisions of Article 21, paragraph 7. The Conference of the Parties serving as the meeting of the Parties to this Protocol shall initiate the consideration of such commitments at least seven years before the end of the first commitment period referred to in paragraph 1 above.

10. Any emission reduction units, or any part of an assigned amount, which a Party acquires from another Party in accordance with the provisions of Article 6 or of Article 17 shall be added to the assigned amount for the acquiring Party.

11. Any emission reduction units, or any part of an assigned amount, which a Party transfers to another Party in accordance with the provisions of Article 6 or of Article 17 shall be subtracted from the assigned amount for the transferring Party.

12. Any certified emission reductions which a Party acquires from another Party in accordance with the provisions of Article 12 shall be added to the assigned amount for the acquiring Party.

13. If the emissions of a Party included in Annex I in a commitment period are less than its assigned amount under this Article, this difference shall, on request of that Party, be added to the assigned amount for that Party for subsequent commitment periods.

14. Each Party included in Annex I shall strive to implement the commitments mentioned in paragraph 1 above in such a way as to minimize adverse social, environmental and economic impacts on developing country Parties, particularly those identified in Article 4, paragraphs 8 and 9, of the Convention. In line with relevant decisions of the Conference of the Parties on the implementation of those paragraphs, the Conference of the Parties serving as the meeting of the Parties to this Protocol shall, at its first session, consider what actions are necessary to minimize the adverse effects of climate change and/or the impacts of response measures on Parties referred to in those paragraphs. Among the issues to be considered shall be the establishment of funding, insurance and transfer of technology.

Article 4

1. Any Parties included in Annex I that have reached an agreement to fulfil their commitments under Article 3 jointly, shall be deemed to have met those commitments provided that their total combined aggregate anthropogenic carbon dioxide equivalent emissions of the greenhouse gases listed in Annex A do not exceed their assigned amounts calculated pursuant to their quantified emission limitation and reduction commitments inscribed in Annex B and in accordance with the provisions of Article 3. The respective emission level allocated to each of the Parties to the agreement shall be set out in that agreement.

2. The Parties to any such agreement shall notify the secretariat of the terms of the agreement on the date of deposit of their instruments of ratification, acceptance or approval of this Protocol, or accession thereto. The secretariat shall in turn inform the Parties and signatories to the Convention of the terms of the agreement.

3. Any such agreement shall remain in operation for the duration of the commitment period specified in Article 3, paragraph 7.

4. If Parties acting jointly do so in the framework of, and together with, a regional economic integration organization, any alteration in the composition of the organization after adoption of this Protocol shall not affect existing commitments under this Protocol. Any alteration in the composition of the organization shall only apply for the purposes of those commitments under Article 3 that are adopted subsequent to that alteration.

5. In the event of failure by the Parties to such an agreement to achieve their total combined level of emission reductions, each Party to that agreement shall be responsible for its own level of emissions set out in the agreement.

6. If Parties acting jointly do so in the framework of, and together with, a regional economic integration organization which is itself a Party to this Protocol, each member

State of that regional economic integration organization individually, and together with the regional economic integration organization acting in accordance with Article 24, shall, in the event of failure to achieve the total combined level of emission reductions, be responsible for its level of emissions as notified in accordance with this Article.

Article 5

1. Each Party included in Annex I shall have in place, no later than one year prior to the start of the first commitment period, a national system for the estimation of anthropogenic emissions by sources and removals by sinks of all greenhouse gases not controlled by the Montreal Protocol. Guidelines for such national systems, which shall incorporate the methodologies specified in paragraph 2 below, shall be decided upon by the Conference of the Parties serving as the meeting of the Parties to this Protocol at its first session.

2. Methodologies for estimating anthropogenic emissions by sources and removals by sinks of all greenhouse gases not controlled by the *Montreal Protocol* shall be those accepted by the Intergovernmental Panel on Climate Change and agreed upon by the Conference of the Parties at its third session. Where such methodologies are not used, appropriate adjustments shall be applied according to methodologies agreed upon by the Conference of the Parties serving as the meeting of the Parties to this Protocol at its first session. Based on the work of, inter alia, the Intergovernmental Panel on Climate Change and advice provided by the Subsidiary Body for Scientific and Technological Advice, the Conference of the Parties serving as the meeting of the Parties to this Protocol shall regularly review and, as appropriate, revise such methodologies and adjustments, taking fully into account any relevant decisions by the Conference of the Parties. Any revision to methodologies or adjustments shall be used only for the purposes of ascertaining compliance with commitments under Article 3 in respect of any commitment period adopted subsequent to that revision.

3. The global warming potentials used to calculate the carbon dioxide equivalence of anthropogenic emissions by sources and removals by sinks of greenhouse gases listed in Annex A shall be those accepted by the Intergovernmental Panel on Climate Change and agreed upon by the Conference of the Parties at its third session. Based on the work of, inter alia, the Intergovernmental Panel on Climate Change and advice provided by the Subsidiary Body for Scientific and Technological Advice, the Conference of the Parties serving as the meeting of the Parties to this Protocol shall regularly review and, as appropriate, revise the global warming potential of each such greenhouse gas, taking fully into account any relevant decisions by the Conference of the Parties. Any revision to a global warming potential shall apply only to commitments under Article 3 in respect of any commitment period adopted subsequent to that revision.

Article 6

1. For the purpose of meeting its commitments under Article 3, any Party included in Annex I may transfer to, or acquire from, any other such Party emission reduction units resulting from projects aimed at reducing anthropogenic emissions by sources or enhancing anthropogenic removals by sinks of greenhouse gases in any sector of the economy, provided that:

(a) Any such project has the approval of the Parties involved;

(b) Any such project provides a reduction in emissions by sources, or an enhancement of removals by sinks, that is additional to any that would otherwise occur;

(c) It does not acquire any emission reduction units if it is not in compliance with its obligations under Articles 5 and 7; and

(d) The acquisition of emission reduction units shall be supplemental to domestic actions for the purposes of meeting commitments under Article 3.

2. The Conference of the Parties serving as the meeting of the Parties to this Protocol may, at its first session or as soon as practicable thereafter, further elaborate guidelines for the implementation of this Article, including for verification and reporting.

3. A Party included in Annex I may authorize legal entities to participate, under its responsibility, in actions leading to the generation, transfer or acquisition under this Article of emission reduction units.

4. If a question of implementation by a Party included in Annex I of the requirements referred to in this Article is identified in accordance with the relevant provisions of Article 8, transfers and acquisitions of emission reduction units may continue to be made after the question has been identified, provided that any such units may not be used by a Party to meet its commitments under Article 3 until any issue of compliance is resolved.

Article 7

1. Each Party included in Annex I shall incorporate in its annual inventory of anthropogenic emissions by sources and removals by sinks of greenhouse gases not controlled by the Montreal Protocol, submitted in accordance with the relevant decisions of the Conference of the Parties, the necessary supplementary information for the purposes of ensuring compliance with Article 3, to be determined in accordance with paragraph 4 below.

2. Each Party included in Annex I shall incorporate in its national communication, submitted under Article 12 of the Convention, the supplementary information necessary to demonstrate compliance with its commitments under this Protocol, to be determined in accordance with paragraph 4 below.

3. Each Party included in Annex I shall submit the information required under paragraph 1 above annually, beginning with the first inventory due under the Convention

for the first year of the commitment period after this Protocol has entered into force for that Party. Each such Party shall submit the information required under paragraph 2 above as part of the first national communication due under the Convention after this Protocol has entered into force for it and after the adoption of guidelines as provided for in paragraph 4 below. The frequency of subsequent submission of information required under this Article shall be determined by the Conference of the Parties serving as the meeting of the Parties to this Protocol, taking into account any timetable for the submission of national communications decided upon by the Conference of the Parties.

4. The Conference of the Parties serving as the meeting of the Parties to this Protocol shall adopt at its first session, and review periodically thereafter, guidelines for the preparation of the information required under this Article, taking into account guidelines for the preparation of national communications by Parties included in Annex I adopted by the Conference of the Parties. The Conference of the Parties serving as the meeting of the Parties to this Protocol shall also, prior to the first commitment period, decide upon modalities for the accounting of assigned amounts.

Article 8

1. The information submitted under Article 7 by each Party included in Annex I shall be reviewed by expert review teams pursuant to the relevant decisions of the Conference of the Parties and in accordance with guidelines adopted for this purpose by the Conference of the Parties serving as the meeting of the Parties to this Protocol under paragraph 4 below. The information submitted under Article 7, paragraph 1, by each Party included in Annex I shall be reviewed as part of the annual compilation and accounting of emissions inventories and assigned amounts. Additionally, the information submitted under Article 7, paragraph 2, by each Party included in Annex I shall be reviewed as part of the review of communications.

2. Expert review teams shall be coordinated by the secretariat and shall be composed of experts selected from those nominated by Parties to the Convention and, as appropriate, by intergovernmental organizations, in accordance with guidance provided for this purpose by the Conference of the Parties.

3. The review process shall provide a thorough and comprehensive technical assessment of all aspects of the implementation by a Party of this Protocol. The expert review teams shall prepare a report to the Conference of the Parties serving as the meeting of the Parties to this Protocol, assessing the implementation of the commitments of the Party and identifying any potential problems in, and factors influencing, the fulfilment of commitments. Such reports shall be circulated by the secretariat to all Parties to the Convention. The secretariat shall list those questions of implementation indicated in such reports for further consideration by the Conference of the Parties serving as the meeting of the Parties to this Protocol.

4. The Conference of the Parties serving as the meeting of the Parties to this Protocol shall adopt at its first session, and review periodically thereafter, guidelines for the review of implementation of this Protocol by expert review teams taking into account the relevant decisions of the Conference of the Parties.

5. The Conference of the Parties serving as the meeting of the Parties to this Protocol shall, with the assistance of the Subsidiary Body for Implementation and, as appropriate, the Subsidiary Body for Scientific and Technological Advice, consider:

(a) The information submitted by Parties under Article 7 and the reports of the expert reviews thereon conducted under this Article; and

(b) Those questions of implementation listed by the secretariat under paragraph 3 above, as well as any questions raised by Parties.

6. Pursuant to its consideration of the information referred to in paragraph 5 above, the Conference of the Parties serving as the meeting of the Parties to this Protocol shall take decisions on any matter required for the implementation of this Protocol.

Article 9

1. The Conference of the Parties serving as the meeting of the Parties to this Protocol shall periodically review this Protocol in the light of the best available scientific information and assessments on climate change and its impacts, as well as relevant technical, social and economic information. Such reviews shall be coordinated with pertinent reviews under the Convention, in particular those required by Article 4, paragraph 2(d), and Article 7, paragraph 2(a), of the Convention. Based on these reviews, the Conference of the Parties serving as the meeting of the Parties to this Protocol shall take appropriate action.

2. The first review shall take place at the second session of the Conference of the Parties serving as the meeting of the Parties to this Protocol. Further reviews shall take place at regular intervals and in a timely manner.

Article 10

All Parties, taking into account their common but differentiated responsibilities and their specific national and regional development priorities, objectives and circumstances, without introducing any new commitments for Parties not included in Annex I, but reaffirming existing commitments under Article 4, paragraph 1, of the Convention, and continuing to advance the implementation of these commitments in order to achieve sustainable development, taking into account Article 4, paragraphs 3, 5 and 7, of the Convention, shall:

(a) Formulate, where relevant and to the extent possible, cost-effective national and, where appropriate, regional programmes to improve the quality of local emission factors, activity data and/or models which reflect the socioeconomic conditions of each

Party for the preparation and periodic updating of national inventories of anthropogenic emissions by sources and removals by sinks of all greenhouse gases not controlled by the *Montreal Protocol*, using comparable methodologies to be agreed upon by the Conference of the Parties, and consistent with the guidelines for the preparation of national communications adopted by the Conference of the Parties;

(b) Formulate, implement, publish and regularly update national and, where appropriate, regional programmes containing measures to mitigate climate change and measures to facilitate adequate adaptation to climate change:

  i. Such programmes would, inter alia, concern the energy, transport and industry sectors as well as agriculture, forestry and waste management. Furthermore, adaptation technologies and methods for improving spatial planning would improve adaptation to climate change; and

  ii. Parties included in Annex I shall submit information on action under this Protocol, including national programmes, in accordance with Article 7; and other Parties shall seek to include in their national communications, as appropriate, information on programmes which contain measures that the Party believes contribute to addressing climate change and its adverse impacts, including the abatement of increases in greenhouse gas emissions, and enhancement of and removals by sinks, capacity building and adaptation measures;

(c) Cooperate in the promotion of effective modalities for the development, application and diffusion of, and take all practicable steps to promote, facilitate and finance, as appropriate, the transfer of, or access to, environmentally sound technologies, know-how, practices and processes pertinent to climate change, in particular to developing countries, including the formulation of policies and programmes for the effective transfer of environmentally sound technologies that are publicly owned or in the public domain and the creation of an enabling environment for the private sector, to promote and enhance the transfer of, and access to, environmentally sound technologies;

(d) Cooperate in scientific and technical research and promote the maintenance and the development of systematic observation systems and development of data archives to reduce uncertainties related to the climate system, the adverse impacts of climate change and the economic and social consequences of various response strategies, and promote the development and strengthening of endogenous capacities and capabilities to participate in international and intergovernmental efforts, programmes and networks on research and systematic observation, taking into account Article 5 of the Convention;

(e) Cooperate in and promote at the international level, and, where appropriate, using existing bodies, the development and implementation of education and training programmes, including the strengthening of national capacity building, in particular human and institutional capacities and the exchange or secondment of personnel to train experts in this field, in particular for developing countries, and facilitate at the national level public awareness of, and public access to information on, climate change. Suitable modalities should be developed to implement these activities through the relevant bodies of the Convention, taking into account Article 6 of the Convention;

(f) Include in their national communications information on programmes and activities undertaken pursuant to this Article in accordance with relevant decisions of the Conference of the Parties; and

(g) Give full consideration, in implementing the commitments under this Article, to Article 4, paragraph 8, of the Convention.

Article 11

1. In the implementation of Article 10, Parties shall take into account the provisions of Article 4, paragraphs 4, 5, 7, 8 and 9, of the Convention.

2. In the context of the implementation of Article 4, paragraph 1, of the Convention, in accordance with the provisions of Article 4, paragraph 3, and Article 11 of the Convention, and through the entity or entities entrusted with the operation of the financial mechanism of the Convention, the developed country Parties and other developed Parties included in Annex II to the Convention shall:

(a) Provide new and additional financial resources to meet the agreed full costs incurred by developing country Parties in advancing the implementation of existing commitments under Article 4, paragraph 1(a), of the Convention that are covered in Article 10, subparagraph (a); and

(b) Also provide such financial resources, including for the transfer of technology, needed by the developing country Parties to meet the agreed full incremental costs of advancing the implementation of existing commitments under Article 4, paragraph 1, of the Convention that are covered by Article 10 and that are agreed between a developing country Party and the international entity or entities referred to in Article 11 of the Convention, in accordance with that Article.

The implementation of these existing commitments shall take into account the need for adequacy and predictability in the flow of funds and the importance of appropriate burden sharing among developed country Parties. The guidance to the entity or entities entrusted with the operation of the financial mechanism of the Convention in relevant decisions of the Conference of the Parties, including those agreed before the adoption of this Protocol, shall apply *mutatis mutandis* to the provisions of this paragraph.

3. The developed country Parties and other developed Parties in Annex II to the Convention may also provide, and developing country Parties avail themselves of, financial resources for the implementation of Article 10, through bilateral, regional and other multilateral channels.

Article 12

1. A clean development mechanism is hereby defined.

2. The purpose of the clean development mechanism shall be to assist Parties not included in Annex I in achieving sustainable development and in contributing to the ultimate objective of the Convention, and to assist Parties included in Annex I in achieving compliance with their quantified emission limitation and reduction commitments under Article 3.

3. Under the clean development mechanism:

(a) Parties not included in Annex I will benefit from project activities resulting in certified emission reductions; and

(b) Parties included in Annex I may use the certified emission reductions accruing from such project activities to contribute to compliance with part of their quantified emission limitation and reduction commitments under Article 3, as determined by the Conference of the Parties serving as the meeting of the Parties to this Protocol.

4. The clean development mechanism shall be subject to the authority and guidance of the Conference of the Parties serving as the meeting of the Parties to this Protocol and be supervised by an executive board of the clean development mechanism.

5. Emission reductions resulting from each project activity shall be certified by operational entities to be designated by the Conference of the Parties serving as the meeting of the Parties to this Protocol, on the basis of:

(a) Voluntary participation approved by each Party involved;

(b) Real, measurable, and long-term benefits related to the mitigation of climate change; and

(c) Reductions in emissions that are additional to any that would occur in the absence of the certified project activity.

6. The clean development mechanism shall assist in arranging funding of certified project activities as necessary.

7. The Conference of the Parties serving as the meeting of the Parties to this Protocol shall, at its first session, elaborate modalities and procedures with the objective of ensuring transparency, efficiency and accountability through independent auditing and verification of project activities.

8. The Conference of the Parties serving as the meeting of the Parties to this Protocol shall ensure that a share of the proceeds from certified project activities is used to cover administrative expenses as well as to assist developing country Parties that are particularly vulnerable to the adverse effects of climate change to meet the costs of adaptation.

9. Participation under the clean development mechanism, including in activities mentioned in paragraph 3(a) above and in the acquisition of certified emission

reductions, may involve private and/or public entities, and is to be subject to whatever guidance may be provided by the executive board of the clean development mechanism.

10. Certified emission reductions obtained during the period from the year 2000 up to the beginning of the first commitment period can be used to assist in achieving compliance in the first commitment period.

Article 13

1. The Conference of the Parties, the supreme body of the Convention, shall serve as the meeting of the Parties to this Protocol.

2. Parties to the Convention that are not Parties to this Protocol may participate as observers in the proceedings of any session of the Conference of the Parties serving as the meeting of the Parties to this Protocol. When the Conference of the Parties serves as the meeting of the Parties to this Protocol, decisions under this Protocol shall be taken only by those that are Parties to this Protocol.

3. When the Conference of the Parties serves as the meeting of the Parties to this Protocol, any member of the Bureau of the Conference of the Parties representing a Party to the Convention but, at that time, not a Party to this Protocol, shall be replaced by an additional member to be elected by and from amongst the Parties to this Protocol.

4. The Conference of the Parties serving as the meeting of the Parties to this Protocol shall keep under regular review the implementation of this Protocol and shall make, within its mandate, the decisions necessary to promote its effective implementation. It shall perform the functions assigned to it by this Protocol and shall:

(a) Assess, on the basis of all information made available to it in accordance with the provisions of this Protocol, the implementation of this Protocol by the Parties, the overall effects of the measures taken pursuant to this Protocol, in particular environmental, economic and social effects as well as their cumulative impacts and the extent to which progress towards the objective of the Convention is being achieved;

(b) Periodically examine the obligations of the Parties under this Protocol, giving due consideration to any reviews required by Article 4, paragraph 2(d), and Article 7, paragraph 2, of the Convention, in the light of the objective of the Convention, the experience gained in its implementation and the evolution of scientific and technological knowledge, and in this respect consider and adopt regular reports on the implementation of this Protocol;

(c) Promote and facilitate the exchange of information on measures adopted by the Parties to address climate change and its effects, taking into account the differing circumstances, responsibilities and capabilities of the Parties and their respective commitments under this Protocol;

(d) Facilitate, at the request of two or more Parties, the coordination of measures adopted by them to address climate change and its effects, taking into account the differing circumstances, responsibilities and capabilities of the Parties and their respective commitments under this Protocol;

(e) Promote and guide, in accordance with the objective of the Convention and the provisions of this Protocol, and taking fully into account the relevant decisions by the Conference of the Parties, the development and periodic refinement of comparable methodologies for the effective implementation of this Protocol, to be agreed on by the Conference of the Parties serving as the meeting of the Parties to this Protocol;

(f) Make recommendations on any matters necessary for the implementation of this Protocol;

(g) Seek to mobilize additional financial resources in accordance with Article 11, paragraph 2;

(h) Establish such subsidiary bodies as are deemed necessary for the implementation of this Protocol;

(i) Seek and utilize, where appropriate, the services and cooperation of, and information provided by, competent international organizations and intergovernmental and non-governmental bodies; and

(j) Exercise such other functions as may be required for the implementation of this Protocol, and consider any assignment resulting from a decision by the Conference of the Parties.

5. The rules of procedure of the Conference of the Parties and financial procedures applied under the Convention shall be applied *mutatis mutandis* under this Protocol, except as may be otherwise decided by consensus by the Conference of the Parties serving as the meeting of the Parties to this Protocol.

6. The first session of the Conference of the Parties serving as the meeting of the Parties to this Protocol shall be convened by the secretariat in conjunction with the first session of the Conference of the Parties that is scheduled after the date of the entry into force of this Protocol. Subsequent ordinary sessions of the Conference of the Parties serving as the meeting of the Parties to this Protocol shall be held every year and in conjunction with ordinary sessions of the Conference of the Parties, unless otherwise decided by the Conference of the Parties serving as the meeting of the Parties to this Protocol.

7. Extraordinary sessions of the Conference of the Parties serving as the meeting of the Parties to this Protocol shall be held at such other times as may be deemed necessary by the Conference of the Parties serving as the meeting of the Parties to this Protocol, or at the written request of any Party, provided that, within six months of the request being communicated to the Parties by the secretariat, it is supported by at least one third of the Parties.

8. The United Nations, its specialized agencies and the International Atomic Energy

Agency, as well as any State member thereof or observers thereto not party to the Convention, may be represented at sessions of the Conference of the Parties serving as the meeting of the Parties to this Protocol as observers. Any body or agency, whether national or international, governmental or non-governmental, which is qualified in matters covered by this Protocol and which has informed the secretariat of its wish to be represented at a session of the Conference of the Parties serving as the meeting of the Parties to this Protocol as an observer, may be so admitted unless at least one third of the Parties present object. The admission and participation of observers shall be subject to the rules of procedure, as referred to in paragraph 5 above.

Article 14

1. The secretariat established by Article 8 of the Convention shall serve as the secretariat of this Protocol.

2. Article 8, paragraph 2, of the Convention on the functions of the secretariat, and Article 8, paragraph 3, of the Convention on arrangements made for the functioning of the secretariat, shall apply *mutatis mutandis* to this Protocol. The secretariat shall, in addition, exercise the functions assigned to it under this Protocol.

Article 15

1. The Subsidiary Body for Scientific and Technological Advice and the Subsidiary Body for Implementation established by Articles 9 and 10 of the Convention shall serve as, respectively, the Subsidiary Body for Scientific and Technological Advice and the Subsidiary Body for Implementation of this Protocol. The provisions relating to the functioning of these two bodies under the Convention shall apply *mutatis mutandis* to this Protocol. Sessions of the meetings of the Subsidiary Body for Scientific and Technological Advice and the Subsidiary Body for Implementation of this Protocol shall be held in conjunction with the meetings of, respectively, the Subsidiary Body for Scientific and Technological Advice and the Subsidiary Body for Implementation of the Convention.

2. Parties to the Convention that are not Parties to this Protocol may participate as observers in the proceedings of any session of the subsidiary bodies. When the subsidiary bodies serve as the subsidiary bodies of this Protocol, decisions under this Protocol shall be taken only by those that are Parties to this Protocol.

3. When the subsidiary bodies established by Articles 9 and 10 of the Convention exercise their functions with regard to matters concerning this Protocol, any member of the Bureaux of those subsidiary bodies representing a Party to the Convention but, at that time, not a party to this Protocol, shall be replaced by an additional member to be elected by and from amongst the Parties to this Protocol.

Article 16

The Conference of the Parties serving as the meeting of the Parties to this Protocol shall, as soon as practicable, consider the application to this Protocol of, and modify as appropriate, the multilateral consultative process referred to in Article 13 of the Convention, in the light of any relevant decisions that may be taken by the Conference of the Parties. Any multilateral consultative process that may be applied to this Protocol shall operate without prejudice to the procedures and mechanisms established in accordance with Article 18.

Article 17

The Conference of the Parties shall define the relevant principles, modalities, rules and guidelines, in particular for verification, reporting and accountability for emissions trading. The Parties included in Annex B may participate in emissions trading for the purposes of fulfilling their commitments under Article 3. Any such trading shall be supplemental to domestic actions for the purpose of meeting quantified emission limitation and reduction commitments under that Article.

Article 18

The Conference of the Parties serving as the meeting of the Parties to this Protocol shall, at its first session, approve appropriate and effective procedures and mechanisms to determine and to address cases of non-compliance with the provisions of this Protocol, including through the development of an indicative list of consequences, taking into account the cause, type, degree and frequency of non-compliance. Any procedures and mechanisms under this Article entailing binding consequences shall be adopted by means of an amendment to this Protocol.

Article 19

The provisions of Article 14 of the Convention on settlement of disputes shall apply *mutatis mutandis* to this Protocol.

Article 20

1. Any Party may propose amendments to this Protocol.

2. Amendments to this Protocol shall be adopted at an ordinary session of the Conference of the Parties serving as the meeting of the Parties to this Protocol. The text of any proposed amendment to this Protocol shall be communicated to the Parties by the secretariat at least six months before the meeting at which it is proposed for adoption. The secretariat shall also communicate the text of any proposed amendments to the Parties and signatories to the Convention and, for information, to the Depositary.

3. The Parties shall make every effort to reach agreement on any proposed amendment to this Protocol by consensus. If all efforts at consensus have been exhausted, and no agreement reached, the amendment shall as a last resort be adopted by a three-fourths majority vote of the Parties present and voting at the meeting. The adopted amendment shall be communicated by the secretariat to the Depositary, who shall circulate it to all Parties for

their acceptance.

4. Instruments of acceptance in respect of an amendment shall be deposited with the Depositary. An amendment adopted in accordance with paragraph 3 above shall enter into force for those Parties having accepted it on the ninetieth day after the date of receipt by the Depositary of an instrument of acceptance by at least three fourths of the Parties to this Protocol.

5. The amendment shall enter into force for any other Party on the ninetieth day after the date on which that Party deposits with the Depositary its instrument of acceptance of the said amendment.

Article 21

1. Annexes to this Protocol shall form an integral part thereof and, unless otherwise expressly provided, a reference to this Protocol constitutes at the same time a reference to any annexes thereto. Any annexes adopted after the entry into force of this Protocol shall be restricted to lists, forms and any other material of a descriptive nature that is of a scientific, technical, procedural or administrative character.

2. Any Party may make proposals for an annex to this Protocol and may propose amendments to annexes to this Protocol.

3. Annexes to this Protocol and amendments to annexes to this Protocol shall be adopted at an ordinary session of the Conference of the Parties serving as the meeting of the Parties to this Protocol. The text of any proposed annex or amendment to an annex shall be communicated to the Parties by the secretariat at least six months before the meeting at which it is proposed for adoption. The secretariat shall also communicate the text of any proposed annex or amendment to an annex to the Parties and signatories to the Convention and, for information, to the Depositary.

4. The Parties shall make every effort to reach agreement on any proposed annex or amendment to an annex by consensus. If all efforts at consensus have been exhausted, and no agreement reached, the annex or amendment to an annex shall as a last resort be adopted by a three-fourths majority vote of the Parties present and voting at the meeting. The adopted annex or amendment to an annex shall be communicated by the secretariat to the Depositary, who shall circulate it to all Parties for their acceptance.

5. An annex, or amendment to an annex other than Annex A or B, that has been adopted in accordance with paragraphs 3 and 4 above shall enter into force for all Parties to this Protocol six months after the date of the communication by the Depositary to such Parties of the adoption of the annex or adoption of the amendment to the annex, except for those Parties that have notified the Depositary, in writing, within that period of their non-acceptance of the annex or amendment to the annex. The annex or amendment to an annex shall enter into force for Parties which withdraw their notification of non-

acceptance on the ninetieth day after the date on which withdrawal of such notification has been received by the Depositary.

6. If the adoption of an annex or an amendment to an annex involves an amendment to this Protocol, that annex or amendment to an annex shall not enter into force until such time as the amendment to this Protocol enters into force.

7. Amendments to Annexes A and B to this Protocol shall be adopted and enter into force in accordance with the procedure set out in Article 20, provided that any amendment to Annex B shall be adopted only with the written consent of the Party concerned.

Article 22

1. Each Party shall have one vote, except as provided for in paragraph 2 below.

2. Regional economic integration organizations, in matters within their competence, shall exercise their right to vote with a number of votes equal to the number of their member States that are Parties to this Protocol. Such an organization shall not exercise its right to vote if any of its member States exercises its right, and *vice versa*.

Article 23

The Secretary-General of the United Nations shall be the Depositary of this Protocol.

Article 24

1. This Protocol shall be open for signature and subject to ratification, acceptance or approval by States and regional economic integration organizations which are Parties to the Convention. It shall be open for signature at United Nations Headquarters in New York from 16 March 1998 to 15 March 1999. This Protocol shall be open for accession from the day after the date on which it is closed for signature. Instruments of ratification, acceptance, approval or accession shall be deposited with the Depositary.

2. Any regional economic integration organization which becomes a Party to this Protocol without any of its member States being a Party shall be bound by all the obligations under this Protocol. In the case of such organizations, one or more of whose member States is a Party to this Protocol, the organization and its member States shall decide on their respective responsibilities for the performance of their obligations under this Protocol. In such cases, the organization and the member States shall not be entitled to exercise rights under this Protocol concurrently.

3. In their instruments of ratification, acceptance, approval or accession, regional economic integration organizations shall declare the extent of their competence with respect to the matters governed by this Protocol. These organizations shall also inform the Depositary, who shall in turn inform the Parties, of any substantial modification in the extent of their competence.

Article 25

1. This Protocol shall enter into force on the ninetieth day after the date on which

not less than 55 Parties to the Convention, incorporating Parties included in Annex I which accounted in total for at least 55 per cent of the total carbon dioxide emissions for 1990 of the Parties included in Annex I, have deposited their instruments of ratification, acceptance, approval or accession.

2. For the purposes of this Article, "the total carbon dioxide emissions for 1990 of the Parties included in Annex I" means the amount communicated on or before the date of adoption of this Protocol by the Parties included in Annex I in their first national communications submitted in accordance with Article 12 of the Convention.

3. For each State or regional economic integration organization that ratifies, accepts or approves this Protocol or accedes thereto after the conditions set out in paragraph 1 above for entry into force have been fulfilled, this Protocol shall enter into force on the ninetieth day following the date of deposit of its instrument of ratification, acceptance, approval or accession.

4. For the purposes of this Article, any instrument deposited by a regional economic integration organization shall not be counted as additional to those deposited by States members of the organization.

Article 26

No reservations may be made to this Protocol.

Article 27

1. At any time after three years from the date on which this Protocol has entered into force for a Party, that Party may withdraw from this Protocol by giving written notification to the Depositary.

2. Any such withdrawal shall take effect upon expiry of one year from the date of receipt by the Depositary of the notification of withdrawal, or on such later date as may be specified in the notification of withdrawal.

3. Any Party that withdraws from the Convention shall be considered as also having withdrawn from this Protocol.

Article 28

The original of this Protocol, of which the Arabic, Chinese, English, French, Russian and Spanish texts are equally authentic, shall be deposited with the Secretary-General of the United Nations.

Done at Kyoto this eleventh day of December one thousand nine hundred and ninety-seven.

IN WITNESS WHEREOF the undersigned, being duly authorized to that effect, have affixed their signatures to this Protocol on the dates indicated.

Annex A

Greenhouse gases

Carbon dioxide (CO_2)

Methane (CH_4)

Nitrous oxide (N_2O)

Hydrofluorocarbons (HFCs)

Perfluorocarbons (PFCs)

Sulphur hexafluoride (SF_6)

Sectors/source categories

Energy

  Fuel combustion

    Energy industries

    Manufacturing industries and construction

    Transport

    Other sectors

    Other

  Fugitive emissions from fuels

    Solid fuels

    Oil and natural gas

    Other

  Industrial processes

    Mineral products

    Chemical industry

    Metal production

    Other production

    Production of halocarbons and sulphur hexafluoride

    Consumption of halocarbons and sulphur hexafluoride

    Other

  Solvent and other product use

  Agriculture

    Enteric fermentation

    Manure management

    Rice cultivation

    Agricultural soils

    Prescribed burning of savannas

    Field burning of agricultural residues

    Other

  Waste

    Solid waste disposal on land

    Wastewater handling

Waste incineration

Other

Annex B

Party	Quantified emission limitation or reduction commitment (percentage of base year or period)	Party	Quantified emission limitation or reduction commitment (percentage of base year or period)
Australia	108	Japan	94
Austria	92	Latvia*	92
Belgium	92	Liechtenstein	92
Bulgaria*	92	Lithuania*	92
Canada	94	Luxembourg	92
Croatia*	95	Monaco	92
Czech Republic*	92	Netherlands	92
Denmark	92	New Zealand	100
Estonia*	92	Norway	101
European Community	92	Poland*	94
Finland	92	Portugal	92
France	92	Romania*	92
Germany	92	Russian Federation*	100
Greece	92	Slovakia*	92
Hungary*	94	Slovenia*	92
Iceland	110	Spain	92
Ireland	92	Sweden	92
Italy	92	Switzerland	92
Ukraine*	100	Britain and Northern Ireland	92
United Kingdom of Great		United States of America	93

* Countries that are undergoing the process of transition to a market economy.

(Source: https://environment.yale.edu/publication-series/documents/downloads/a-g/AppxKyoto.pdf)

三、注解(Notes)

1. International Civil Aviation Organization

《国际民用航空公约》,通称《芝加哥公约》。1944年11月1日,52个国家参加了在芝加哥召开的国际会议,签订了《国际民用航空公约》,按照公约规定成立了临时国际民航组织。1947年4月4日,《芝加哥公约》正式生效。1947年5月13日,国际民航组织正式成为联合国的一个专门机构。我国是国际民航组织的创始国之一,1944 年签署了《国际民用航空公约》,1946 年正式成为会员国。

2. International Maritime Organization

国际海事组织是联合国负责海上航行安全和防止船舶造成海洋污染的一个专门机构,总部设在英国伦敦。该组织最早成立于 1959 年 1 月 6 日,原名"政府间海事协商组织",1982 年 5 月更名为国际海事组织,截至 2012 年 9 月,已有 171 个正式成员。

3. Intergovernmental Panel on Climate Change

联合国政府间气候变化专门委员会(IPCC)是世界气象组织(World Meteorological Organization,WMO)及联合国环境规划署(United Nations Environment Programme,UNEP)于 1988 年联合建立的政府间机构。联合国政府间气候变化专门委员会的作用是在全面、客观、公开和透明的基础上,为决策人提供对气候变化的科学评估,评估天气变化所带来的影响和潜在威胁,并提供适应或减缓气候变迁影响的相关建议。

四、相关词汇(Key Words and Phrases)

1.	meteorological	[ˌmiːtɪərəˈlɒdʒɪkəl]	adj.	气象的;气象学的
2.	affirmative	[əˈfɜːmətɪv]	adj.	肯定的;积极的
			n.	肯定;赞成的一方
3.	notification	[ˌnəʊtɪfɪˈkeɪʃn]	n.	通知;通告;[法]告示
4.	elaborate	[ɪˈlæb(ə)rət]	adj.	精心制作的;详尽的
			v.	精心制作;详细阐述
5.	fiscal	[ˈfɪsk(ə)l]	adj.	会计的,财政的;国库的
6.	exemption	[ɪɡˈzempʃn]	n.	免除,豁免;免税
7.	comparability	[ˌkɒmpərəˈbɪləti]	n.	相似性;可比较性
8.	verifiable	[ˈvɛrəfaɪəbl]	adj.	可证实的;能作证的;可检验的
9.	subsequent	[ˈsʌbsɪkw(ə)nt]	adj.	随后的
10.	initiate	[ɪˈnɪʃɪeɪt]	vt.	开始,创始;发起
			adj.	新加入的;接受初步知识的
11.	subtract	[səbˈtrækt]	vt.	减去;扣掉
12.	equivalent	[ɪˈkwɪv(ə)l(ə)nt]	adj.	(在价值、数量等方面)相等的
			n.	对等的人(或事物)
13.	signatory	[ˈsɪɡnət(ə)rɪ]	n.	(协议的)签名人,签约国
			adj.	签署的,签约的
14.	integration	[ˌɪntɪˈɡreɪʃ(ə)n]	n.	集成;综合
15.	ascertain	[ˌæsəˈteɪn]	vt.	确定;查明;探知
16.	compliance	[kəmˈplaɪəns]	n.	顺从,服从;符合;屈从;可塑性

17. subsidiary	[səbˈsɪdɪərɪ]	adj.	辅助的，次要的；附属的；子公司的
18. consensus	[kənˈsensəs]	n.	一致；舆论；合意；复数 consensuses
19. compilation	[kɒmpɪˈleɪʃ(ə)n]	n.	编译；编辑；汇编
20. circulate	[ˈsɜːkjʊleɪt]	vi.	传播，流传；循环；流通
21. pertinent	[ˈpɜːtɪnənt]	adj.	相关的，相干的；中肯的；切题的
22. reaffirming	[riːəˈfɜːm]	vt.	再肯定，重申；再断言
23. secondment	[sɪˈkɒndmənt]	n.	借调，暂借
24. mitigation	[mɪtɪˈgeɪʃ(ə)n]	n.	减轻；缓和；平静
25. vulnerable	[ˈvʌlnərəbl]	adj.	易受攻击的，易受…的攻击；易受伤害的；有弱点的
26. *mutatis mutandis*			加上必要的变更；细节上做必要的修改

五、长难句(Difficult Sentences)

1. The Parties included in Annex I shall, individually or jointly, ensure that their aggregate anthropogenic carbon dioxide equivalent emissions of the greenhouse gases listed in Annex A do not exceed their assigned amounts, calculated pursuant to their quantified emission limitation and reduction commitments inscribed in Annex B and in accordance with the provisions of this Article, with a view to reducing their overall emissions of such gases by at least 5 per cent below 1990 levels in the commitment period 2008 to 2012. (Article 3, 1)

解析：句子的主干是 The parties ensure that…，其中 ensure 由副词 individually 和 jointly 修饰。整个宾语从句的主语是 their aggregate anthropogenic carbon dioxide equivalent emissions of the greenhouse gases，谓语是 do not exceed，宾语为 assigned amounts，其后有两个由 calculated pursuant to 和 in accordance with 引导的后置定语起修饰、限定的作用。句子最后是表示目的的介词短语 with a view to。

译文：附件一所列缔约方应单独或共同确保其在附件 A 中所列温室气体的人为二氧化碳当量排放总量不超过附件 B 中据本条约规定所载其量化的限制计算出的分配数量和减少排放承诺，以期在 2008 年至 2012 年承诺期内这些气体的总排放量比 1990 年水平至少减少 5%。

2. Prior to the first session of the Conference of the Parties serving as the meeting of the Parties to this Protocol, each Party included in Annex I shall provide, for consideration by the Subsidiary Body for Scientific and Technological Advice, data to establish its level of carbon stocks in 1990 and to enable an estimate to be made of its changes in carbon stocks in subsequent years. (Article 3, 4)

解析：句子开始是一个由 prior to 引导的介词短语，其中，现在分词 serving 作定语修饰 the first session of the Conference of the Parties。句子的主语是 each Party，谓语和宾语是 shall provide data，其后有两个并列 to 引导的不定式表示目的。for consideration by the Subsidiary Body for Scientific and Technological Advice 为插入语。

译文：在本公约第一届缔约方会议举行之前，附件一所列各缔约方应提供数据供所属科技咨询机构审议，以便确定其1990年的碳储量水平，并能对其以后各年的碳储量变化进行预估。

3. In line with relevant decisions of the Conference of the Parties on the implementation of those paragraphs, the Conference of the Parties serving as the meeting of the Parties to this Protocol shall, at its first session, consider what actions are necessary to minimize the adverse effects of climate change and/or the impacts of response measures on Parties referred to in those paragraphs. (Article 3, 14)

解析：本句以介词短语 in line with 开始。in line with 的意思是：依照，符合，与……保持一致。主语是 the Conference of the Parties，谓语是 shall consider，宾语是 what 引导的名词性从句。名词性从句的宾语是两个，一个是 adverse effects，另一个是 the impacts of response measures。

译文：依照本公约缔约方会议关于履行这些条款的相关决定，作为本公约规定的缔约方会议，应在第一届会议上审议采取何种必要行动以最大限度地减少气候变化的不利影响和/或上述条款中提到的对应措施对缔约方产生的影响。

4. If Parties acting jointly do so in the framework of, and together with, a regional economic integration organization which is itself a Party to this Protocol, each member State of that regional economic integration organization individually, and together with the regional economic integration organization acting in accordance with Article 24, shall, in the event of failure to achieve the total combined level of emission reductions, be responsible for its level of emissions as notified in accordance with this Article. (Article 4, 6)

解析：该句是一个含有由 if 引导的条件从句的复合句，句子结构是 If parties do so, each member shall be responsible for...。主句的主语为 each member，谓语是 shall be responsible for …。If 引导的从句中 Parties 为主语，分词 acting jointly 修饰限定 Parties，谓语为 do so，有两个限制，即 in the framework of a regional economic integration organization 和 together with a regional economic integration organization。后面 which 引导的定语从句修饰限定 a regional economic integration organization。In the event of 表示条件，意思是倘若，如果。

译文：如缔约方在一个本身为议定书缔约方的区域经济一体化组织的框架内并与该组织一起共同行事，该区域经济一体化组织的每一个成员国单独地并与按照第二十四条行事的区域经济一体化组织一起，如未能达到总的合并减少排放水平,则应对依本条所通知的其排放水平负责。

5. If a question of implementation by a Party included in Annex I of the requirements referred to in this Article is identified in accordance with the relevant provisions of Article 8, transfers and acquisitions of emission reduction units may continue to be made after the question has been identified, provided that any such units may not be used by a Party to meet its commitments under Article 3 until any issue of compliance is resolved. (Article 6, 4)

解析:这是 if 引导的条件从句,句子主干是 If a question of implementation is identified, transfers and acquisition of emission reduction units may continue to be made。Provided 意思为"倘若/如果"或"但",作用相当于 if 或 but,在法律英语中应用广泛,如该短语前有主句,则它表示的是与之前陈述相反的"例外",法律界经常称这类句子为"但书"(proviso)。

译文:如依第八条有关规定查明附件一所列缔约方在履行本条所指的要求存在问题时,减少排放单位的转让和收购工作在查明问题后可继续进行,但在任何守约问题得到解决之前,缔约方不可使用任何减少排放单位来履行其依第三条的承诺。

6. All parties shall formulate, where relevant and to the extent possible, cost-effective national and, where appropriate, regional programmes to improve the quality of local emission factors, activity data and/or models which reflect the socioeconomic conditions of each Party for the preparation and periodic updating of national inventories of anthropogenic emissions by sources and removals by sinks of all greenhouse gases not controlled by the *Montreal Protocol*, using comparable methodologies to be agreed upon by the Conference of the Parties, and consistent with the guidelines for the preparation of national communications adopted by the Conference of the Parties. (Article 10, a)

解析:formulate 所引导的宾语 programmes 是由两个 where 引导的地点状语从句来修饰。to 引导的不定式表示制定方案的目的;而 which 引导的从句用来修饰 emission factors, activity data models。现在分词 using 表示伴随。

译文:所有缔约方应在相关时并在可能的范围内,制定符合成本效益的国家方案以及在适当情况下的区域方案,以改进可反映每一缔约方社会经济状况的地方排放因素、活动数据和/或模式的质量,用以编制和定期更新《蒙特利尔协定书》未予管制的温室气体的各种源的人为排放和各种汇的清除的国家清单,同时采用将由本公约缔约方会议议定的可比方法,并与本公约缔约方会议通过的国家信息通报编制指南相一致。

六、课后练习(Exercises)

1. Skimming and Scanning

Directions: Reading **Article 3** from Kyoto Protocol to the United Nations Framework Convention on Climate Change. At the end of the passage, there are six statements. Each statement contains information given in one of the paragraphs of the passage. Identify the paragraph from which the information is derived. Each paragraph is marked with a letter. You may choose a paragraph more than once. Answer the questions by writing the corresponding letter in the bracket in front of each statement.

A. The Parties included in Annex I shall, individually or jointly, ensure that their aggregate anthropogenic carbon dioxide equivalent emissions of the greenhouse gases listed in Annex A do not exceed their assigned amounts, calculated pursuant to their quantified emission limitation and reduction commitments inscribed in Annex B and in accordance with the provisions of this Article, with a view to reducing their overall emissions of such gases by at least 5 per cent below 1990 levels in the commitment period 2008 to 2012.

B. Each Party included in Annex I shall, by 2005, have made demonstrable progress in achieving its commitments under this Protocol.

C. The net changes in greenhouse gas emissions by sources and removals by sinks resulting from direct human-induced land-use change and forestry activities, limited to afforestation, reforestation and deforestation since 1990, measured as verifiable changes in carbon stocks in each commitment period, shall be used to meet the commitments under this Article of each Party included in Annex I. The greenhouse gas emissions by sources and removals by sinks associated with those activities shall be reported in a transparent and verifiable manner and reviewed in accordance with Articles 7 and 8.

D. Prior to the first session of the Conference of the Parties serving as the meeting of the Parties to this Protocol, each Party included in Annex I shall provide, for consideration by the Subsidiary Body for Scientific and Technological Advice, data to establish its level of carbon stocks in 1990 and to enable an estimate to be made of its changes in carbon stocks in subsequent years. The Conference of the Parties serving as the meeting of the Parties to this Protocol shall, at its first session or as soon as practicable thereafter, decide upon modalities, rules and guidelines as to how, and which, additional human-induced activities related to changes in greenhouse gas emissions by sources and removals by sinks in the agricultural soils and the land-use change and forestry categories shall be added to, or subtracted from, the assigned amounts for Parties included in Annex I, taking into account uncertainties, transparency in reporting, verifiability, the methodological work of the Intergovernmental Panel on Climate Change, the advice provided by the Subsidiary Body for Scientific and Technological Advice in accordance with Article 5 and the decisions of the Conference of the Parties. Such a decision shall apply in the second and subsequent commitment periods. A Party may choose to apply such a decision on these additional human-induced activities for its first commitment period, provided that these activities have taken place since 1990.

E. The Parties included in Annex I undergoing the process of transition to a market economy whose base year or period was established pursuant to decision 9/ cp. 2 of the Conference of the Parties at its second session shall use that base year or period for the implementation of their commitments under this Article. Any other Party included in Annex I undergoing the process of transition to a market economy which has not yet submitted its first national communication under Article 12 of the Convention may also notify the Conference of the Parties serving as the meeting of the Parties to this Protocol that it intends to use a historical base year or period other than 1990 for the implementation of its commitments under this Article. The Conference of the Parties serving as the meeting of the Parties to this Protocol shall decide on the acceptance of such notification.

F. Taking into account Article 4, paragraph 6, of the Convention, in the implementation of their commitments under this Protocol other than those under this Article, a certain degree of flexibility shall be allowed by the Conference of the Parties serving as the meeting of the Parties to this Protocol to the Parties included in Annex I undergoing the process of transition to a market economy.

G. In the first quantified emission limitation and reduction commitment period, from 2008 to 2012, the assigned amount for each Party included in Annex I shall be equal to the percentage inscribed for it in Annex B of its aggregate anthropogenic carbon dioxide equivalent emissions of the greenhouse gases listed in Annex A in 1990, or the base year or period determined in accordance with paragraph 5 above, multiplied by five. Those Parties included in Annex I for whom land-use change and forestry constituted a net source of greenhouse gas emissions in 1990 shall include in their 1990 emissions base year or period the aggregate anthropogenic carbon dioxide equivalent emissions by sources minus removals by sinks in 1990 from land-use change for the purposes of calculating their assigned amount.

H. Any Party included in Annex I may use 1995 as its base year for hydrofluorocarbons（氢氟碳化物）, perfluorocarbons（全氟碳化物）and sulphur hexafluoride（六氟化硫）, for the purposes of the calculation referred to in paragraph 7 above.

I. Commitments for subsequent periods for Parties included in Annex I shall be established in amendments to Annex B to this Protocol, which shall be adopted in accordance with the provisions of Article 21, paragraph 7. The Conference of the Parties serving as the meeting of the Parties to this Protocol shall initiate the consideration of such commitments at least seven years before the end of the first commitment period referred to in paragraph 1 above.

J. Any emission reduction units, or any part of an assigned amount, which a Party acquires from another Party in accordance with the provisions of Article 6 or of Article 17 shall be added to the assigned amount for the acquiring Party.

K. Any emission reduction units, or any part of an assigned amount, which a Party transfers to another Party in accordance with the provisions of Article 6 or of Article 17 shall be subtracted from the assigned amount for the transferring Party.

L. Any certified emission reductions which a Party acquires from another Party in accordance with the provisions of Article 12 shall be added to the assigned amount for the acquiring Party.

M. If the emissions of a Party included in Annex I in a commitment period are less than its assigned amount under this Article, this difference shall, on request of that Party, be added to the assigned amount for that Party for subsequent commitment periods.

N. Each Party included in Annex I shall strive to implement the commitments mentioned in paragraph 1 above in such a way as to minimize adverse social, environmental and economic impacts on developing country Parties, particularly those identified in Article 4, paragraphs 8 and 9, of the Convention. In line with relevant decisions of the Conference of the Parties on the implementation of those paragraphs, the Conference of the Parties serving as the meeting of the Parties to this Protocol shall, at its first session, consider what actions are necessary to minimize the adverse effects of climate change and/or the impacts of response measures on Parties referred to in those paragraphs. Among the issues to be considered shall be the establishment of funding, insurance and transfer of technology.

(_____) (1) The net change in greenhouse emission due to human-induced land-use change and forestry activities can be used as verifiable changes to measure the carbon stocks change in each commitment.

(_____) (2) If any Party transfers its emission reduction units to another Party, the reduced amount of carbon emission shall be subtracted from its assigned amount.

(_____) (3) All the Parties shall make sure that they will reduce their overall emission of greenhouse gas by at least 5% below 1990 levels in the commitment period 2008-2012.

(_____) (4) Each Party shall make great efforts to implement the commitments to minimize negative social, environmental and economic impacts on developing country Parties.

(_____) (5) All Parties shall at its first session decide upon rules and guidelines as to the greenhouse gas emission change by the human-induced activities and take account into uncertainties, transparency in reporting and other issues.

(_____) (6) To the parties undergoing the transition to a market economy, they will be given a certain degree of flexibility in implementing their commitments.

2. Reading Comprehension

Directions: Read **Article 10** and **Article 12** from Kyoto Protocol to the United Nations Framework Convention on Climate Change, and decide whether the following statements are True or False. Write T for True or F for False in the bracket in front of each statement.

A. Questions 1-3 are based on **Article 10**.

(1) (_____) All parties should formulate and regularly update national and regional environmental protection programs excluded those in energy, transport and industry sectors.

(2) (_____) Developing countries should be given priority to formulate, facilitate the transfer of environmentally sound technologies and practices.

(3) (_____) Education and training programs should be carried out especially in developing countries to facilitate public awareness of climate change.

B. Questions 4-6 are based on **Article 12.**

(4) (_____) The purpose of the clean development mechanism is to assist Parties included in Annex I in achieving sustainable development.

(5) (_____) Real, measurable, and long-term benefits related to the mitigation of climate change can be used as proof to show that the project activity has reduced emission.

(6) (_____) Those developing countries that are particularly vulnerable to the adverse effects of climate change need not to pay the administrative expense.

3. Extensive Reading

Directions: In this section, there was a passage with ten blanks. You are required to select one word for each blank from a list of choices given in a word bank following the passage. Read the passage through carefully before making your choices. Each choice in the blank is identified by a letter. You may not use any of the words in the blank more than once.

China has called for pilot programs that aim to promote a low-carbon economy. Seven cities and provinces-namely Beijing, Tianjin, Shanghai, Chongqing, Guangdong, Hubei and Shenzhen-will become the first batch of pilot areas that start a carbon emission rights exchange.

The new concept of carbon trading is designed to (1) _____ the European Union's Emissions Trading System. The exchange will set a (2) _____ amount of carbon dioxide that participating firms are allowed to emit every year and grant each firm an emission quota. In addition to establishing carbon exchanges in cities, the Plan also calls for the building of pilot low-carbon development zones and residential communities, in a move to create a cluster effect among both businesses and consumers.

China's rush to try new carbon trading experiments has (3) _____ the country's sense of urgency to gain a say in the global "green" competition. When carbon emissions become more costly, the ability of producing less carbon has gradually grown into a new (4) _____ advantage in the global economic race.

However, China's (5) _____ of the innovative carbon exchange program could run into some roadblocks due to the lack of a legal framework and expertise. Without a national law on carbon emissions in place, it will take local governments some time to work out an effective enforcement system. The failure of the previous (6) _____ carbon exchanges has proved that businesses lack the self-motivation to participate in carbon trading. Therefore, (7) _____ regulations with punishment specified are highly necessary for the success of carbon exchanges.

China also lacks the expertise in carbon emission measurement. The measurement in the past mainly took electricity and coal consumption into account, but missed many other types of emissions, such as those from agriculture. The lack of accuracy in carbon emission measurement will directly affect the fair distribution of emission permits to companies.

The shortage of experienced carbon trading designers and administrators could become another (8) _____. "We need people who know environmental science, as well as economics…there are very few people in China with those qualifications."an official said.

The good news is that China has decided to include greenhouse emission measures into the government statistical indicators system, and ordered pilot cities to establish dedicated funds that (9) _____ financial support for the implementation of the new program. Foreign companies with knowledge in the related field will likely find a new "blue ocean" during China's (10) _____ to the low-carbon age.

A. feasible	B. lacked	C. voluntary	D. revealed	E. ensure
F. implementation	G. transaction	H. comparative	I. transition	J. concern
K. maximum	L. contribution	M. resemble	N. application	O. emission

4. Vocabulary Expanding

Directions: In this section, there are ten sentences from Kyoto Protocol to the United Nations Framework Convention on Climate Change. You are required to complete these sentences with the proper form of the words given in the brackets.

1. In the event of failure by the Parties to such an agreement to achieve their total combined level of _____ reductions, each Party to that agreement shall be responsible for its own level set out in the agreement. (emit)

2. Each Party shall implement research on and increase use _____ forms of energy, of carbon dioxide sequestration technologies and of advanced and innovative environmentally sound technology. (new)

3. Parties shall take steps to share their experience and exchange information on such policies and measures including developing ways of improving their comparability, _____ and effectiveness. (transparent)

4. Each Party included in Annex I shall, by 2005, have made _____ progress

in achieving its commitments under this protocol. (demonstrate)

5. Each Party in achieving its qualified emission limitation and reduction _____, shall implement such policies and measures in accordance with its national circumstances. (commit)

6. Taking into account of the Convention, in the implementation of their commitments under this Protocol other than those under this Article, a certain degree of _____ will be allowed by the Conference of the Parties. (flexible)

7. Certified emission reductions obtained during the period from the year 2000 up to the beginning of the first commitment period can be used to assist in achieving _____ in the first commitment period. (comply)

8. The acquisition of emission reduction units shall be _____ to domestic actions for the purposes of meeting commitments under Article 3. (supplement)

9. The Conference of the Parties serving as the meeting of the Parties to this Protocol shall adopt at its first session and review _____ thereafter, guidelines for the preparation of the information required under this Article. (period)

10. All Parties shall take all practical steps to promote, facilitate and finance the transfer of _____ sound technologies. (environment)

七、思考题(Questions for Discussion)

1. What makes up "Intergovernmental Panel on Climate Change"?

2. What is ultimate objective of *Kyoto Protocol* to the *United Nations Framework Convention on Climate Change*?

3. What shall each Party do to achieve its qualified emission limitation and reduction commitments?

4. Who can attend the Conference as observers besides those Parties covered by this Protocol?

八、拓展学习(Further Studies)

Directions: Surf the Internet and find more information about the following topics before or after class. Present to the class some successful projects to illustrate the application of these concepts to practice.

1. What measures has Chinese government taken to implement the *Kyoto Protocol*?

2. What contributions did China make in promoting the development of renewable energy?

3. Small changes could reduce carbon emission to a great extent. What can we do to make a difference to save our planet?

九、模拟联合国大会(Model United Nations Practice)

Directions: Work in teams and simulate the institutions and committees of the United Nations, featuring delegates of the UN members and the six committees of the General Assembly, negotiating issues of carbon emission in the world and working out resolutions. Students are suggested to focus on the following topics:

1. How to reduce carbon emission in developing countries?

2. Some developed countries including the United States and Canada have opted out of the *Kyoto Protocol*. What shall UN do to guide those countries?

3. How to raise the public awareness of environmental protection?

第三章

联合国防治荒漠化公约

United Nations Convention to Combat Desertification in Countries Experiencing Serious Drought and/or Desertification, Particularly in Africa

一、背景知识(Background)

《联合国防治荒漠化公约》是1994年6月7日在巴黎通过的,并于1996年12月正式生效。该公约的全称为《联合国关于在发生严重干旱和/或沙漠化的国家特别是在非洲防治沙漠化的公约》,截止到2017年第十三次缔约方大会,缔约方已达196个。公约的核心目标是由各国政府共同制定国家级、次区域级和区域级行动方案,并与捐助方、地方社区和非政府组织合作,以对抗应对荒漠化的挑战。《联合国防治荒漠化公约》(本章以下简称《公约》)是联合国环境与发展大会框架下的三大环境公约之一。2005年5月2日至11日,《公约》履约审查委员会第三次会议在德国波恩举行,审查了非洲国家的履约情况。2005年10月17日至28日,《公约》第七次缔约方大会(COP7)在肯尼亚首都内罗毕召开。期间还召开了高级别会议、履约审查委员会第四次会议、科技委员会第七次会议和议员圆桌会议。我国自1994年签署《公约》以来,2002年开始实施《中华人民共和国防沙治沙法》,2006年制定了履约方案。

二、公约原文(The Text of the Convention)

United Nations Convention to Combat Desertification in Countries Experiencing Serious Drought and/or Desertification, Particularly in Africa

Prologue
The Parties to this Convention,

Affirming that human beings in affected or threatened areas are at the centre of concerns to combat desertification and mitigate the effects of drought,

Reflecting the urgent concern of the international community, including States and international organizations, about the adverse impacts of desertification and drought,

Aware that arid, semi-arid and dry sub-humid areas together account for a significant proportion of the Earth's land area and are the habitat and source of livelihood for a large segment of its population,

Acknowledging that desertification and drought are problems of global dimension in that they affect all regions of the world and that joint action of the international community is needed to combat desertification and/or mitigate the effects of drought,

Noting the high concentration of developing countries, notably the least developed countries, among those experiencing serious drought and/or desertification, and the particularly tragic consequences of these phenomena in Africa,

Noting also that desertification is caused by complex interactions among physical, biological, political, social, cultural and economic factors,

Considering the impact of trade and relevant aspects of international economic relations on the ability of affected countries to combat desertification adequately,

Conscious that sustainable economic growth, social development and poverty eradication are priorities of affected developing countries, particularly in Africa, and are essential to meeting sustainability objectives,

Mindful that desertification and drought affect sustainable development through their interrelationships with important social problems such as poverty, poor health and nutrition, lack of food security, and those arising from migration, displacement of persons and demographic dynamics,

Appreciating the significance of the past efforts and experience of States and international organizations in combating desertification and mitigating the effects of drought, particularly in implementing the *Plan of Action to Combat Desertification* which was adopted at the United Nations Conference on Desertification in 1977,

Realizing that, despite efforts in the past, progress in combating desertification and mitigating the effects of drought has not met expectations and that a new and more effective approach is needed at all levels within the framework of sustainable development,

Recognizing the validity and relevance of decisions adopted at the United Nations Conference on Environment and Development, particularly of Agenda 21 and its chapter 12, which provide a basis for combating desertification,

Reaffirming in this light the commitments of developed countries as contained in paragraph 13 of chapter 33 of Agenda 21,

Recalling General Assembly resolution 47/188, particularly the priority in it prescribed for Africa, and all other relevant United Nations resolutions, decisions and programmes on desertification and drought, as well as relevant declarations by African countries and those from other regions,

Reaffirming the *Rio Declaration on Environment and Development* which states, in its Principle 2, that States have, in accordance with the *Charter of the United Nations* and the principles of international law, the sovereign right to exploit their own resources pursuant to their own environmental and developmental policies, and the responsibility to ensure that activities within their jurisdiction or control do not cause damage to the environment of other States or of areas beyond the limits of national jurisdiction,

Recognizing that national Governments play a critical role in combating desertification and mitigating the effects of drought and that progress in that respect depends on local implementation of action programmes in affected areas,

Recognizing also the importance and necessity of international cooperation and partnership in combating desertification and mitigating the effects of drought,

Recognizing further the importance of the provision to affected developing countries, particularly in Africa, of effective means, *inter alia* substantial financial resources, including new and additional funding, and access to technology, without which it will be difficult for them to implement fully their commitments under this Convention,

Expressing concern over the impact of desertification and drought on affected countries in Central Asia and the Transcaucasus,

Stressing the important role played by women in regions affected by desertification and/or drought, particularly in rural areas of developing countries, and the importance of ensuring the full participation of both men and women at all levels in programmes to combat desertification and mitigate the effects of drought,

Emphasizing the special role of non-governmental organizations and other major groups in programmes to combat desertification and mitigate the effects of drought,

Bearing in mind the relationship between desertification and other environmental problems of global dimension facing the international and national communities,

Bearing also in mind the contribution that combating desertification can make to achieving the objectives of the *United Nations Framework Convention on Climate Change*, the *Convention on Biological Diversity* and other related environmental conventions,

Believing that strategies to combat desertification and mitigate the effects of drought will be most effective if they are based on sound systematic observation and rigorous scientific knowledge and if they are continuously re-evaluated,

Recognizing the urgent need to improve the effectiveness and coordination of international cooperation to facilitate the implementation of national plans and priorities,

Determined to take appropriate action in combating desertification and mitigating the effects of drought for the benefit of present and future generations,

Have agreed as follows:

PART I INTRODUCTION

Article 1 Use of terms

For the purposes of this Convention:

(a) "desertification" means land degradation in arid, semi-arid and dry sub-humid areas resulting from various factors, including climatic variations and human activities;

(b) "combating desertification" includes activities which are part of the integrated development of land in arid, semi-arid and dry sub-humid areas for sustainable development which are aimed at:

　　i. prevention and/or reduction of land degradation;

　　ii. rehabilitation of partly degraded land; and

　　iii. reclamation of desertified land;

(c) "drought" means the naturally occurring phenomenon that exists when precipitation has been significantly below normal recorded levels, causing serious hydrological imbalances that adversely affect land resource production systems;

(d) "mitigating the effects of drought" means activities related to the prediction of drought and intended to reduce the vulnerability of society and natural systems to drought as it relates to combating desertification;

(e) "land" means the terrestrial bio-productive system that comprises soil, vegetation, other biota, and the ecological and hydrological processes that operate within the system;

(f) "land degradation" means reduction or loss, in arid, semi-arid and dry sub-humid areas, of the biological or economic productivity and complexity of rainfed cropland, irrigated cropland, or range, pasture, forest and woodlands resulting from land uses or from a process or combination of processes, including processes arising from human activities and habitation patterns, such as:

　　i. soil erosion caused by wind and/or water;

　　ii. deterioration of the physical, chemical and biological or economic properties of soil; and

　　iii. long-term loss of natural vegetation;

(g) "arid, semi-arid and dry sub-humid areas" means areas, other than polar and sub-polar regions, in which the ratio of annual precipitation to potential evapotranspiration falls within the range from 0.05 to 0.65;

(h) "affected areas" means arid, semi-arid and/or dry sub-humid areas affected or threatened by desertification;

(i) "affected countries" means countries whose lands include, in whole or in part, affected areas;

(j) "regional economic integration organization" means an organization constituted by sovereign States of a given region which has competence in respect of matters governed by this Convention and has been duly authorized, in accordance with its internal procedures, to sign, ratify, accept, approve or accede to this Convention;

(k) "developed country Parties" means developed country Parties and regional economic integration organizations constituted by developed countries.

Article 2　Objective

1. The objective of this Convention is to combat desertification and mitigate the effects of drought in countries experiencing serious drought and/or desertification, particularly in Africa, through effective action at all levels, supported by international cooperation and partnership arrangements, in the framework of an integrated approach which is consistent with Agenda 21, with a view to contributing to the achievement of sustainable development in affected areas.

2. Achieving this objective will involve long-term integrated strategies that focus simultaneously, in affected areas, on improved productivity of land, and the rehabilitation, conservation and sustainable management of land and water resources, leading to improved living conditions, in particular at the community level.

Article 3　Principles

In order to achieve the objective of this Convention and to implement its provisions, the Parties shall be guided, *inter alia*, by the following:

(a) the Parties should ensure that decisions on the design and implementation of programmes to combat desertification and/or mitigate the effects of drought are taken with the participation of populations and local communities and that an enabling environment is created at higher levels to facilitate action at national and local levels;

(b) the Parties should, in a spirit of international solidarity and partnership, improve cooperation and coordination at subregional, regional and international levels, and better focus financial, human, organizational and technical resources where they are needed;

(c) the Parties should develop, in a spirit of partnership, cooperation among all levels of government, communities, non-governmental organizations and landholders to establish a better understanding of the nature and value of land and scarce water resources in affected areas and to work towards their sustainable use; and

(d) the Parties should take into full consideration the special needs and circumstances of affected developing country Parties, particularly the least developed among them.

PART Ⅱ　GENERAL PROVISIONS

Article 4　General obligations

1. The Parties shall implement their obligations under this Convention, individually or jointly, either through existing or prospective bilateral and multilateral arrangements or a combination thereof, as appropriate, emphasizing the need to coordinate efforts and develop a coherent long-term strategy at all levels.

2. In pursuing the objective of this Convention, the Parties shall:

(a) adopt an integrated approach addressing the physical, biological and socio-economic aspects of the processes of desertification and drought;

(b) give due attention, within the relevant international and regional bodies, to the situation of affected developing country Parties with regard to international trade, marketing arrangements and debt with a view to establishing an enabling international economic environment conducive to the promotion of sustainable development;

(c) integrate strategies for poverty eradication into efforts to combat desertification and mitigate the effects of drought;

(d) promote cooperation among affected country Parties in the fields of environmental protection and the conservation of land and water resources, as they relate to desertification and drought;

(e) strengthen subregional, regional and international cooperation;

(f) cooperate within relevant intergovernmental organizations;

(g) determine institutional mechanisms, if appropriate, keeping in mind the need to avoid duplication; and

(h) promote the use of existing bilateral and multilateral financial mechanisms and arrangements that mobilize and channel substantial financial resources to affected developing country Parties in combating desertification and mitigating the effects of drought.

3. Affected developing country Parties are eligible for assistance in the implementation of the Convention.

Article 5 Obligations of affected country Parties

In addition to their obligations pursuant to Article 4, affected country Parties undertake to:

(a) give due priority to combating desertification and mitigating the effects of drought, and allocate adequate resources in accordance with their circumstances and capabilities;

(b) establish strategies and priorities, within the framework of sustainable development plans and/or policies, to combat desertification and mitigate the effects of drought;

(c) address the underlying causes of desertification and pay special attention to the socio economic factors contributing to desertification processes;

(d) promote awareness and facilitate the participation of local populations, particularly women and youth, with the support of non-governmental organizations, in efforts to combat desertification and mitigate the effects of drought; and

(e) provide an enabling environment by strengthening, as appropriate, relevant existing legislation and, where they do not exist, enacting new laws and establishing long-term policies and action programmes.

Article 6 Obligations of developed country Parties

In addition to their general obligations pursuant to Article 4, developed country

Parties undertake to:

(a) actively support, as agreed, individually or jointly, the efforts of affected developing country Parties, particularly those in Africa, and the least developed countries, to combat desertification and mitigate the effects of drought;

(b) provide substantial financial resources and other forms of support to assist affected developing country Parties, particularly those in Africa, effectively to develop and implement their own long-term plans and strategies to combat desertification and mitigate the effects of drought;

(c) promote the mobilization of new and Additional funding pursuant to Article 20, paragraph 2 (b);

(d) encourage the mobilization of funding from the private sector and other non-governmental sources; and

(e) promote and facilitate access by affected country Parties, particularly affected developing country Parties, to appropriate technology, knowledge and know-how.

Article 7 Priority for Africa

In implementing this Convention, the Parties shall give priority to affected African country Parties, in the light of the particular situation prevailing in that region, while not neglecting affected developing country Parties in other regions.

Article 8 Relationship with other conventions

1. The Parties shall encourage the coordination of activities carried out under this Convention and, if they are Parties to them, under other relevant international agreements, particularly the *United Nations Framework Convention on Climate Change* and the *Convention on Biological Diversity*, in order to derive maximum benefit from activities under each agreement while avoiding duplication of effort. The Parties shall encourage the conduct of joint programmes, particularly in the fields of research, training, systematic observation and information collection and exchange, to the extent that such activities may contribute to achieving the objectives of the agreements concerned.

2. The provisions of this Convention shall not affect the rights and obligations of any Party deriving from a bilateral, regional or international agreement into which it has entered prior to the entry into force of this Convention for it.

Part Ⅲ ACTION PROGRAMMES, SCIENTIFIC AND TECHNICAL COOPERATION AND SUPPORTING MEASURES

Section 1 Action programmes

Article 9 Basic approach

1. In carrying out their obligations pursuant to Article 5, Affected developing

country Parties and any other affected country Party in the framework of its regional implementation annex or, otherwise, that has notified the Permanent Secretariat in writing of its intention to prepare a national action programme, shall, as appropriate, prepare, make public and implement national action programmes, utilizing and building, to the extent possible, on existing relevant successful plans and programmes, and subregional and regional action programmes, as the central element of the strategy to combat desertification and mitigate the effects of drought. Such programmes shall be updated through a continuing participatory process on the basis of lessons from field action, as well as the results of research. The preparation of national action programmes shall be closely interlinked with other efforts to formulate national policies for sustainable development.

2. In the provision by developed country Parties of different forms of assistance under the terms of Article 6, priority shall be given to supporting, as agreed, national, subregional and regional action programmes of affected developing country Parties, particularly those in Africa, either directly or through relevant multilateral organizations or both.

3. The Parties shall encourage organs, funds and programmes of the United Nations system and other relevant intergovernmental organizations, academic institutions, the scientific community and non-governmental organizations in a position to cooperate, in accordance with their mandates and capabilities, to support the elaboration, implementation and follow-up of action programmes.

Article 10 National action programmes

1. The purpose of national action programmes is to identify the factors contributing to desertification and practical measures necessary to combat desertification and mitigate the effects of drought.

2. National action programmes shall specify the respective roles of government, local communities and land users and the resources available and needed. They shall, *inter alia*:

(a) incorporate long-term strategies to combat desertification and mitigate the effects of drought, emphasize implementation and be integrated with national policies for sustainable development;

(b) allow for modifications to be made in response to changing circumstances and be sufficiently flexible at the local level to cope with different socioeconomic, biological and geophysical conditions;

(c) give particular attention to the implementation of preventive measures for lands that are not yet degraded or which are only slightly degraded;

(d) enhance national climatological, meteorological and hydrological capabilities and the means to provide for drought early warning;

(e) promote policies and strengthen institutional frameworks which develop cooperation and coordination, in a spirit of partnership, between the donor community, governments at all levels, local populations and community groups, and facilitate access by local populations to appropriate information and technology;

(f) provide for effective participation at the local, national and regional levels of non-governmental organizations and local populations, both women and men, particularly resource users, including farmers and pastoralists and their representative organizations, in policy planning, decision-making, and implementation and review of national action programmes; and

(g) require regular review of, and progress reports on, their implementation.

3. National action programmes may include, *inter alia*, some or all of the following measures to prepare for and mitigate the effects of drought:

(a) establishment and/or strengthening, as appropriate, of early warning systems, including local and national facilities and joint systems at the subregional and regional levels, and mechanisms for assisting environmentally displaced persons;

(b) strengthening of drought preparedness and management, including drought contingency plans at the local, national, subregional and regional levels, which take into consideration seasonal to interannual climate predictions;

(c) establishment and/or strengthening, as appropriate, of food security systems, including storage and marketing facilities, particularly in rural areas;

(d) establishment of alternative livelihood projects that could provide incomes in drought prone areas; and

(e) development of sustainable irrigation programmes for both crops and livestock.

4. Taking into account the circumstances and requirements specific to each affected country Party, national action programmes include, as appropriate, *inter alia*, measures in some or all of the following priority fields as they relate to combating desertification and mitigating the effects of drought in affected areas and to their populations: promotion of alternative livelihoods and improvement of national economic environments with a view to strengthening programmes aimed at the eradication of poverty and at ensuring food security; demographic dynamics; sustainable management of natural resources; sustainable agricultural practices; development and efficient use of various energy sources; institutional and legal frameworks; strengthening of capabilities for assessment and systematic observation, including hydrological and meteorological services, and capacity building, education and public awareness.

Article 11 Subregional and regional action programmes

Affected country Parties shall consult and cooperate to prepare, as appropriate, in accordance with relevant regional implementation annexes, subregional and/or regional action programmes to harmonize, complement and increase the efficiency of national programmes. The provisions of Article 10 shall apply *mutatis mutandis* to subregional and regional programmes. Such cooperation may include agreed joint programmes for the sustainable management of transboundary natural resources, scientific and technical cooperation, and strengthening of relevant institutions.

Article 12 International cooperation

Affected country Parties, in collaboration with other Parties and the international community, should cooperate to ensure the promotion of an enabling international environment in the implementation of the Convention. Such cooperation should also cover fields of technology transfer as well as scientific research and development, information collection and dissemination and financial resources.

Article 13 Support for the elaboration and implementation of action programmes

1. Measures to support action programmes pursuant to Article 9 include, *inter alia*:

(a) financial cooperation to provide predictability for action programmes, allowing for necessary long-term planning;

(b) elaboration and use of cooperation mechanisms which better enable support at the local level, including action through non-governmental organizations, in order to promote the replicability of successful pilot programme activities where relevant;

(c) increased flexibility in project design, funding and implementation in keeping with the experimental, iterative approach indicated for participatory action at the local community level; and

(d) as appropriate, administrative and budgetary procedures that increase the efficiency of cooperation and of support programmes.

2. In providing such support to affected developing country Parties, priority shall be given to African country Parties and to least developed country Parties.

Article 14 Coordination in the elaboration and implementation of action programmes

1. The Parties shall work closely together, directly and through relevant intergovernmental organizations, in the elaboration and implementation of action programmes.

2. The Parties shall develop operational mechanisms, particularly at the national and field levels, to ensure the fullest possible coordination among developed country Parties, developing country Parties and relevant intergovernmental and non-governmental organi-zations, in order to avoid duplication, harmonize interventions and approaches, and maximize the impact of assistance. In affected developing country Parties, priority will be given to coordinating activities related to international cooperation in order to maximize the efficient use of resources, to ensure responsive assistance, and to facilitate the implementation of national action programmes and priorities under this Convention.

Article 15 Regional implementation annexes

Elements for incorporation in action programmes shall be selected and adapted to the socio economic, geographical and climatic factors applicable to affected country

Parties or regions, as well as to their level of development. Guidelines for the preparation of action programmes and their exact focus and content for particular subregions and regions are set out in the regional implementation annexes.

Section 2 Scientific and technical cooperation

Article 16 Information collection, analysis and exchange

The Parties agree, according to their respective capabilities, to integrate and coordinate the collection, analysis and exchange of relevant short-term and long-term data and information to ensure systematic observation of land degradation in affected areas and to understand better and assess the processes and effects of drought and desertification. This would help accomplish, *inter alia*, early warning and advance planning for periods of adverse climatic variation in a form suited for practical application by users at all levels, including especially local populations. To this end, they shall, as appropriate:

(a) facilitate and strengthen the functioning of the global network of institutions and facilities for the collection, analysis and exchange of information, as well as for systematic observation at all levels, which shall, *inter alia*:

　　i. aim to use compatible standards and systems;

　　ii. encompass relevant data and stations, including in remote areas;

　　iii. use and disseminate modern technology for data collection, transmission and assessment on land degradation; and

　　iv. link national, subregional and regional data and information centres more closely with global information sources;

(b) ensure that the collection, analysis and exchange of information address the needs of local communities and those of decision makers, with a view to resolving specific problems, and that local communities are involved in these activities;

(c) support and further develop bilateral and multilateral programmes and projects aimed at defining, conducting, assessing and financing the collection, analysis and exchange of data and information, including, *inter alia*, integrated sets of physical, biological, social and economic indicators;

(d) make full use of the expertise of competent intergovernmental and non-governmental organizations, particularly to disseminate relevant information and experiences among target groups in different regions;

(e) give full weight to the collection, analysis and exchange of socio economic data, and their integration with physical and biological data;

(f) exchange and make fully, openly and promptly available information from all publicly available sources relevant to combating desertification and mitigating the effects of drought; and

(g) subject to their respective national legislation and/or policies, exchange information on local and traditional knowledge, ensuring adequate protection for it and providing appropriate return from the benefits derived from it, on an equitable basis and on mutually agreed terms, to the local populations concerned.

Article 17 Research and development

1. The Parties undertake, according to their respective capabilities, to promote technical and scientific cooperation in the fields of combating desertification and mitigating the effects of drought through appropriate national, subregional, regional and international institutions. To this end, they shall support research activities that:

(a) contribute to increased knowledge of the processes leading to desertification and drought and the impact of, and distinction between, causal factors, both natural and human, with a view to combating desertification and mitigating the effects of drought, and achieving improved productivity as well as sustainable use and management of resources;

(b) respond to well defined objectives, address the specific needs of local populations and lead to the identification and implementation of solutions that improve the living standards of people in affected areas;

(c) protect, integrate, enhance and validate traditional and local knowledge, know-how and practices, ensuring, subject to their respective national legislation and/or policies, that the owners of that knowledge will directly benefit on an equitable basis and on mutually agreed terms from any commercial utilization of it or from any technological development derived from that knowledge;

(d) develop and strengthen national, subregional and regional research capabilities in affected developing country Parties, particularly in Africa, including the development of local skills and the strengthening of appropriate capacities, especially in countries with a weak research base, giving particular attention to multidisciplinary and participative socioeconomic research;

(e) take into account, where relevant, the relationship between poverty, migration caused by environmental factors, and desertification;

(f) promote the conduct of joint research programmes between national, subregional, regional and international research organizations, in both the public and private sectors, for the development of improved, affordable and accessible technologies for sustainable development through effective participation of local populations and communities; and

(g) enhance the availability of water resources in affected areas, by means of, *inter alia*, cloud-seeding.

2. Research priorities for particular regions and subregions, reflecting different local conditions, should be included in action programmes. The Conference of the Parties shall review research priorities periodically on the advice of the Committee on Science and Technology.

Article 18 Transfer, acquisition, adaptation and development of technology

1. The Parties undertake, as mutually agreed and in accordance with their respective national legislation and/or policies, to promote, finance and/or facilitate the financing of the transfer, acquisition, adaptation and development of environmentally sound, economically viable and socially acceptable technologies relevant to combating desertification and/or mitigating the effects of drought, with a view to contributing to the achievement of sustainable development in affected areas. Such cooperation shall be conducted bilaterally or multilaterally, as appropriate, making full use of the expertise of intergovernmental and non-governmental organizations. The Parties shall, in particular:

(a) fully utilize relevant existing national, subregional, regional and international information systems and clearing-houses for the dissemination of information on available technologies, their sources, their environmental risks and the broad terms under which they may be acquired;

(b) facilitate access, in particular by affected developing country Parties, on favourable terms, including on concessional and preferential terms, as mutually agreed, taking into account the need to protect intellectual property rights, to technologies most suitable to practical application for specific needs of local populations, paying special attention to the social, cultural, economic and environmental impact of such technology;

(c) facilitate technology cooperation among affected country Parties through financial assistance or other appropriate means;

(d) extend technology cooperation with affected developing country Parties, including, where relevant, joint ventures, especially to sectors which foster alternative livelihoods; and

(e) take appropriate measures to create domestic market conditions and incentives, fiscal or otherwise, conducive to the development, transfer, acquisition and adaptation of suitable technology, knowledge, know-how and practices, including measures to ensure adequate and effective protection of intellectual property rights.

2. The Parties shall, according to their respective capabilities, and subject to their respective national legislation and/or policies, protect, promote and use in particular relevant traditional and local technology, knowledge, know-how and practices and, to that end, they undertake to:

(a) make inventories of such technology, knowledge, know-how and practices and their potential uses with the participation of local populations, and disseminate such information, where appropriate, in cooperation with relevant intergovernmental and non-governmental organizations;

(b) ensure that such technology, knowledge, know-how and practices are adequately protected and that local populations benefit directly, on an equitable basis and as mutually agreed, from any commercial utilization of them or from any technological development derived therefrom;

(c) encourage and actively support the improvement and dissemination of such technology, knowledge, know-how and practices or of the development of new technology based on them; and

(d) facilitate, as appropriate, the adaptation of such technology, knowledge, know-how and practices to wide use and integrate them with modern technology, as appropriate.

Section 3　Supporting measures

Article 19　Capacity building, education and public awareness

1. The Parties recognize the significance of capacity building- that is to say, institution building, training and development of relevant local and national capacities in efforts to combat desertification and mitigate the effects of drought. They shall promote, as appropriate, capacity building:

(a) through the full participation at all levels of local people, particularly at the local level, especially women and youth, with the cooperation of non-governmental and local organizations;

(b) by strengthening training and research capacity at the national level in the field of desertification and drought;

(c) by establishing and/or strengthening support and extension services to disseminate relevant technology methods and techniques more effectively, and by training field agents and members of rural organizations in participatory approaches for the conservation and sustainable use of natural resources;

(d) by fostering the use and dissemination of the knowledge, know-how and practices of local people in technical cooperation programmes, wherever possible;

(e) by adapting, where necessary, relevant environmentally sound technology and traditional methods of agriculture and pastoralism to modern socioeconomic conditions;

(f) by providing appropriate training and technology in the use of alternative energy sources, particularly renewable energy resources, aimed particularly at reducing dependence on wood for fuel;

(g) through cooperation, as mutually agreed, to strengthen the capacity of affected developing country Parties to develop and implement programmes in the field of collection, analysis and exchange of information pursuant to Article 16;

(h) through innovative ways of promoting alternative livelihoods, including training in new skills;

(i) by training of decision makers, managers, and personnel who are responsible for the collection and analysis of data for the dissemination and use of early warning information on drought conditions and for food production;

(j) through more effective operation of existing national institutions and legal frameworks and, where necessary, creation of new ones, along with strengthening of strategic planning and management; and

(k) by means of exchange visitor programmes to enhance capacity building in affected country Parties through a long-term, interactive process of learning and study.

2. Affected developing country Parties shall conduct, in cooperation with other Parties and competent intergovernmental and non-governmental organizations, as appropriate, an interdisciplinary review of available capacity and facilities at the local and national levels, and the potential for strengthening them.

3. The Parties shall cooperate with each other and through competent intergovernmental organizations, as well as with non-governmental organizations, in undertaking and supporting public awareness and educational programmes in both affected and, where relevant, unaffected country Parties to promote understanding of the causes and effects of desertification and drought and of the importance of meeting the objective of this Convention. To that end, they shall:

(a) organize awareness campaigns for the general public;

(b) promote, on a permanent basis, access by the public to relevant information, and wide public participation in education and awareness activities;

(c) encourage the establishment of associations that contribute to public awareness;

(d) develop and exchange educational and public awareness material, where possible in local languages, exchange and second experts to train personnel of affected developing country Parties in carrying out relevant education and awareness programmes, and fully utilize relevant educational material available in competent international bodies;

(e) assess educational needs in affected areas, elaborate appropriate school curricula and expand, as needed, educational and adult literacy programmes and opportunities for all, in particular for girls and women, on the identification, conservation and sustainable use and management of the natural resources of affected areas; and

(f) develop interdisciplinary participatory programmes integrating desertification and drought awareness into educational systems and in non-formal, adult, distance and practical educational programmes.

4. The Conference of the Parties shall establish and/or strengthen networks of regional education and training centres to combat desertification and mitigate the effects of drought. These networks shall be coordinated by an institution created or designated for that purpose, in order to train scientific, technical and management personnel and to strengthen existing institutions responsible for education and training in affected country Parties, where appropriate, with a view to harmonizing programmes and to organizing exchanges of experience among them. These networks shall cooperate closely with relevant intergovernmental and non-governmental organizations to avoid duplication of effort.

Article 20 Financial resources

1. Given the central importance of financing to the achievement of the objective of the Convention, the Parties, taking into account their capabilities, shall make every effort to ensure that adequate financial resources are available for programmes to combat desertification and mitigate the effects of drought.

2. In this connection, developed country Parties, while giving priority to affected African country Parties without neglecting affected developing country Parties in other regions, in accordance with Article 7, undertake to:

(a) mobilize substantial financial resources, including grants and concessional loans, in order to support the implementation of programmes to combat desertification and mitigate the effects of drought;

(b) promote the mobilization of adequate, timely and predictable financial resources, including new and additional funding from the Global Environment Facility of the agreed incremental costs of those activities concerning desertification that relate to its four focal areas, in conformity with the relevant provisions of the Instrument establishing the Global Environment Facility;

(c) facilitate through international cooperation the transfer of technology, knowledge and know-how; and

(d) explore, in cooperation with affected developing country Parties, innovative methods and incentives for mobilizing and channelling resources, including those of foundations, non-governmental organizations and other private sector entities, particularly debt swaps and other innovative means which increase financing by reducing the external debt burden of affected developing country Parties, particularly those in Africa.

3. Affected developing country Parties, taking into account their capabilities, undertake to mobilize adequate financial resources for the implementation of their national action programmes.

4. In mobilizing financial resources, the Parties shall seek full use and continued qualitative improvement of all national, bilateral and multilateral funding sources and mechanisms, using consortia, joint programmes and parallel financing, and shall seek to involve private sector funding sources and mechanisms, including those of non-governmental organizations. To this end, the Parties shall fully utilize the operational mechanisms developed pursuant to Article 14.

5. In order to mobilize the financial resources necessary for affected developing country Parties to combat desertification and mitigate the effects of drought, the Parties shall:

(a) rationalize and strengthen the management of resources already allocated for combating desertification and mitigating the effects of drought by using them more effectively and efficiently, assessing their successes and shortcomings, removing hindrances to their effective use and, where necessary, reorienting programmes in light of the integrated long-term approach adopted pursuant to this Convention;

(b) give due priority and attention within the governing bodies of multilateral financial institutions, facilities and funds, including regional development banks and funds, to supporting affected developing country Parties, particularly those in Africa, in activities which advance implementation of the Convention, notably action programmes they undertake in the framework of regional implementation annexes; and

(c) examine ways in which regional and subregional cooperation can be strengthened to support efforts undertaken at the national level.

6. Other Parties are encouraged to provide, on a voluntary basis, knowledge, know-how and techniques related to desertification and/or financial resources to affected developing country Parties.

7. The full implementation by affected developing country Parties, particularly those in Africa, of their obligations under the Convention will be greatly assisted by the fulfilment by developed country Parties of their obligations under the Convention, including in particular those regarding financial resources and transfer of technology. In fulfilling their obligations, developed country Parties should take fully into account that economic and social development and poverty eradication are the first priorities of affected developing country Parties, particularly those in Africa.

Article 21 Financial mechanisms

1. The Conference of the Parties shall promote the availability of financial mechanisms and shall encourage such mechanisms to seek to maximize the availability of funding for affected developing country Parties, particularly those in Africa, to implement the Convention. To this end, the Conference of the Parties shall consider for adoption *inter alia* approaches and policies that:

(a) facilitate the provision of necessary funding at the national, subregional, regional and global levels for activities pursuant to relevant provisions of the Convention;

(b) promote multiple-source funding approaches, mechanisms and arrangements and their assessment, consistent with Article 20;

(c) provide on a regular basis, to interested Parties and relevant intergovernmental and non-governmental organizations, information on available sources of funds and on funding patterns in order to facilitate coordination among them;

(d) facilitate the establishment, as appropriate, of mechanisms, such as national desertification funds, including those involving the participation of non-governmental organizations, to channel financial resources rapidly and efficiently to the local level in affected developing country Parties; and

(e) strengthen existing funds and financial mechanisms at the subregional and regional levels, particularly in Africa, to support more effectively the implementation of the Convention.

2. The Conference of the Parties shall also encourage the provision, through various mechanisms within the United Nations system and through multilateral financial institutions, of support at the national, subregional and regional levels to activities that enable developing country Parties to meet their obligations under the Convention.

3. Affected developing country Parties shall utilize, and where necessary, establish and/or strengthen, national coordinating mechanisms, integrated in national development programmes, that would ensure the efficient use of all available financial resources. They shall also utilize participatory processes involving non-governmental organizations, local groups and the private sector, in raising funds, in elaborating as well as implementing programmes and in assuring access to funding by groups at the local level. These actions can be enhanced by improved coordination and flexible programming on the part of those providing assistance.

4. In order to increase the effectiveness and efficiency of existing financial mechanisms, a Global Mechanism to promote actions leading to the mobilization and channelling of substantial financial resources, including for the transfer of technology, on a grant basis, and/or on concessional or other terms, to affected developing country Parties, is hereby established. This Global Mechanism shall function under the authority and guidance of the Conference of the Parties and be accountable to it.

5. The Conference of the Parties shall identify, at its first ordinary session, an organization to house the Global Mechanism. The Conference of the Parties and the organization it has identified shall agree upon modalities for this Global Mechanism to ensure *inter alia* that such Mechanism:

(a) identifies and draws up an inventory of relevant bilateral and multilateral cooperation programmes that are available to implement the Convention;

(b) provides advice, on request, to Parties on innovative methods of financing and sources of financial assistance and on improving the coordination of cooperation activities at the national level;

(c) provides interested Parties and relevant intergovernmental and non-governmental organizations with information on available sources of funds and on funding patterns in order to facilitate coordination among them; and

(d) reports to the Conference of the Parties, beginning at its second ordinary session, on its activities.

6. The Conference of the Parties shall, at its first session, make appropriate arrangements with the organization it has identified to house the Global Mechanism for the administrative operations of such Mechanism, drawing to the extent possible on existing budgetary and human resources.

7. The Conference of the Parties shall, at its third ordinary session, review the

policies, operational modalities and activities of the Global Mechanism accountable to it pursuant to paragraph 4, taking into account the provisions of Article 7. On the basis of this review, it shall consider and take appropriate action.

PART Ⅳ INSTITUTIONS

Article 22 Conference of the Parties

1. A Conference of the Parties is hereby established.

2. The Conference of the Parties is the supreme body of the Convention. It shall make, within its mandate, the decisions necessary to promote its effective implementation. In particular, it shall:

(a) regularly review the implementation of the Convention and the functioning of its institutional arrangements in the light of the experience gained at the national, subregional, regional and international levels and on the basis of the evolution of scientific and technological knowledge;

(b) promote and facilitate the exchange of information on measures adopted by the Parties, and determine the form and timetable for transmitting the information to be submitted pursuant to Article 26, review the reports and make recommendations on them;

(c) establish such subsidiary bodies as are deemed necessary for the implementation of the Convention;

(d) review reports submitted by its subsidiary bodies and provide guidance to them;

(e) agree upon and adopt, by consensus, rules of procedure and financial rules for itself and any subsidiary bodies;

(f) adopt amendments to the Convention pursuant to Articles 30 and 31;

(g) approve a programme and budget for its activities, including those of its subsidiary bodies, and undertake necessary arrangements for their financing;

(h) as appropriate, seek the cooperation of, and utilize the services of and information provided by, competent bodies or agencies, whether national or international, intergovernmental or non-governmental;

(i) promote and strengthen the relationship with other relevant conventions while avoiding duplication of effort; and

(j) exercise such other functions as may be necessary for the achievement of the objective of the Convention.

3. The Conference of the Parties shall, at its first session, adopt its own rules of procedure, by consensus, which shall include decision-making procedures for matters not already covered by decision-making procedures stipulated in the Convention. Such procedures may include specified majorities required for the adoption of particular

decisions.

4. The first session of the Conference of the Parties shall be convened by the interim secretariat referred to in Article 35 and shall take place not later than one year after the date of entry into force of the Convention. Unless otherwise decided by the Conference of the Parties, the second, third and fourth ordinary sessions shall be held yearly, and thereafter, ordinary sessions shall be held every two years.

5. Extraordinary sessions of the Conference of the Parties shall be held at such other times as may be decided either by the Conference of the Parties in ordinary session or at the written request of any Party, provided that, within three months of the request being communicated to the Parties by the Permanent Secretariat, it is supported by at least one third of the Parties.

6. At each ordinary session, the Conference of the Parties shall elect a Bureau. The structure and functions of the Bureau shall be determined in the rules of procedure. In appointing the Bureau, due regard shall be paid to the need to ensure equitable geographical distribution and adequate representation of affected country Parties, particularly those in Africa.

7. The United Nations, its specialized agencies and any State member thereof or observers thereto not Party to the Convention, may be represented at sessions of the Conference of the Parties as observers. Any body or agency, whether national or international, governmental or non-governmental, which is qualified in matters covered by the Convention, and which has informed the Permanent Secretariat of its wish to be represented at a session of the Conference of the Parties as an observer, may be so admitted unless at least one third of the Parties present object. The admission and participation of observers shall be subject to the rules of procedure adopted by the Conference of the Parties.

8. The Conference of the Parties may request competent national and international organizations which have relevant expertise to provide it with information relevant to Article 16, paragraph (g), Article 17, paragraph 1 (c) and Article 18, paragraph 2 (b).

Article 23　Permanent Secretariat

1. A Permanent Secretariat is hereby established.

2. The functions of the Permanent Secretariat shall be:

(a) to make arrangements for sessions of the Conference of the Parties and its subsidiary bodies established under the Convention and to provide them with services as required;

(b) to compile and transmit reports submitted to it;

(c) to facilitate assistance to affected developing country Parties, on request, particularly those in Africa, in the compilation and communication of information required under the Convention;

(d) to coordinate its activities with the secretariats of other relevant international bodies and conventions;

(e) to enter, under the guidance of the Conference of the Parties, into such administrative and contractual arrangements as may be required for the effective discharge of its functions;

(f) to prepare reports on the execution of its functions under this Convention and present them to the Conference of the Parties; and

(g) to perform such other secretariat functions as may be determined by the Conference of the Parties.

3. The Conference of the Parties, at its first session, shall designate a Permanent Secretariat and make arrangements for its functioning.

Article 24　Committee on Science and Technology

1. A Committee on Science and Technology is hereby established as a subsidiary body of the Conference of the Parties to provide it with information and advice on scientific and technological matters relating to combating desertification and mitigating the effects of drought. The Committee shall meet in conjunction with the ordinary sessions of the Conference of the Parties and shall be multidisciplinary and open to the participation of all Parties. It shall be composed of government representatives competent in the relevant fields of expertise. The Conference of the Parties shall decide, at its first session, on the terms of reference of the Committee.

2. The Conference of the Parties shall establish and maintain a roster of independent experts with expertise and experience in the relevant fields. The roster shall be based on nominations received in writing from the Parties, taking into account the need for a multidisciplinary approach and broad geographical representation.

3. The Conference of the Parties may, as necessary, appoint ad hoc panels to provide it, through the Committee, with information and advice on specific issues regarding the state of the art in fields of science and technology relevant to combating desertification and mitigating the effects of drought. These panels shall be composed of experts whose names are taken from the roster, taking into account the need for a multidisciplinary approach and broad geographical representation. These experts shall have scientific backgrounds and field experience and shall be appointed by the Conference of the Parties on the recommendation of the Committee. The Conference of the Parties shall decide on the terms of reference and the modalities of work of these panels.

Article 25　Networking of institutions, agencies and bodies

1. The Committee on Science and Technology shall, under the supervision of the

Conference of the Parties, make provision for the undertaking of a survey and evaluation of the relevant existing networks, institutions, agencies and bodies willing to become units of a network. Such a network shall support the implementation of the Convention.

2. On the basis of the results of the survey and evaluation referred to in paragraph 1, the Committee on Science and Technology shall make recommendations to the Conference of the Parties on ways and means to facilitate and strengthen networking of the units at the local, national and other levels, with a view to ensuring that the thematic needs set out in Articles 16 to 19 are addressed.

3. Taking into account these recommendations, the Conference of the Parties shall:

(a) identify those national, subregional, regional and international units that are most appropriate for networking, and recommend operational procedures, and a time frame, for them; and

(b) identify the units best suited to facilitating and strengthening such networking at all levels.

PART V PROCEDURES

Article 26 Communication of information

1. Each Party shall communicate to the Conference of the Parties for consideration at its ordinary sessions, through the Permanent Secretariat, reports on the measures which it has taken for the implementation of the Convention. The Conference of the Parties shall determine the timetable for submission and the format of such reports.

2. Affected country Parties shall provide a description of the strategies established pursuant to Article 5 and of any relevant information on their implementation.

3. Affected country Parties which implement action programmes pursuant to Articles 9 to 15 shall provide a detailed description of the programmes and of their implementation.

4. Any group of affected country Parties may make a joint communication on measures taken at the subregional and/or regional levels in the framework of action programmes.

5. Developed country Parties shall report on measures taken to assist in the preparation and implementation of action programmes, including information on the financial resources they have provided, or are providing, under the Convention.

6. Information communicated pursuant to paragraphs 1 to 4 shall be transmitted by the Permanent Secretariat as soon as possible to the Conference of the Parties and to any relevant subsidiary body.

7. The Conference of the Parties shall facilitate the provision to affected developing countries, particularly those in Africa, on request, of technical and financial support in compiling and communicating information in accordance with this article, as well as identifying the technical and financial needs associated with action programmes.

Article 27 Measures to resolve questions on implementation

The Conference of the Parties shall consider and adopt procedures and institutional mechanisms for the resolution of questions that may arise with regard to the implementation of the Convention.

Article 28 Settlement of disputes

1. Parties shall settle any dispute between them concerning the interpretation or application of the Convention through negotiation or other peaceful means of their own choice.

2. When ratifying, accepting, approving, or acceding to the Convention, or at any time thereafter, a Party which is not a regional economic integration organization may declare in a written instrument submitted to the Depositary that, in respect of any dispute concerning the interpretation or application of the Convention, it recognizes one or both of the following means of dispute settlement as compulsory in relation to any Party accepting the same obligation:

(a) arbitration in accordance with procedures adopted by the Conference of the Parties in an annex as soon as practicable;

(b) submission of the dispute to the International Court of Justice.

3. A Party which is a regional economic integration organization may make a declaration with like effect in relation to arbitration in accordance with the procedure referred to in paragraph 2 (a).

4. A declaration made pursuant to paragraph 2 shall remain in force until it expires in accordance with its terms or until three months after written notice of its revocation has been deposited with the Depositary.

5. The expiry of a declaration, a notice of revocation or a new declaration shall not in any way affect proceedings pending before an arbitral tribunal or the International Court of Justice unless the Parties to the dispute otherwise agree.

6. If the Parties to a dispute have not accepted the same or any procedure pursuant to paragraph 2 and if they have not been able to settle their dispute within twelve months following notification by one Party to another that a dispute exists between them, the dispute shall be submitted to conciliation at the request of any Party to the dispute, in accordance with procedures adopted by the Conference of the Parties in an annex as soon as practicable.

Article 29 Status of annexes

1. Annexes form an integral part of the Convention and, unless expressly provided otherwise, a reference to the Convention also constitutes a reference to its annexes.

2. The Parties shall interpret the provisions of the annexes in a manner that is in conformity with their rights and obligations under the articles of this Convention.

Article 30 Amendments to the Convention

1. Any Party may propose amendments to the Convention.

2. Amendments to the Convention shall be adopted at an ordinary session of the Conference of the Parties. The text of any proposed amendment shall be communicated to the Parties by the Permanent Secretariat at least six months before the meeting at which it is proposed for adoption. The Permanent Secretariat shall also communicate proposed amendments to the signatories to the Convention.

3. The Parties shall make every effort to reach agreement on any proposed amendment to the Convention by consensus. If all efforts at consensus have been exhausted and no agreement reached, the amendment shall, as a last resort, be adopted by a two-thirds majority vote of the Parties present and voting at the meeting. The adopted amendment shall be communicated by the Permanent Secretariat to the Depositary, who shall circulate it to all Parties for their ratification, acceptance, approval or accession.

4. Instruments of ratification, acceptance, approval or accession in respect of an amendment shall be deposited with the Depositary. An amendment adopted pursuant to paragraph 3 shall enter into force for those Parties having accepted it on the ninetieth day after the date of receipt by the Depositary of an instrument of ratification, acceptance, approval or accession by at least two thirds of the Parties to the Convention which were Parties at the time of the adoption of the amendment.

5. The amendment shall enter into force for any other Party on the ninetieth day after the date on which that Party deposits with the Depositary its instrument of ratification, acceptance or approval of, or accession to the said amendment.

6. For the purposes of this Article and Article 31, "Parties present and voting" means Parties present and casting an affirmative or negative vote.

Article 31 Adoption and amendment of annexes

1. Any additional annex to the Convention and any amendment to an annex shall be proposed and adopted in accordance with the procedure for amendment of the Convention set forth in Article 30, provided that, in adopting an additional regional implementation annex or amendment to any regional implementation annex, the majority provided for in that article shall include a two-thirds majority vote of the Parties of the region concerned present and voting. The adoption or amendment of an annex shall be communicated by the Depositary to all Parties.

2. An annex, other than an additional regional implementation annex, or an amendment to an annex, other than an amendment to any regional implementation annex, that has been adopted in accordance with paragraph 1, shall enter into force for all Parties to the Convention six months after the date of communication by the Depositary to

such Parties of the adoption of such annex or amendment, except for those Parties that have notified the Depositary in writing within that period of their non-acceptance of such annex or amendment. Such annex or amendment shall enter into force for Parties which withdraw their notification of non-acceptance on the ninetieth day after the date on which withdrawal of such notification has been received by the Depositary.

3. An additional regional implementation annex or amendment to any regional implementation annex that has been adopted in accordance with paragraph 1, shall enter into force for all Parties to the Convention six months after the date of the communication by the Depositary to such Parties of the adoption of such annex or amendment, except with respect to:

(a) any Party that has notified the Depositary in writing, within such six month period, of its non-acceptance of that additional regional implementation annex or of the amendment to the regional implementation annex, in which case such annex or amendment shall enter into force for Parties which withdraw their notification of non-acceptance on the ninetieth day after the date on which withdrawal of such notification has been received by the Depositary; and

(b) any Party that has made a declaration with respect to additional regional implementation annexes or amendments to regional implementation annexes in accordance with Article 34, paragraph 4, in which case any such annex or amendment shall enter into force for such a Party on the ninetieth day after the date of deposit with the Depositary of its instrument of ratification, acceptance, approval or accession with respect to such annex or amendment.

4. If the adoption of an annex or an amendment to an annex involves an amendment to the Convention, that annex or amendment to an annex shall not enter into force until such time as the amendment to the Convention enters into force.

Article 32 Right to vote

1. Except as provided for in paragraph 2, each Party to the Convention shall have one vote.

2. Regional economic integration organizations, in matters within their competence, shall exercise their right to vote with a number of votes equal to the number of their member States that are Parties to the Convention. Such an organization shall not exercise its right to vote if any of its member States exercises its right, and *vice versa*.

PART VI FINAL PROVISIONS

Article 33 Signature

This Convention shall be opened for signature at Paris, on 14–15 October 1994, by States Members of the United Nations or any of its specialized agencies or that are

Parties to the Statute of the International Court of Justice and by regional economic integration organizations. It shall remain open for signature, thereafter, at the United Nations Headquarters in New York until 13 October 1995.

Article 34 Ratification, acceptance, approval and accession

1. The Convention shall be subject to ratification, acceptance, approval or accession by States and by regional economic integration organizations. It shall be open for accession from the day after the date on which the Convention is closed for signature. Instruments of ratification, acceptance, approval or accession shall be deposited with the Depositary.

2. Any regional economic integration organization which becomes a Party to the Convention without any of its member States being a Party to the Convention shall be bound by all the obligations under the Convention. Where one or more member States of such an organization are also Party to the Convention, the organization and its member States shall decide on their respective responsibilities for the performance of their obligations under the Convention. In such cases, the organization and the member States shall not be entitled to exercise rights under the Convention concurrently.

3. In their instruments of ratification, acceptance, approval or accession, regional economic integration organizations shall declare the extent of their competence with respect to the matters governed by the Convention. They shall also promptly inform the Depositary, who shall in turn inform the Parties, of any substantial modification in the extent of their competence.

4. In its instrument of ratification, acceptance, approval or accession, any Party may declare that, with respect to it, any additional regional implementation annex or any amendment to any regional implementation annex shall enter into force only upon the deposit of its instrument of ratification, acceptance, approval or accession with respect thereto.

Article 35 Interim arrangements

The secretariat functions referred to in Article 23 will be carried out on an interim basis by the secretariat established by the General Assembly of the United Nations in its resolution 47/188 of 22 December 1992, until the completion of the first session of the Conference of the Parties.

Article 36 Entry into force

1. The Convention shall enter into force on the ninetieth day after the date of deposit of the fiftieth instrument of ratification, acceptance, approval or accession.

2. For each State or regional economic integration organization ratifying, accepting, approving or acceding to the Convention after the deposit of the fiftieth instrument of ratification, acceptance, approval or accession, the Convention shall enter into force on the ninetieth day after the date of deposit by such State or regional economic integration

organization of its instrument of ratification, acceptance, approval or accession.

3. For the purposes of paragraphs 1 and 2, any instrument deposited by a regional economic integration organization shall not be counted as additional to those deposited by States members of the organization.

Article 37　Reservations

No reservations may be made to this Convention.

Article 38　Withdrawal

1. At any time after three years from the date on which the Convention has entered into force for a Party, that Party may withdraw from the Convention by giving written notification to the Depositary.

2. Any such withdrawal shall take effect upon expiry of one year from the date of receipt by the Depositary of the notification of withdrawal, or on such later date as may be specified in the notification of withdrawal.

Article 39　Depositary

The Secretary-General of the United Nations shall be the Depositary of the Convention.

Article 40　Authentic texts

The original of the present Convention, of which the Arabic, Chinese, English, French, Russian and Spanish texts are equally authentic, shall be deposited with the Secretary-General of the United Nations.

IN WITNESS WHEREOF the undersigned, being duly authorized to that effect, have signed the present Convention.

DONE AT Paris, this 17th day of June one thousand nine hundred and ninety-four.

(Source: https://moew.government.bg/static/media/ups/tiny/file/KVESMS/conventions_full/Convention_desertification_en.pdf)

三、注解(Notes)

1. The Plan of Action to Combat Desertification

1977年8月29日至9月9日，联合国在肯尼亚首都内罗毕召开世界荒漠化问题会议，有94个国家代表参加。这次会议明确了土地荒漠化是世界上最严重的环境问题。与会国签署了一项防治荒漠化的全球共同行动方案，即《防治沙漠化行动计划》，目标是到2000年使全球性的荒漠化问题基本得到解决。

2. The Rio Declaration on Environment and Development

《里约环境与发展宣言》指出：和平、发展和保护环境是互相依存、不可分割的，世界各国应在环境与发展领域加强国际合作，为建立一种新的、公平的全球伙伴关系而努力。呼吁为签订尊重大家的利益和维护全球环境与发展体系完整的国际协定而努力,认识到我们的地球家园的大自然的完整性和互相依存性。

四、相关词汇(Key Words and Phrases)

1. amendment	[əˈmendmənt]	n.	修正案;改善;改正
2. arbitration	[ˌɑːbɪˈtreɪʃ(ə)n]	n.	公断,仲裁
3. authentic	[ɔːˈθentɪk]	adj.	真正的,真实的;可信的;有效的
4. consortia	[kənˈsɔːrʃə]	n.	联盟;合作;公会
5. degradation	[ˌdegrəˈdeɪʃ(ə)n]	n.	退化;降格,降级
6. depositary	[dɪˈpɒzɪt(ə)rɪ]	n.	受托人
7. desertification	[dɪˌzɜːtɪfɪˈkeɪʃn]	n.	(土壤)荒漠化
8. disseminate	[dɪˈsemɪneɪt]	vt. & vi.	宣传,传播;散布
9. duplication	[ˌdjuːplɪˈkeɪʃn]	n.	复制;副本;重复
10. expire	[ɪkˈspaɪə]	vi.	期满;终止;名词形式为 expiry
11. hindrance	[ˈhɪndr(ə)ns]	n.	障碍;妨碍;妨害;阻碍物
12. hydrological	[ˌhaɪdrəˈlɑdʒɪkəl]	adj.	水文学的,水文的
13. iterative	[ˈɪt(ə)rətɪv]	adj.	[数]迭代的;重复的,反复的
14. precipitation	[prɪˌsɪpɪˈteɪʃn]	n.	降水,降水量(包括雨、雪、冰等)
15. pursuant	[pəˈsjuːənt]	adj.	依据的;追赶的;随后的
16. rehabilitation	[ˌriːhəˌbɪlɪˈteɪʃən]	n.	复原
17. revocation	[ˌrevəˈkeɪʃən]	n.	取消;撤回;废除
18. terrestrial	[təˈrestrɪəl]	adj.	地球的;陆地的,[生物]陆生的;人间的
		n.	陆地生物;地球上的人
19. subject to			使服从;使遭受;受…管制

五、长难句(Difficult Sentences)

1. In carrying out their obligations pursuant to Article 5, affected developing country Parties and any other affected country Party in the framework of its regional implementation annex or, otherwise, that has notified the Permanent Secretariat in writing of its intention to prepare a national action programme, shall, as appropriate, prepare, make public and implement national action programmes, utilizing and building, to the extent possible, on existing relevant successful plans and programmes, and subregional and regional action programmes, as the central element of the strategy to combat desertification and mitigate the effects of drought. (Article 9, 1)

解析：that 引导的定语从句修饰 affected developing country Parties and any other affected country。as appropriate 和 to the extent possible 均为插入语。

译文：为履行第 5 条规定的义务，受影响发展中国家缔约方和在区域执行附件框架内，或以书面通知常设秘书处打算制定国家行动方案的任何其他受影响国家缔约方应尽可能利用现有的、相关的、成功的计划和方案，并在其基础上，酌情制定、公布和实施国家行动方案，并制定、公布和实施分区域和区域行动方案，将它们作为防治荒漠化、缓解干旱影响战略的中心内容。

2. The Parties agree, according to their respective capabilities, to integrate and coordinate the collection, analysis and exchange of relevant short-term and long-term data and information to ensure systematic observation of land degradation in affected areas and to understand better and assess the processes and effects of drought and desertification. (Article 16, Information collection, analysis and exchange)

解析：according to their respective capabilities 为插入语。to ensure 和 to understand 为并列成分，表示目的。

译文：缔约方同意根据各自能力综合和协调有关长、短期数据及信息的收集、分析和交流工作，确保系统性地观察受影响地区土地退化情况，更好地了解和评价干旱和荒漠化的过程和影响。

3. … protect, integrate, enhance and validate traditional and local knowledge, know-how and practices, ensuring, subject to their respective national legislation and/or policies, that the owners of that knowledge will directly benefit on an equitable basis and on mutually agreed terms from any commercial utilization of it or from any technological development derived from that knowledge. (Article 17, 1-c)

解析：subject to their respective national legislation and/or policies 是插入语，应单独理解。

译文：保护、整合、增强和验证传统的和地方的知识、技术和做法。在遵守其各国家法律和/或政策的前提下，确保知识的所有者将在公平基础上根据双方共同商定的条件，直接从知识的任何商业利用或从知识衍生的任何技术发展中受益。

4. Affected developing country Parties shall utilize, and where necessary, establish and/or strengthen, national coordinating mechanisms, integrated in national development programmes, that would ensure the efficient use of all available financial resources. (Article 21, 3)

解析：and where necessary 为插入语。integrated in national development programmes 及 that 引导的从句均用来修饰 national coordinating mechanisms。

译文：受影响国家缔约方应利用，在需要时建立和/或加强即将并入国家发展方案的国家协调机制，以便保证有效使用所有可获得的资金资源。

六、课后练习(Exercises)

1. Skimming and Scanning

Directions: Read the following passage excerpted from United Nations Convention to Combat Desertification in Countries Experiencing Serious Drought and/or Desertification, Particularly in Africa. At the end of the passage, there are six statements. Each statement contains information given in one of the paragraphs of the passage. Identify the paragraph from which the information is derived. Each paragraph is marked with a letter. You may choose a paragraph more than once. Answer the questions by writing the corresponding letter in the bracket in front of each statement.

The Parties to this Convention,

A. Affirming that human beings in affected or threatened areas are at the centre of concerns to combat desertification and mitigate the effects of drought, reflecting the urgent concern of the international community, including States and international organizations, about the adverse impacts of desertification and drought, aware that arid, semi-arid and dry sub-humid areas together account for a significant proportion of the Earth's land area and are the habitat and source of livelihood for a large segment of its population, acknowledging that desertification and drought are problems of global dimension in that they affect all regions of the world and that joint action of the international community is needed to combat desertification and/or mitigate the effects of drought,

B. Noting the high concentration of developing countries, notably the least developed countries, among those experiencing serious drought and/or desertification, and the particularly tragic consequences of these phenomena in Africa, noting also that desertification is caused by complex interactions among physical, biological, political, social, cultural and economic factors,

C. Considering the impact of trade and relevant aspects of international economic relations on the ability of affected countries to combat desertification adequately, conscious that sustainable economic growth, social development and poverty eradication are priorities of affected developing countries, particularly in Africa, and are essential to meeting sustainability objectives, mindful that desertification and drought affect sustainable development through their interrelationships with important social problems such as poverty, poor health and nutrition, lack of food security, and those arising from migration, displacement of persons and demographic dynamics,

D. Appreciating the significance of the past efforts and experience of States and international organizations in combating desertification and mitigating the effects of drought, particularly in implementing the *Plan of Action to Combat Desertification* which was adopted at the *United Nations Conference on Desertification* in 1977, realizing that, despite efforts in the past, progress in combating desertification and mitigating the effects of drought has not met expectations and that a new and more effective approach is needed at all levels within the framework of sustainable development,

E. Recognizing the validity and relevance of decisions adopted at the United Nations Conference on Environment and Development, particularly of Agenda 21 and its chapter 12, which provide a basis for combating desertification, reaffirming in this light the commitments of developed countries as contained in paragraph 13 of chapter 33 of Agenda 21, recalling General Assembly resolution 47/188, particularly the priority in it prescribed for Africa, and all other relevant United Nations resolutions, decisions and programmes on desertification and drought, as well as relevant declarations by African countries and those from other regions,

F. Reaffirming the Rio Declaration on Environment and Development which states, in its Principle 2, that States have, in accordance with the Charter of the United Nations and the principles of international law, the sovereign right to exploit their own resources pursuant to their own environmental and developmental policies, and the responsibility to ensure that activities within their jurisdiction or control do not cause damage to the environment of other States or of areas beyond the limits of national jurisdiction,

G. Recognizing that national Governments play a critical role in combating desertification and mitigating the effects of drought and that progress in that respect depends on local implementation of action programmes in affected areas, recognizing also the importance and necessity of international cooperation and partnership in combating desertification and mitigating the effects of drought, recognizing further the importance of the provision to affected developing countries, particularly in Africa, of effective means, *inter alia* substantial financial resources, including new and additional funding, and access to technology, without which it will be difficult for them to implement fully their commitments under this Convention,

H. Expressing concern over the impact of desertification and drought on affected countries in Central Asia and the Transcaucasus, stressing the important role played by women in regions affected by desertification and/or drought, particularly in rural areas of developing countries, and the importance of ensuring the full participation of both men and women at all levels in programmes to combat desertification and mitigate the effects of drought,

I. Emphasizing the special role of non-governmental organizations and other major groups in programmes to combat desertification and mitigate the effects of drought, bearing in mind the relationship between desertification and other environmental problems of global dimension facing the international and national communities, bearing also in mind the contribution that combating desertification can make to achieving the objectives of the *United Nations Framework Convention on Climate Change*, the

Convention on Biological Diversity and other related environmental conventions,

J. Believing that strategies to combat desertification and mitigate the effects of drought will be most effective if they are based on sound systematic observation and rigorous scientific knowledge and if they are continuously re-evaluated,

K. Recognizing the urgent need to improve the effectiveness and coordination of international cooperation to facilitate the implementation of national plans and priorities, determined to take appropriate action in combating desertification and mitigating the effects of drought for the benefit of present and future generations …

(_____) (1) A large portion of the Earth's land area is arid, semi-arid and dry sub-humid.

(_____) (2) To implement fully their commitments under this Convention, it is important to provide effective means to affected developing countries, particularly in Africa.

(_____) (3) It is stressed that the full participation of both men and women at all levels in programmes to combat desertification and mitigate the effects of drought should be ensured.

(_____) (4) The affected developing countries, particularly in Africa should take priorities to sustainable economic growth, social development and poverty eradication to meeting sustainability objectives.

(_____) (5) According to the Charter of the United Nations and the principles of international law, the sovereign right to exploit their own resources pursuant to their own environmental and developmental policies are ensured.

(_____) (6) Non-governmental organizations and other major groups in programmes play the special role in combating desertification and mitigating the effects of drought.

2. Reading Comprehension

Directions: Read **Article 10-National action programmes** and **Article 19-Capacity building, education and public awareness** from United Nations Convention to Combat Desertification in Countries Experiencing Serious Drought and/or Desertification, Particularly in Africa, and decide whether the following statements are True or False. Write T for True or F for False in the bracket in front of each statement.

A. Questions 1 to 3 are based on **Article 10-National action programmes.**

(1) (_____) The purpose of national action programmes is to classify the factors contributing to desertification and practical measures necessary to combat desertification and mitigate the effects of drought.

(2) (_____) National action programmes shall be integrated with local policies for sustainable development.

(3) (_____) drought contingency plans at the local, national, subregional and

regional levels should be taken into consideration seasonal in the National action programmes

B. Questions 4 to 6 are based on **Article 19-Capacity building, education and public awareness.**

(4)(_____) To combat desertification, capacity building — that is to say, institution building, training and development of relevant local and national capacities is of significance.

(5)(_____) The networks of regional education and training centres to combat desertification and mitigate the effects of drought shall be established to train scientific, technical and management personnel and responsible for education and training in affected country Parties.

(6)(_____) Competent intergovernmental organizations shall cooperate with non-governmental organizations to promote understanding of the causes and effects of desertification and drought.

3. Extensive Reading

Directions: In this section, there is a passage with ten blanks. You are required to select one word for each blank from a list of choices given in a word bank following the passage. Read the passage through carefully before making your choices. Each choice in the bank is identified by a letter. You may not use any of the words in the bank more than once.

Desertification, also called desertization, the process by which natural or human causes reduce the biological productivity of drylands (arid and semiarid lands). Declines in productivity may be the result of climate change, deforestation, overgrazing, poverty, political instability, unsustainable irrigation practices, or (1)_____ of these factors. The concept does not refer to the physical (2)_____ of existing deserts but rather to the various processes that threaten all dryland (3)_____, including deserts as well as grasslands and scrublands.

Slightly less than half of Earth's ice-free land surface — approximately 52 million square km (about 20 million square miles) — is drylands, and these drylands cover some of the world's poorest countries. The United Nations Environment Programme (UNEP) notes that desertification has (4)_____ 36 million square km (14 million square miles) of land and is a major international concern. According to the United Nations Convention to Combat Desertification, the lives of 250 million people are affected by (5)_____, and as many as 135 million people may be displaced by desertification by 2045, making it one of the most severe environmental (6)_____ facing humanity.

Africa is the continent most affected by desertification, and one of the most obvious natural (7)_____ on the landmass is the southern edge of the Sahara Desert. The countries that lie on the edge of the Sahara are among the poorest in the world, and they are (8) _____ to periodic droughts that devastate their peoples. African drylands (which include the Sahara, the Kalahari, and the grasslands of East Africa) span 20 million square km (about 7.7 million square miles), some 65 percent of the continent. One-third of Africa's drylands are largely (9) _____ arid deserts, while the remaining two-thirds support two-thirds of the continent's burgeoning human population. As Africa's population increases, the productivity of the land supporting this population (10) _____. Some one-fifth of the irrigated cropland, three-fifths of the rain-fed cropland, and three-fourths of the rangeland have been at least moderately harmed by desertification.

A. affected	B. borders	C. expansion	D. subject
E. combinations	F. challenges	G. declines	H. desertification
I. attached	J. contentment	K. deserted	L. uninhabited
M. ecosystems	N. vacuum	O. ecosystems	P. resemblance

4. Vocabulary Expanding

Directions: In this section, there are ten sentences from the United Nations Convention to Combat Desertification in Countries Experiencing Serious Drought and/or Desertification, Particularly in Africa. You are required to complete sentences with the proper form of the words given in brackets.

(1) The Parties should ensure that decisions on the design and implementation of programmes to combat desertification and/or mitigate the effects of drought are taken with the _____ of populations and local communities and that an enabling environment is created at higher levels to facilitate action at national and local levels. (participate)

(2) The Parties should develop, in a spirit of partnership, cooperation among all levels of government, communities, non-governmental organizations and landholders to establish a better understanding of the nature and value of land and scarce water resources in affected areas and to work towards their _____ use. (sustain)

(3) The Parties shall implement their obligations under this Convention, individually or jointly, either through existing or _____ bilateral and multilateral arrangements or a combination thereof, as appropriate, emphasizing the need to coordinate efforts and develop a coherent long-term strategy at all levels. (prospect)

(4) In pursuing the objective of this Convention, the Parties shall promote the use of existing bilateral and multilateral financial mechanisms and arrangements that _____ and channel substantial financial resources to affected developing country Parties in combating desertification and mitigating the effects of drought. (mobile)

(5) In addition to their obligations pursuant to Article 4, affected country Parties undertake to establish strategies and _____, within the framework of sustainable

development plans and/or policies, to combat desertification and mitigate the effects of drought. (prior)

(6) In addition to their general obligations pursuant to Article 4, developed country Parties undertake to: provide substantial _____ resources and other forms of support to assist affected developing country Parties, particularly those in Africa, effectively to develop and implement their own long-term plans and strategies to combat desertification and mitigate the effects of drought. (finance)

(7) The provisions of this Convention shall not affect the rights and obligations of any Party deriving from a bilateral, _____ or international agreement into which it has entered prior to the entry into force of this Convention for it. (region)

(8) The Parties shall encourage organs, funds and programmes of the United Nations system and other relevant _____ organizations, academic institutions, the scientific community and non-governmental organizations in a position to cooperate, in accordance with their mandates and capabilities, to support the elaboration, implementation and follow-up of action programmes. (government)

(9) Affected country Parties, in collaboration with other Parties and the international community, should cooperate to ensure the promotion of an enabling international environment in the _____ of the Convention. Such cooperation should also cover fields of technology transfer as well as scientific research and development, information collection and dissemination and financial resources. (implement)

(10) The Parties agree, according to their respective capabilities, to integrate and coordinate the collection, analysis and exchange of relevant short-term and long-term data and information to ensure _____ observation of land degradation in affected areas and to understand better and assess the processes and effects of drought and desertification. (system)

七、思考题(Questions for Discussion)

Directions: Work in groups and answer the following questions.

1. What is the background and significance of the *United Nations Convention to Combat Desertification in Countries Experiencing Serious Drought and/or Desertification, Particularly in Africa*?

2. What are the shared characteristics between the *United Nations Convention to Combat Desertification in Countries Experiencing Serious Drought and/or Desertification, Particularly in Africa* and *United Nations Framework Convention on Climate Change*?

3. What are the troubles and difficulties in implementation of the *United Nations Convention to Combat Desertification in Countries Experiencing Serious Drought and/or Desertification, Particularly in Africa*?

八、拓展学习(Further Studies)

Directions: Surf the Internet and find more information about the following topics before or after class. Present to the class some successful projects to illustrate the application of these concepts to practice.

1. Implementation of the United Nations Convention to Combat Desertification in Countries Experiencing Serious Drought and/or Desertification, Particularly in Africa in foreign countries.

2. Efforts in Implementation of the *United Nations Convention to Combat Desertification in Countries Experiencing Serious Drought and/or Desertification, Particularly in Africa* in China.

九、模拟联合国大会(Model United Nations Practice)

Directions: Work in teams and simulate the institutions and committees of the United Nations, featuring delegates of the UN members and the six committees of the General Assembly, negotiating issues of desertification in the world and working out resolutions. Students are suggested to focus on the following topics:

1. What are the main reasons for desertification?
2. What are the functions of forestry in combating desertification?
3. How to solve drought and water shortage problems around the world?

第四章

国际湿地公约

Convention on Wetlands of International Importance especially as Waterfowl Habitat

一、背景知识(Background)

《国际湿地公约》全称为《关于特别是作为水禽栖息地的国际重要湿地公约》,简称《湿地公约》或拉姆萨公约(英文简称 RAMSAR)。1971年2月2日,来自18个国家的代表在伊朗南部海滨小城拉姆萨签署,1975年12月21日生效,1982年3月12日议定书修正。《湿地公约》是关于湿地及其生物多样性保护的多边国际公约,旨在保护和合理利用全球湿地。其宗旨是承认人类与环境的相互依存关系,并通过协调一致的国际行动确保作为众多水禽繁殖栖息地的湿地得到良好的保护而不至于丧失。秘书处设在瑞士格兰德。缔约方会议为《湿地公约》最高机构,每三年举行一次会议,审议成员国和国际组织共同关心的湿地保护问题,通过决议或决定的方式,确定工作计划和努力方向。我国于1992年2月20日递交加入书,1992年7月31日正式对我国生效。履约主管部门为国家林业和草原局。湿地公约是全球第一部政府间多边环境公约,截止到2019年已有170个缔约方。《湿地公约》主张以湿地保护和"明智利用"为原则,在不损坏湿地生态系统的范围之内可持续利用湿地。1996年3月,《湿地公约》常务委员会第19次会议决定,从1997年起,将每年的2月2日定为"世界湿地日"。

二、公约原文(The Text of the Convention)

Convention on Wetlands of International Importance especially as Waterfowl Habitat

Ramsar, Iran, 2. 2. 1971

as amended by the Protocol of 3. 12. 1982

and the Amendments of 28. 5. 1987

Paris, 13 July 1994

Director, Office of International Standards and Legal Affairs

United Nations Educational, Scientific and Cultural Organization (UNESCO)

The Contracting Parties,

RECOGNIZING the interdependence of Man and his environment;

CONSIDERING the fundamental ecological functions of wetlands as regulators of water regimes and as habitats supporting a characteristic flora and fauna, especially waterfowl;

BEING CONVINCED that wetlands constitute a resource of great economic, cultural, scientific, and recreational value, the loss of which would be irreparable;

DESIRING to stem the progressive encroachment on and loss of wetlands now and in the future;

RECOGNIZING that waterfowl in their seasonal migrations may transcend frontiers and so should be regarded as an international resource;

BEING CONFIDENT that the conservation of wetlands and their flora and fauna can be ensured by combining far-sighted national policies with coordinated international action;

Have agreed as follows:

Article 1

1. For the purpose of this Convention wetlands are areas of marsh, fen, peatland or water, whether natural or artificial, permanent or temporary, with water that is static or flowing, fresh, brackish or salt, including areas of marine water the depth of which at low tide does not exceed six metres.

2. For the purpose of this Convention waterfowl are birds ecologically dependent on wetlands.

Article 2

1. Each Contracting Party shall designate suitable wetlands within its territory for inclusion in a List of Wetlands of International Importance, hereinafter referred to as

"the List" which is maintained by the bureau established under Article 8. The boundaries of each wetland shall be precisely described and also delimited on a map and they may incorporate riparian and coastal zones adjacent to the wetlands, and islands or bodies of marine water deeper than six metres at low tide lying within the wetlands, especially where these have importance as waterfowl habitat.

2. Wetlands should be selected for the List on account of their international significance in terms of ecology, botany, zoology, limnology or hydrology. In the first instance wetlands of international importance to waterfowl at any season should be included.

3. The inclusion of a wetland in the List does not prejudice the exclusive sovereign rights of the Contracting Party in whose territory the wetland is situated.

4. Each Contracting Party shall designate at least one wetland to be included in the List when signing this Convention or when depositing its instrument of ratification or accession, as provided in Article 9.

5. Any Contracting Party shall have the right to add to the List further wetlands situated within its territory, to extend the boundaries of those wetlands already included by it in the List, or, because of its urgent national interests, to delete or restrict the boundaries of wetlands already included by it in the List and shall, at the earliest possible time, inform the organization or government responsible for the continuing bureau duties specified in Article 8 of any such changes.

6. Each Contracting Party shall consider its international responsibilities for the conservation, management and wise use of migratory stocks of waterfowl, both when designating entries for the List and when exercising its right to change entries in the List relating to wetlands within its territory.

Article 3

1. The Contracting Parties shall formulate and implement their planning so as to promote the conservation of the wetlands included in the List, and as far as possible the wise use of wetlands in their territory.

2. Each Contracting Party shall arrange to be informed at the earliest possible time if the ecological character of any wetland in its territory and included in the List has changed, is changing or is likely to change as the result of technological developments, pollution or other human interference. Information on such changes shall be passed without delay to the organization or government responsible for the continuing bureau duties specified in Article 8.

Article 4

1. Each Contracting Party shall promote the conservation of wetlands and waterfowl by establishing nature reserves on wetlands, whether they are included in the List or

not, and provide adequately for their wardening.

2. Where a Contracting Party in its urgent national interest, deletes or restricts the boundaries of a wetland included in the List, it should as far as possible compensate for any loss of wetland resources, and in particular it should create additional nature reserves for waterfowl and for the protection, either in the same area or elsewhere, of an adequate portion of the original habitat.

3. The Contracting Parties shall encourage research and the exchange of data and publications regarding wetlands and their flora and fauna.

4. The Contracting Parties shall endeavour through management to increase waterfowl populations on appropriate wetlands.

5. The Contracting Parties shall promote the training of personnel competent in the fields of wetland research, management and wardening.

Article 5

The Contracting Parties shall consult with each other about implementing obligations arising from the Convention especially in the case of a wetland extending over the territories of more than one Contracting Party or where a water system is shared by Contracting Parties. They shall at the same time endeavour to coordinate and support present and future policies and regulations concerning the conservation of wetlands and their flora and fauna.

Article 6

1. There shall be established a Conference of the Contracting Parties to review and promote the implementation of this Convention. The Bureau referred to in Article 8, paragraph 1, shall convene ordinary meetings of the Conference of the Contracting Parties at intervals of not more than three years, unless the Conference decides otherwise, and extraordinary meetings at the written requests of at least one third of the Contracting Parties. Each ordinary meeting of the Conference of the Contracting Parties shall determine the time and venue of the next ordinary meeting.

2. The Conference of the Contracting Parties shall be competent:

(a) to discuss the implementation of this Convention;

(b) to discuss additions to and changes in the List;

(c) to consider information regarding changes in the ecological character of wetlands included in the List provided in accordance with paragraph 2 of Article 3;

(d) to make general or specific recommendations to the Contracting Parties regarding the conservation, management and wise use of wetlands and their flora and fauna;

(e) to request relevant international bodies to prepare reports and statistics on matters which are essentially international in character affecting wetlands;

(f) to adopt other recommendations, or resolutions, to promote the functioning of this Convention.

3. The Contracting Parties shall ensure that those responsible at all levels for wetlands management shall be informed of, and take into consideration, recommendations of such Conferences concerning the conservation, management and wise use of wetlands and their flora and fauna.

4. The Conference of the Contracting Parties shall adopt rules of procedure for each of its meetings.

5. The Conference of the Contracting Parties shall establish and keep under review the financial regulations of this Convention. At each of its ordinary meetings, it shall adopt the budget for the next financial period by a two-third majority of Contracting Parties present and voting.

6. Each Contracting Party shall contribute to the budget according to a scale of contributions adopted by unanimity of the Contracting Parties present and voting at a meeting of the ordinary Conference of the Contracting Parties.

Article 7

1. The representatives of the Contracting Parties at such Conferences should include persons who are experts on wetlands or waterfowl by reason of knowledge and experience gained in scientific, administrative or other appropriate capacities.

2. Each of the Contracting Parties represented at a Conference shall have one vote, recommendations, resolutions and decisions being adopted by a simple majority of the Contracting Parties present and voting, unless otherwise provided for in this Convention.

Article 8

1. The International Union for Conservation of Nature and Natural Resources shall perform the continuing bureau duties under this Convention until such time as another organization or government is appointed by a majority of two-thirds of all Contracting Parties.

2. The continuing bureau duties shall be, *inter alia*:

(a) to assist in the convening and organizing of Conferences specified in Article 6;

(b) to maintain the *List of Wetlands of International Importance* and to be informed by the Contracting Parties of any additions, extensions, deletions or restrictions concerning wetlands included in the List provided in accordance with paragraph 5 of Article 2;

(c) to be informed by the Contracting Parties of any changes in the ecological character of wetlands included in the List provided in accordance with paragraph 2 of Article 3;

(d) to forward notification of any alterations to the List, or changes in character of wetlands included therein, to all Contracting Parties and to arrange for these matters to be discussed at the next Conference;

(e) to make known to the Contracting Party concerned, the recommendations of the Conferences in respect of such alterations to the List or of changes in the character of wetlands included therein.

Article 9

1. This Convention shall remain open for signature indefinitely.

2. Any member of the United Nations or of one of the Specialized Agencies or of the International Atomic Energy Agency or Party to the Statute of the International Court of Justice may become a Party to this Convention by:

(a) signature without reservation as to ratification;

(b) signature subject to ratification followed by ratification;

(c) accession.

3. Ratification or accession shall be effected by the deposit of an instrument of ratification or accession with the Director-General of the United Nations Educational, Scientific and Cultural Organization (hereinafter referred to as "the Depositary")

Article 10

1. This Convention shall enter into force four months after seven States have become Parties to this Convention in accordance with paragraph 2 of Article 9.

2. Thereafter this Convention shall enter into force for each Contracting Party four months after the day of its signature without reservation as to ratification, or its deposit of an instrument of ratification or accession.

Article 10 bis

1. This Convention may be amended at a meeting of the Contracting Parties convened for that purpose in accordance with this article.

2. Proposals for amendment may be made by any Contracting Party.

3. The text of any proposed amendment and the reasons for it shall be communicated to the organization or government performing the continuing bureau duties under the Convention (hereinafter referred to as "the Bureau") and shall promptly be communicated by the Bureau to all Contracting Parties. Any comments on the text by the Contracting Parties shall be communicated to the Bureau within three months of the date on which the amendments were communicated to the Contracting Parties by the Bureau. The Bureau shall, immediately after the last day for submission of comments, communicate to the Contracting Parties all comments submitted by that day.

4. A meeting of Contracting Parties to consider an amendment communicated in accordance with paragraph 3 shall be convened by the Bureau upon the written request of one third of the Contracting Parties. The Bureau shall consult the Parties concerning the time and venue of the meeting.

5. Amendments shall be adopted by a two-thirds majority of the Contracting Parties present and voting.

6. An amendment adopted shall enter into force for the Contracting Parties which have accepted it on the first day of the fourth month following the date on which two thirds of the Contracting Parties have deposited an instrument of acceptance with the Depositary. For each Contracting Party which deposits an instrument of acceptance after the date on which two thirds of the Contracting Parties have deposited an instrument of acceptance, the amendment shall enter into force on the first day of the fourth month following the date of the deposit of its instrument of acceptance.

Article 11

1. This Convention shall continue in force for an indefinite period.

2. Any Contracting Party may denounce this Convention after a period of five years from the date on which it entered into force for that party by giving written notice thereof to the Depositary. Denunciation shall take effect four months after the day on which notice thereof is received by the Depositary.

Article 12

1. The Depositary shall inform all States that have signed and acceded to this Convention as soon as possible of:

(a) signatures to the Convention;

(b) deposits of instruments of ratification of this Convention;

(c) deposits of instruments of accession to this Convention;

(d) the date of entry into force of this Convention;

(e) notifications of denunciation of this Convention.

2. When this Convention has entered into force, the Depositary shall have it registered with the Secretariat of the United Nations in accordance with Article 102 of the Charter.

IN WITNESS WHEREOF, the undersigned, being duly authorized to that effect, have signed this Convention.

DONE at Ramsar this 2nd day of February 1971, in a single original in the English, French, German and Russian languages, all texts being equally authentic* which shall be deposited with the Depositary which shall send true copies thereof to all Contracting Parties.

*Pursuant to the *Final Act of the Conference* to conclude the Protocol, the Depositary provided the second Conference of the Contracting Parties with official versions of the Convention in the Arabic, Chinese and Spanish languages, prepared in consultation with interested Governments and with the assistance of the Bureau.

(Source: https://www.ramsar.org/sites/default/files/documents/libary/scam_

certified_ e. polf)

三、注解(Notes)

1. The International Union for Conservation of Nature and Natural Resources

国际自然保护联盟(IUCN)是由主权国家、政府机构和非政府组织共同参与组成的一个国际组织。国际自然保护联盟于1948年10月5日在联合国教科文组织和法国政府在法国的枫丹白露联合举行的会议上成立,当时名为国际自然保护协会,1956年6月在爱丁堡改为现名。总部设在瑞士的格朗。国际自然保护联盟是由来自180多个国家的1000多名国际知名的科学家和专家为其下属的6个全球性的委员会工作。在世界62个国家设有办事处,服务于500多个项目。旨在促进解决世界范围内的自然资源的保护和合理利用问题,是当前世界上涉及自然和自然资源保护问题的主要国际研究协调组织。

2. The International Atomic Energy Agency

国际原子能机构(IAEA)是国际原子能领域的政府间科学技术合作组织,同时兼管地区原子安全及测量检查,于1954年12月由第9届联大通过决议设立并于1957年7月成立,是联合国的一个专门机构,总部设在维也纳。现任总干事巴拉迪（埃及人）于1997年12月1日任职,至1999年年底,共有130个成员国。1984年1月1日中国正式成为国际原子能机构成员国,1984年6月,机构理事会接纳中国为指定理事国。

国际原子能机构的宗旨是"加速扩大原子能对全世界和平、健康和繁荣的贡献",并"确保由机构本身,或经机构请求、或在其监督管制下提供的协助不致用于推进任何军事目的"。由35国组成的理事会为该组织最高执行机构;秘书处由总干事领导下的专业人员和工作人员组成,总干事由理事会任命,6名副总干事负责6个独立的部门;下设科学咨询委员会、技术援助委员会、行政和预算委员会和保障委员会;每年召开一次由全体成员国代表组成的大会;出版物有《核聚变》《国际原子能机构通报》。

四、相关词汇(Key Words and Phrases)

1. depositary [dɪˈpɒzɪt(ə)rɪ] n. 受托人
2. waterfowl [ˈwɔːtəfaʊl] n. 水禽;[鸟]水鸟
3. delimited [diˈlimitid] v. 划定…的界限;限定(delimit 的过去分词)
   adj. 划定界限的;被限定了的
4. riparian [raɪˈpeərɪən] adj. 河边的,水滨的
   n. 河岸拥有人
5. adjacent [əˈdʒeɪs(ə)nt] adj. 邻近的;毗连的;接近的

6. botany	[ˈbɒt(ə)nɪ]	n.	植物学；精纺毛纱；细羊毛	
7. hydrology	[haɪˈdrɒlədʒɪ]	n.	水文学，水文地理学	
8. sovereign	[ˈsɒvrɪn]	adj.	至高无上的；有主权的；拥有最高统治权的	
		n.	君主；独立国；最高统治者	
9. designate	[ˈdezɪgneɪt]	vt.	指定；指派；标出；把…定名为	
		adj.	指定的；选定的	
10. migratory	[ˈmaɪgrət(ə)rɪ]	adj.	迁移的；流浪的	
11. compensate	[ˈkɒmpenseɪt]	vi.	补偿，赔偿；抵消	
		vt.	补偿，赔偿；付报酬	
12. flora	[ˈflɔrə]	n.	植物；群落	
13. unanimity	[juːnəˈnɪmɪtɪ]	n.	同意，全体一致	
14. submission	[səbˈmɪʃ(ə)n]	n.	投降；屈服，服从；谦恭，柔顺；提交，呈递	
15. procedure	[prəˈsiːdʒə]	n.	程序，手续；步骤	
16. venue	[ˈvenjuː]	n.	审判地；集合地；会场，场所	
17. extension	[ɪkˈstenʃ(ə)n; ek-]	n.	伸展，扩大；延长，延期	

五、长难句（Difficult Sentences）

1. For the purpose of this Convention wetlands are areas of marsh, fen, peatland or water, whether natural or artificial, permanent or temporary, with water that is static or flowing, fresh, brackish or salt, including areas of marine water the depth of which at low tide does not exceed six metres. （Article 1, 1）

解析：that 引导的定语从句修饰 water；the depth of which 相当于 whose depth，修饰前面的 marine water。

译文：本公约定义湿地为天然或人造、永久或暂时之死水或流水、淡水、微咸或咸水沼泽地、泥炭地或水域，包括低潮时水深不超过6米的海水区。

2. Each Contracting Party shall designate suitable wetlands within its territory for inclusion in a List of Wetlands of International Importance, hereinafter referred to as "the List" which is maintained by the bureau established under Article 8. （Article 2, 1）

解析：hereinafter 意为：以下，下文地（adv.）；which 引导从句修饰"the List"。

译文：每个缔约国应指定其领土内适当湿地列入《具有国际意义的湿地目录》（下称《目录》），该《目录》由根据第8条设立的办事处保管。

3. The Contracting Parties shall formulate and implement their planning so as to promote the conservation of the wetlands included in the List, and as far as possible the wise use of wetlands in their territory. （Article 3, 1）

解析：so as to 表目的；to promote the conservation 意为"促进，以促进……"；as

far as possible 尽可能。这一短语引导的 the wise use of 与前文的 the conservation of 为并列成分。

译文：各缔约国应制定和执行规划，以促进对列入《目录》的湿地的保护，并尽可能地合理使用其领土内的湿地。

4. Each of the Contracting Parties represented at a Conference shall have one vote, recommendations, resolutions and decisions being adopted by a simple majority of the Contracting Parties present and voting, unless otherwise provided for in this Convention. (Article 7, 2)

解析：being adopted by 现在分词引导的被动语态作定语修饰前文的 recommendations, resolutions and decisions，意为"为……所采纳"。present and voting 作定语修饰 the Contracting Parties。Unless 引导的让步状语从句。

译文：出席会议的每一缔约国有一票表决权；建议、决议和决定由出席会议及参加投票的缔约国的简单多数通过，除非本公约另作其他规定。

六、课后练习(Exercises)

1. Skimming and Scanning

Directions: Read the following passage excerpted from Convention on Wetlands of International Importance especially as Waterfowl Habitat At the end of the passage, there are six statements. Each statement contains information given in one of the paragraphs of the passage. Identify the paragraph from which the information is derived. Each paragraph is marked with a letter. You may choose a paragraph more than once. Answer the questions by writing the corresponding letter in the bracket in front of each statement.

A. For the purpose of this Convention wetlands are areas of marsh, fen, peatland or water, whether natural or artificial, permanent or temporary, with water that is static or flowing, fresh, brackish or salt, including areas of marine water the depth of which at low tide does not exceed six metres. For the purpose of this Convention waterfowl are birds ecologically dependent on wetlands.

B. Each Contracting Party shall designate suitable wetlands within its territory for inclusion in a List of Wetlands of International Importance, hereinafter referred to as "the List" which is maintained by the bureau established under Article 8. The boundaries of each wetland shall be precisely described and also delimited on a map and they may incorporate riparian and coastal zones adjacent to the wetlands, and islands or bodies of marine water deeper than six metres at low tide lying within the wetlands, especially where these have importance as waterfowl habitat.

C. Wetlands should be selected for the List on account of their international significance in terms of ecology, botany, zoology, limnology or hydrology. In the first instance wetlands of international importance to waterfowl at any season should be included. The inclusion of a wetland in the List does not prejudice the exclusive sovereign rights of the Contracting Party in whose territory the wetland is situated.

D. Each Contracting Party shall designate at least one wetland to be included in the List when signing this Convention or when depositing its instrument of ratification or accession, as provided in Article 9. Any Contracting Party shall have the right to add to the List further wetlands situated within its territory, to extend the boundaries of those wetlands already included by it in the List, or, because of its urgent national interests, to delete or restrict the boundaries of wetlands already included by it in the List and shall, at the earliest possible time, inform the organization or government responsible for the continuing bureau duties specified in Article 8 of any such changes.

E. Each Contracting Party shall consider its international responsibilities for the conservation, management and wise use of migratory stocks of waterfowl, both when designating entries for the List and when exercising its right to change entries in the List relating to wetlands within its territory.

F. The Contracting Parties shall formulate and implement their planning so as to promote the conservation of the wetlands included in the List, and as far as possible the wise use of wetlands in their territory.

G. Each Contracting Party shall arrange to be informed at the earliest possible time if the ecological character of any wetland in its territory and included in the List has changed, is changing or is likely to change as the result of technological developments, pollution or other human interference. Information on such changes shall be passed without delay to the organization or government responsible for the continuing bureau duties specified in Article 8.

H. Each Contracting Party shall promote the conservation of wetlands and waterfowl by establishing nature reserves on wetlands, whether they are included in the List or not, and provide adequately for their wardening.

I. Where a Contracting Party in its urgent national interest, deletes or restricts the boundaries of a wetland included in the List, it should as far as possible compensate for any loss of wetland resources, and in particular it should create additional nature reserves for waterfowl and for the protection, either in the same area or elsewhere, of an adequate portion of the original habitat.

J. The Contracting Parties shall encourage research and the exchange of data and publications regarding wetlands and their flora and fauna. The Contracting Parties shall endeavour through management to increase waterfowl populations on appropriate wetlands. The Contracting Parties shall promote the training of personnel competent in the fields of wetland research, management and wardening.

K. The Contracting Parties shall consult with each other about implementing obligations arising from the Convention especially in the case of a wetland extending over the territories of more than one Contracting Party or where a water system is shared by Contracting Parties. They shall at the same time endeavour to coordinate and support present and future policies and regulations concerning the conservation of wetlands and their flora and fauna.

(_____) (1) For each Contracting Party, at least one wetland should be designated to be included in the *List of Wetlands of International Importance* when signing this Convention.

(_____) (2) The Contracting Parties are encouraged to promote the training of personnel competent in the fields of wetland research, management and wardening.

(_____) (3) Wetlands of international importance to waterfowl at any season should be taken priority in selection for the *List of Wetlands of International Importance*.

(_____) (4) Wetlands are defined to be areas of marsh, fen, peatland or water, whether natural or artificial, permanent or temporary, with water that is static or flowing, fresh, brackish or salt, including areas of marine water the depth of which at low tide does not exceed six metres for the purpose of this Convention.

(_____) (5) The international responsibilities for the conservation, management and wise use of migratory stocks of waterfowl, both when designating entries for the List and when exercising its right to change entries in the List relating to wetlands within its territory should be taken for each Contracting Party.

(_____) (6) Information on such changes as ecological character of any wetland in its territory and changes in the List of Wetlands of International Importance shall be passed without delay to the organization or government responsible for the continuing bureau duties specified in Article 8.

2. Reading Comprehension

Directions: Read **Article 9** and **Article 10 bis** from Convention on Wetlands of International Importance especially as Waterfowl Habitat, and decide whether the following statements are True or False. Write T for True or F for False in the bracket in front of each statement.

A. Questions 1 to 3 are based on **Article 9**.

(1) (_____) Any country is welcome to sign and become a Party to this Convention without ratification.

(2) (_____) For any member of the United Nations, the accession to this Convention is not subject to ratification and reservation.

(3) (_____) The Director-General of the United Nations Educational, Scientific and Cultural Organization is responsible for the deposit of an instrument of ratification or accession.

B. Questions 4 to 6 are based on **Article 10 bis**.

(4) (_____) The amendment for this convention may be made by any Contra-

cting Party.

(5) (_____) The Contracting Parties shall make comments on the proposed amendment and communicate to the Bureau within three months of the date on which the amendments were communicated to the Contracting Parties by the Bureau.

(6) (_____) Any proposed amendment shall be adopted by a two-thirds majority of the Contracting Parties.

3. Extensive Reading

Directions: In this section, there is a passage with ten blanks. You are required to select one word for each blank from a list of choices given in a word bank following the passage. Read the passage through carefully before making your choices. Each choice in the bank is identified by a letter. You may not use any of the words in the bank more than once.

Wetlands are vital for human survival. They are among the world's most productive environments; cradles of biological (1) _____ that provide the water and productivity upon which countless species of plants and animals depend for survival. Wetlands are indispensable for the countless benefits or "ecosystem services" that they provide humanity, (2) _____ from freshwater supply, food and building materials, and biodiversity, to flood control, groundwater recharge, and climate change mitigation. Yet study after study demonstrates that wetland area and quality continue to (3) _____ in most regions of the world. As a result, the ecosystem services that wetlands provide to people are compromised.

Managing wetlands is a global challenge and the Convention presently counts 170 countries as Contracting Parties, which recognize the value of having one international treaty (4) _____ to a single ecosystem. The Convention uses a (5) _____ definition of wetlands. This includes all lakes and rivers, underground aquifers, swamps and marshes, wet grasslands, peatlands, oases, estuaries, deltas and tidal flats, mangroves and other coastal areas, coral reefs, and all human-made sites such as fish ponds, rice paddies, reservoirs and salt pans.

At the centre of the Ramsar philosophy is the "wise use" of wetlands. When they accede to the Convention, Contracting Parties commit to work towards the wise use of all the wetlands and water resources in their territory, through national plans, policies and legislation, management actions and public education. The Convention (6) _____ wise use of wetlands as "the maintenance of their ecological character, achieved through the implementation of ecosystem approaches, within the context of (7) _____ development". Wise use can thus be seen as the conservation and sustainable use of wetlands and all the services they provide, for the benefit of people and nature. Contracting Parties commit to work towards the wise use of all the wetlands and water resources in their territory, through national plans, policies and legislation, management actions and public education.

In 1990 the Contracting Parties adopted Guidelines for the (8) _____ of the wise use concept. The Guidelines emphasized the importance of adopting national wetland policies, either (9) _____ or as a component of wider initiatives such as national environmental action plans; developing programmes covering wetland inventory, monitoring, research, training, education and public awareness and developing (10) _____ management plans at wetland sites.

A. dedicated	B. primarily	C. diversity	D. implication	E. defines
F. integrated	G. sustainable	H. implementation	I. arranges	J. ranging
K. extending	L. broad	M. separately	N. descend	O. decline

4. Vocabulary Expanding

Directions: In this section, there are ten sentences from Convention on Wetlands of International Importance especially as Waterfowl Habitat. You are required to complete these sentences with the proper form of the words given in the brackets.

(1) The Contracting Parties consider the fundamental ecological functions of wetlands as regulators of water regimes and as habitats supporting a _____ flora and fauna, especially waterfowl. (character)

(2) The continuing bureau duties shall be to make known to the Contracting Party concerned, the recommendations of the Conferences in respect of such _____ to the List or of changes in the character of wetlands included therein. (alter)

(3) This Convention shall enter into force for each Contracting Party four months after the day of its signature without reservation as to ratification, or its deposit of an instrument of ratification or _____. (access)

(4) The Contracting Parties desire to stem the _____ encroachment on and loss of wetlands now and in the future. (progress)

(5) The Contracting Parties shall consult with each other about _____ obligations arising from the Convention especially in the case of a wetland extending over the territories of more than one Contracting Party or where a water system is shared by Contracting Parties. (implement)

(6) The _____ of a wetland in the List does not prejudice the exclusive sovereign rights of the Contracting Party in whose territory the wetland is situated. (include)

(7) The Contracting Parties are convinced that wetlands constitute a resource of great economic, cultural, scientific, and recreational value, the loss of which would be _____. (reparable)

(8) Each Contracting Party shall consider its international responsibilities for the conservation, management and wise use of _____ stocks of waterfowl, both when designating entries for the List and when exercising its right to change entries in the List

relating to wetlands within its territory. (migrate)

(9) Each Contracting Party shall promote the conservation of wetlands and waterfowl by establishing nature reserves on wetlands, whether they are included in the List or not, and provide _____ for their wardening. (adequate)

(10) The Contracting Parties recognize that waterfowl in their _____ migrations may transcend frontiers and so should be regarded as an international resource. (season)

七、思考题(Questions for Discussion)

Directions: Work in groups and answer the following questions.

1. What is the background of establishment of the World Wetlands Day?
2. When and where was the Convention formally established and what actions have been done with regard to the Convention?
3. What is the objective of the Convention?
4. What are the basic concepts about wetlands according to the Convention? Give some examples.

八、拓展学习(Further Studies)

Directions: Surf the Internet and find more information on the following topics before or after class. Present to the class some successful projects to illustrate the application of these concepts to practice.

1. What efforts does China make in Implementation of the *Convention on Wetlands of International Importance especially as Waterfowl Habitat*?
2. Can you name some of the *List of Wetlands of International* Importance in China?
3. What is the theme of the World Wetlands Day in 2019?

九、模拟联合国大会(Model United Nations Practice)

Directions: Work in teams and simulate the institutions and committees of the United Nations, featuring delegates of the UN members and the six committees of the General Assembly, negotiating issues of wetland protection in the world and working out resolutions. Students are suggested to focus on the following topics:

1. What is the current situation of global wetland protection?
2. What roles could wetlands play in poverty alleviation?
3. How could a country develop and protect water resources?

第五章

生物多样性公约

Convention on Biological Diversity

一、背景知识(Background)

《生物多样性公约》是一项有法律约束力的公约,旨在保护濒临灭绝的植物和动物,最大程度地保护地球上多种多样的生物资源,以造福于当代和子孙后代。该公约规定,发达国家将以赠送或转让的方式向发展中国家提供新的补充资金以补偿它们为保护生物资源而日益增加的费用,应以更实惠的方式向发展中国家转让技术,从而为保护世界上的生物资源提供便利;签约国应为本国境内的植物和野生动物编目造册,制订计划保护濒危的动植物;建立金融机构以帮助发展中国家实施清点和保护动植物的计划;使用另一个国家自然资源的国家要与那个国家分享研究成果、盈利和技术。该公约于1992年6月1日由联合国环境规划署发起的政府间谈判委员会第七次会议在内罗毕通过,1992年6月5日由签约国在巴西里约热内卢举行的联合国环境与发展大会上签署。公约于1993年12月29日正式生效。常设秘书处设在加拿大的蒙特利尔。联合国《生物多样性公约》缔约国大会是全球履行该公约的最高决策机构,一切有关履行《生物多样性公约》的重大决定都要经过缔约国大会的通过。中国于1992年6月11日签署该公约,1992年11月7日批准,1993年1月5日交存加入书。《生物多样性公约》第十五次缔约方大会(COP15)定于2020年10月中下旬在中国昆明召开。

(Source:https://baike.baidu.com)

二、公约原文(The Text of the Convention)

Convention on Biological Diversity

Preamble
The Contracting Parties,
Conscious of the intrinsic value of biological diversity and of the ecological, gen-

etic, social, economic, scientific, educational, cultural, recreational and aesthetic values of biological diversity and its components,

Conscious also of the importance of biological diversity for evolution and for maintaining life sustaining systems of the biosphere,

Affirming that the conservation of biological diversity is a common concern of humankind,

Reaffirming that States have sovereign rights over their own biological resources,

Reaffirming also that States are responsible for conserving their biological diversity and for using their biological resources in a sustainable manner,

Concerned that biological diversity is being significantly reduced by certain human activities,

Aware of the general lack of information and knowledge regarding biological diversity and of the urgent need to develop scientific, technical and institutional capacities to provide the basic understanding upon which to plan and implement appropriate measures,

Noting that it is vital to anticipate, prevent and attack the causes of significant reduction or loss of biological diversity at source,

Noting also that where there is a threat of significant reduction or loss of biological diversity, lack of full scientific certainty should not be used as a reason for postponing measures to avoid or minimize such a threat,

Noting further that the fundamental requirement for the conservation of biological diversity is the in-situ conservation of ecosystems and natural habitats and the maintenance and recovery of viable populations of species in their natural surroundings,

Noting further that ex-situ measures, preferably in the country of origin, also have an important role to play,

Recognizing the close and traditional dependence of many indigenous and local communities embodying traditional lifestyles on biological resources, and the desirability of sharing equitably benefits arising from the use of traditional knowledge, innovations and practices relevant to the conservation of biological diversity and the sustainable use of its components,

Recognizing also the vital role that women play in the conservation and sustainable use of biological diversity and affirming the need for the full participation of women at all levels of policy-making and implementation for biological diversity conservation,

Stressing the importance of, and the need to promote, international, regional and global cooperation among States and intergovernmental organizations and the non-governmental sector for the conservation of biological diversity and the sustainable use of its components,

Acknowledging that the provision of new and additional financial resources and appropriate access to relevant technologies can be expected to make a substantial difference in the world's ability to address the loss of biological diversity,

Acknowledging further that special provision is required to meet the needs of developing countries, including the provision of new and additional financial resources and appropriate access to relevant technologies,

Noting in this regard the special conditions of the least developed countries and small island States,

Acknowledging that substantial investments are required to conserve biological diversity and that there is the expectation of a broad range of environmental, economic and social benefits from those investments,

Recognizing that economic and social development and poverty eradication are the first and overriding priorities of developing countries,

Aware that conservation and sustainable use of biological diversity is of critical importance for meeting the food, health and other needs of the growing world population, for which purpose access to and sharing of both genetic resources and technologies are essential,

Noting that, ultimately, the conservation and sustainable use of biological diversity will strengthen friendly relations among States and contribute to peace for humankind,

Desiring to enhance and complement existing international arrangements for the conservation of biological diversity and sustainable use of its components, and

Determined to conserve and sustainably use biological diversity for the benefit of present and future generations.

Have agreed as follows:

Article 1 Objectives

The objectives of this Convention, to be pursued in accordance with its relevant provisions, are the conservation of biological diversity, the sustainable use of its components and the fair and equitable sharing of the benefits arising out of the utilization of genetic resources, including by appropriate access to genetic resources and by appropriate transfer of relevant technologies, taking into account all rights over those resources and to technologies, and by appropriate funding.

Article 2 Use of terms

For the purposes of this Convention:

"Biological diversity" means the variability among living organisms from all sources including, *inter alia*, terrestrial, marine and other aquatic ecosystems and the ecological complexes of which they are part: this includes diversity within species, between species and of ecosystems.

"Biological resources" includes genetic resources, organisms or parts thereof, populations, or any other biotic component of ecosystems with actual or potential use or value for humanity.

"Biotechnology" means any technological application that uses biological systems, living organisms, or derivatives thereof, to make or modify products or processes for specific use.

"Country of origin of genetic resources" means the country which possesses those genetic resources in in-situ conditions.

"Country providing genetic resources" means the country supplying genetic resources collected from in-situ sources, including populations of both wild and domesticated species, or taken from ex-situ sources, which may or may not have originated in that country.

"Domesticated or cultivated species" means species in which the evolutionary process has been influenced by humans to meet their needs.

"Ecosystem" means a dynamic complex of plant, animal and micro-organism communities and their non-living environment interacting as a functional unit.

"Ex-situ conservation" means the conservation of components of biological diversity outside their natural habitats.

"Genetic material" means any material of plant, animal, microbial or other origin containing functional units of heredity.

"Genetic resources" means genetic material of actual or potential value.

"Habitat" means the place or type of site where an organism or population naturally occurs.

"In-situ conditions" means conditions where genetic resources exist within ecosystems and natural habitats, and, in the case of domesticated or cultivated species, in the surroundings where they have developed their distinctive properties.

"*In-situ* conservation" means the conservation of ecosystems and natural habitats and the maintenance and recovery of viable populations of species in their natural surroundings and, in the case of domesticated or cultivated species, in the surroundings where they have developed their distinctive properties.

"Protected area" means a geographically defined area which is designated or regulated and managed to achieve specific conservation objectives.

"Regional economic integration organization" means an organization constituted by sovereign States of a given region, to which its member States have transferred competence in respect of matters governed by this Convention and which has been duly authorized, in accordance with its internal procedures, to sign, ratify, accept, approve or accede to it.

"Sustainable use" means the use of components of biological diversity in a way and at a rate that does not lead to the long-term decline of biological diversity, thereby maintaining its potential to meet the needs and aspirations of present and future generations.

"Technology" includes biotechnology.

Article 3　Principle

States have, in accordance with the *Charter of the United Nations* and the principles of international law, the sovereign right to exploit their own resources pursuant to their own environmental policies, and the responsibility to ensure that activities within their jurisdiction or control do not cause damage to the environment of other States or of areas beyond the limits of national jurisdiction.

Article 4　Jurisdictional scope

Subject to the rights of other States, and except as otherwise expressly provided in this Convention, the provisions of this Convention apply, in relation to each Contracting Party:

(a) In the case of components of biological diversity, in areas within the limits of its national jurisdiction; and

(b) In the case of processes and activities, regardless of where their effects occur, carried out under its jurisdiction or control, within the area of its national jurisdiction or beyond the limits of national jurisdiction.

Article 5　Cooperation

Each Contracting Party shall, as far as possible and as appropriate, cooperate with other Contracting Parties, directly or where appropriate, through competent international organizations, in respect of areas beyond national jurisdiction and on other matters of mutual interest, for the conservation and sustainable use of biological diversity.

Article 6　General measures for conservation and sustainable use

Each Contracting Party shall, in accordance with its particular conditions and capabilities:

(a) Develop national strategies, plans or programmes for the conservation and sustainable use of biological diversity or adapt for this purpose existing strategies, plans or programmes which shall reflect, *inter alia*, the measures set out in this Convention relevant to the Contracting Party concerned; and

(b) Integrate, as far as possible and as appropriate, the conservation and sustainable use of biological diversity into relevant sectoral or cross-sectoral plans, programmes and policies.

Article 7　Identification and monitoring

Each Contracting Party shall, as far as possible and as appropriate, in particular for the purposes of Articles 8 to 10:

(a) Identify components of biological diversity important for its conservation and sustainable use having regard to the indicative list of categories set down in Annex I;

(b) Monitor, through sampling and other techniques, the components of biological diversity identified pursuant to subparagraph (a) above, paying particular attention to those requiring urgent conservation measures and those which offer the greatest potential for sustainable use;

(c) Identify processes and categories of activities which have or are likely to have significant adverse impacts on the conservation and sustainable use of biological diversity, and monitor their effects through sampling and other techniques; and

(d) Maintain and organize, by any mechanism data, derived from identification and monitoring activities pursuant to subparagraphs (a), (b) and (c) above.

Article 8 *In-situ* Conservation

Each Contracting Party shall, as far as possible and as appropriate:

(a) Establish a system of protected areas or areas where special measures need to be taken to conserve biological diversity;

(b) Develop, where necessary, guidelines for the selection, establishment and management of protected areas or areas where special measures need to be taken to conserve biological diversity;

(c) Regulate or manage biological resources important for the conservation of biological diversity whether within or outside protected areas, with a view to ensuring their conservation and sustainable use;

(d) Promote the protection of ecosystems, natural habitats and the maintenance of viable populations of species in natural surroundings;

(e) Promote environmentally sound and sustainable development in areas adjacent to protected areas with a view to furthering protection of these areas;

(f) Rehabilitate and restore degraded ecosystems and promote the recovery of threatened species, *inter alia*, through the development and implementation of plans or other management strategies;

(g) Establish or maintain means to regulate, manage or control the risks associated with the use and release of living modified organisms resulting from biotechnology which are likely to have adverse environmental impacts that could affect the conservation and sustainable use of biological diversity, taking also into account the risks to human health;

(h) Prevent the introduction of, control or eradicate those alien species which threaten ecosystems, habitats or species;

(i) Endeavour to provide the conditions needed for compatibility between present uses and the conservation of biological diversity and the sustainable use of its components;

(j) Subject to its national legislation, respect, preserve and maintain knowledge, innovations and practices of indigenous and local communities embodying traditional lifestyles relevant for the conservation and sustainable use of biological diversity and promote their wider application with the approval and involvement of the holders of such knowledge, innovations and practices and encourage the equitable sharing of the benefits arising from the utilization of such knowledge, innovations and practices;

(k) Develop or maintain necessary legislation and/or other regulatory provisions for the protection of threatened species and populations;

(l) Where a significant adverse effect on biological diversity has been determined pursuant to Article 7, regulate or manage the relevant processes and categories of activities; and

(m) Cooperate in providing financial and other support for in-situ conservation outlined in subparagraphs (a) to (l) above, particularly to developing countries.

Article 9 *Ex-situ* conservation

Each Contracting Party shall, as far as possible and as appropriate, and predominantly for the purpose of complementing *in-situ* measures:

(a) Adopt measures for the ex-situ conservation of components of biological diversity, preferably in the country of origin of such components;

(b) Establish and maintain facilities for *ex-situ* conservation of and research on plants, animals and micro-organisms, preferably in the country of origin of genetic resources;

(c) Adopt measures for the recovery and rehabilitation of threatened species and for their reintroduction into their natural habitats under appropriate conditions;

(d) Regulate and manage collection of biological resources from natural habitats for ex-situ conservation purposes so as not to threaten ecosystems and in-situ populations of species, except where special temporary ex-situ measures are required under subparagraph (c) above; and

(e) Cooperate in providing financial and other support for *ex-situ* conservation outlined in subparagraphs (a) to (d) above and in the establishment and maintenance of ex-situ conservation facilities in developing countries.

Article 10 Sustainable use of components of biological diversity

Each Contracting Party shall, as far as possible and as appropriate:

(a) Integrate consideration of the conservation and sustainable use of biological resources into national decision-making;

(b) Adopt measures relating to the use of biological resources to avoid or minimize adverse impacts on biological diversity;

(c) Protect and encourage customary use of biological resources in accordance with traditional cultural practices that are compatible with conservation or sustainable use requirements;

(d) Support local populations to develop and implement remedial action in degraded areas where biological diversity has been reduced; and

(e) Encourage cooperation between its governmental authorities and its private sector in developing methods for sustainable use of biological resources.

Article 11   Incentive measures

Each Contracting Party shall, as far as possible and as appropriate, adopt economically and socially sound measures that act as incentives for the conservation and sustainable use of components of biological diversity.

Article 12   Research and training

The Contracting Parties, taking into account the special needs of developing countries, shall:

(a) Establish and maintain programmes for scientific and technical education and training in measures for the identification, conservation and sustainable use of biological diversity and its components and provide support for such education and training for the specific needs of developing countries;

(b) Promote and encourage research which contributes to the conservation and sustainable use of biological diversity, particularly in developing countries, *inter alia*, in accordance with decisions of the Conference of the Parties taken in consequence of recommendations of the Subsidiary Body on Scientific, Technical and Technological Advice; and

(c) In keeping with the provisions of Articles 16, 13 and 20 promote and cooperate in the use of scientific advances in biological diversity research in developing methods for conservation and sustainable use of biological resources.

Article 13   Public education and awareness

The Contracting Parties shall:

(a) Promote and encourage the measures required for, the well as its propagation through in educational programmes; and understanding of the importance of and conservation of biological diversity, as media, and the inclusion of these topics;

(b) Cooperate, as appropriate, with other States and international organizations in developing educational and public awareness programmes, with respect to conservation and sustainable use of biological diversity.

Article 14   Impact assessment and minimizing adverse impacts

1. Each Contracting Party, as far as possible and as appropriate, shall:

(a) Introduce appropriate procedures requiring environmental impact assessment of its proposed projects that are likely to have significant adverse effects on biological diversity with a view to avoiding or minimizing such effects and, where appropriate, allow for public participation in such procedures;

(b) Introduce appropriate arrangements to ensure that the environmental consequences of its programmes and policies that are likely to have significant adverse impacts on biological diversity are duly taken into account;

(c) Promote, on the basis of reciprocity, notification, exchange of information and consultation on activities under their jurisdiction or control which are likely to significantly affect adversely the biological diversity of other States or areas beyond the limits of national jurisdiction, by encouraging the conclusion of bilateral, regional or multilateral arrangements, as appropriate;

(d) In the case of imminent or grave danger or damage, originating under its jurisdiction or control, to biological diversity within the area under jurisdiction of other States or in areas beyond the limits of national jurisdiction, notify immediately the potentially affected States of such danger or damage, as well as initiate action to prevent or minimize such danger or damage; and

(e) Promote national arrangements for emergency responses to activities or events, whether caused naturally or otherwise, which present a grave and imminent danger to biological diversity and encourage international cooperation to supplement such national efforts and, where appropriate and agreed by the States or regional economic Integration organizations concerned, to establish joint contingency plans.

2. The Conference of the Parties shall examine, on the basis of studies to be carried out, the issue of liability and redress, including restoration and compensation, for damage to biological diversity, except where such liability is a purely internal matter.

Article 15 Access to genetic resources

1. Recognizing the sovereign rights of States over their natural resources, the authority to determine access to genetic resources rests with the national governments and is subject to national legislation.

2. Each Contracting Party shall endeavor to create renditions to facilitate access to genetic resources for environmentally sound uses by other Contracting Parties and not to impose restrictions that run counter to the objectives of this Convention.

3. For the purpose of this Convention, the genetic resources being provided by a Contracting Party, as referred to in this Article and Articles 16 and 19, are only those that are provided by Contracting Parties that are countries of origin of such resources or by the Parties that have acquired the genetic resources in accordance with this Convention.

4. Access, where granted, shall be on mutually agreed terms and subject to the provisions of this Article.

5. Access to genetic resources shall be subject to prior informed consent of the Contracting Party providing such resources, unless otherwise determined by that Party.

6. Each Contracting Party shall endeavor to develop and carry out scientific research based on genetic resources provided by other Contracting Parties with the full

participation of, and where possible in, such Contracting Parties.

7. Each Contracting Party shall take legislative, administrative or policy measures, as appropriate, and in accordance with Articles 16 and 19 and, where necessary, through the financial mechanism established by Articles 20 and 21 with the aim of sharing in a fair and equitable way the results of research and development and the benefits arising from the commercial and other utilization of genetic resources with the Contracting Party providing such resources. Such sharing shall be upon mutually agreed terms.

Article 16 Access to and transfer of technology

1. Each Contracting Party, recognizing that technology includes biotechnology, and that both access to and transfer of technology among Contracting Parties are essential elements for the attainment of the objectives of this Convention, undertakes subject to the provisions of this Article to provide and/or facilitate access for and transfer to other Contracting Parties of technologies that are relevant to the conservation and sustainable use of biological diversity or make use of genetic resources and do not cause significant damage to the environment.

2. Access to and transfer of technology referred to in paragraph 1 above to developing countries shall be provided and/or facilitated under fair and most favorable terms, including on concessional and preferential terms where mutually agreed, and, where necessary, in accordance withthe financial mechanism established by Articles 20 and 21. In the case of technology subject to patents and other intellectual property rights, such access and transfer shall be provided on terms which recognize and are consistent with the adequate and effective protection of intellectual property rights. The application of this paragraph shall be consistent with paragraphs 3, 4 and 5 below.

3. Each Contracting Party shall take legislative, administrative or policy measures, as appropriate, with the aim that Contracting Parties, in particular those that are developing countries, which provide genetic resources are provided access to and transfer of technology which makes use of those resources, on mutually agreed terms, including technology protected by patents and other intellectual property rights, where necessary, through the provisions of Articles 20 and 21 and in accordance with international law and consistent with paragraphs 4 and 5 below.

4. Each Contracting Party shall take legislative, administrative or policy measures, as appropriate, with the aim that the private sector facilitates access to, joint development and transfer of technology referred to in paragraph 1 above for the benefit of both governmental institutions and the private sector of developing countries and in this regard shall abide by the obligations included in paragraphs 1, 2 and 3 above.

5. The Contracting Parties, recognizing that patents and other intellectual property rights may have an influence on the implementation of this Convention, shall cooperate in this regard subject to national legislation and international law in order to ensure that

such rights are supportive of and do not run counter to its objectives.

Article 17　Exchange of information

1. The Contracting Parties shall facilitate the exchange of information, from all publicly available sources, relevant to the conservation and sustainable use of biological diversity, taking into account the special needs of developing countries.

2. Such exchange of information shall include exchange of results of technical, scientific and socio-economic research, as well as information on training and surveying programmes, specialized knowledge, indigenous and traditional knowledge as such and in combination with the technologies referred to in Article 16, paragraph 1. It shall also, where feasible, include repatriation of information.

Article 18　Technical and scientific cooperation

1. The Contracting Parties shall promote international technical and scientific cooperation in the field of conservation and sustainable use of biological diversity, where necessary, through the appropriate international and national institutions.

2. Each Contracting Party shall promote technical and scientific cooperation with other Contracting Parties, in particular developing countries, in implementing this Convention, *inter alia*, through the development and implementation of national policies. In promoting such cooperation, special attention should be given to the development and strengthening of national capabilities, by means of human resources development and institution building.

3. The Conference of the Parties, at its first meeting, shall determine how to establish a clearing-house mechanism to promote and facilitate technical and scientific cooperation.

4. The Contracting Parties shall, in accordance with national legislation and policies, encourage and develop methods of cooperation for the development and use of technologies, including indigenous and traditional technologies, in pursuance of the objectives of this Convention. For this purpose, the Contracting Parties shall also promote cooperation in the training of personnel and exchange of experts.

5. The Contracting Parties shall, subject to mutual agreement, promote the establishment of joint research programmes and joint ventures for the development of technologies relevant to the objectives of this Convention.

Article 19　Handling of biotechnology and distribution of its benefits

1. Each Contracting Party shall take legislative, administrative or policy measures, as appropriate, to provide for the affective participation in biotechnological research activities by those Contracting Parties, especially developing countries, which provide the genetic resources for such research, and where feasible in such Contracting Parties.

2. Each Contracting Party shall take all practicable measures to promote and

advance priority access on a fair and equitable basis by Contracting Parties, especially developing countries, to the results and benefits arising from biotechnologies based upon genetic resources provided by those Contracting Parties. Such access shall be on mutually agreed terms.

3. The Parties shall consider the need for and modalities of a protocol setting out appropriate procedures, including, in particular, advance informed agreement, in the field of the safe transfer, handling and use of any living modified organism resulting from biotechnology that may have adverse effect on the conservation and sustainable use of biological diversity.

4. Each Contracting Party shall, directly or by requiring any natural or legal person under its jurisdiction providing the organisms referred to in paragraph 3 above, provide any available information about the use and safety regulations required by that Contracting Party in handling such organisms, as well as any available information on the potential adverse impact of the specific organisms concerned to the Contracting Party into which those organisms are to be introduced.

Article 20 Financial resources

1. Each Contracting Party undertakes to provide, in accordance with its capabilities, financial support and incentives in respect of those national activities which are intended to achieve the objectives of this Convention, in accordance with its national plans, priorities and programmes.

2. The developed country Parties shall provide new and additional financial resources to enable developing country Parties to meet the agreed full incremental costs to them of implementing measures which fulfil the obligations of this Convention and to benefit from its provisions and which costs are agreed between a developing country Party and the institutional structure referred to in Article 21, in accordance with policy, strategy, programme priorities and eligibility criteria and an indicative list of incremental costs established by the Conference of the Parties. Other Parties, including countries undergoing the process of transition to a market economy, may voluntarily assume the obligations of the developed country Parties. For the purpose of this Article, the Conference of the Parties, shall at its first meeting establish a list of developed country Parties and other Parties which voluntarily assume the obligations of the developed country Parties. The Conference of the Parties shall periodically review and if necessary amend the list. Contributions from other countries and sources on a voluntary basis would also be encouraged. The implementation of these commitments shall take into account the need for adequacy, predictability and timely flow of funds and the importance of burden-sharing among the contributing Parties included in the list.

3. The developed country Parties may also provide, and developing country Parties avail themselves of, financial resources related to the implementation of this Convention

through bilateral, regional and other multilateral channels.

4. The extent to which developing country Parties will effectively implement their commitments under this Convention will depend on the effective implementation by developed country Parties of their commitments under this Convention related to financial resources and transfer of technology and will take fully into account the fact that economic and social development and eradication of poverty are the first and overriding priorities of the developing country Parties.

5. The Parties shall take full account of the specific needs and special situation of least developed countries in their actions with regard to funding and transfer of technology.

6. The Contracting Parties shall also take into consideration the special conditions resulting from the dependence on, distribution and location of biological diversity within developing country Parties, in particular small island States.

7. Consideration shall also be given to the special situation of developing countries, including those that are most environmentally vulnerable, such as those with arid and semi-arid zones, coastal and mountainous areas.

Article 21 Financial mechanism

1. There shall be a mechanism for the provision of financial resources to developing country Parties for purposes of this Convention on a grant or concessional basis the essential elements of which are described in this Article. The mechanism shall function under the authority and guidance of, and be accountable to the Conference of the Parties for purposes of this Convention. The operations of the mechanism shall be carried out by such institutional structure as may be decided upon by the Conference of the Parties at its first meeting. For purposes of this Convention, the Conference of the Parties shall determine the policy, strategy, programme priorities and eligibility criteria relating to the access to and utilization of such resources. The contributions shall be such as to take into account the need for predictability, adequacy and timely flow of funds referred to in Article 20 in accordance with the amount of resources needed to be decided periodically by the Conference of the Parties and the importance of burden-sharing among the contributing Parties included in the list referred to in Article 20, paragraph 2. Voluntary contributions may also be made by the developed country Parties and by other countries and sources. The mechanism shall operate within a democratic and transparent system of governance.

2. Pursuant to the objectives of this Convention, the Conference of the Parties shall at its first meeting determine the policy, strategy and programme priorities, as well as detailed criteria and guidelines for eligibility for access to and utilization of the financial resources including monitoring and evaluation on a regular basis of such utilization. The Conference of the Parties shall decide on the arrangements to give effect to paragraph 1 above after consultation with the institutional structure entrusted with the

operation of the financial mechanism.

3. The Conference of the Parties shall review the effectiveness of the mechanism established under this Article, including the criteria and guidelines referred to in paragraph 2 above, not less than two years after the entry into force of this Convention and thereafter on a regular basis. Based on such review, it shall take appropriate action to improve the effectiveness of the mechanism if necessary.

4. The Contracting Parties shall consider strengthening existing financial institutions to provide financial resources for the conservation and sustainable use of biological diversity.

Article 22 Relationship with other international conventions

1. The provisions of this Convention shall not affect the rights and obligations of any Contracting Party deriving from any existing international agreement, except where the exercise of those rights and obligations would cause a serious damage or threat to biological diversity.

2. Contracting Parties shall implement this Convention with respect to the marine environment consistently with the rights and obligations of States under the law of the sea.

Article 23 Conference of the Parties

1. A Conference of the Parties is hereby established. The first meeting of the conference of the Parties shall be convened by the Executive Director of the United Nations Environment Programme not later than one year after the entry into force of this Convention. Thereafter, ordinary meetings of the Conference of the Parties shall be held at regular intervals to be determined by the Conference at its first meeting.

2. Extraordinary meetings of the Conference of the Parties shall be held at such other times as may be deemed necessary by the Conference, or at the written request of any Party, provided that, within six months of the request being communicated to them by the Secretariat, it is supported by at least one third of the Parties.

3. The Conference of the Parties shall by consensus agree upon and adopt rules of procedure for itself and for any subsidiary body it may establish as well as financial rules governing the funding of The Secretariat. At each ordinary meeting, it shall adopt a budget for the financial period until the next ordinary meeting.

4. The Conference of the Parties shall keep under review the implementation of this Convention, and, for this purpose, shall:

(a) Establish the form and the intervals for transmitting the information to be submitted in accordance with Article 26 and consider such information as well as reports submitted by any subsidiary body;

(b) Review scientific, technical and technological advice on biological diversity provided in accordance with Article 25;

(c) Consider and adopt, as required, protocols in accordance with Article 28;

(d) Consider and adopt, as required, in accordance with Articles 29 and 30, amendments to this Convention and its annexes;

(e) Consider amendments to any protocol, as well as to any annexes thereto, and, if so decided, recommend their adoption to the parties to the protocol concerned;

(f) Consider and adopt, as required, in accordance with Article 30, additional annexes to this Convention;

(g) Establish such subsidiary bodies, particularly to provide scientific and technical advice, as are deemed necessary for the implementation of this Convention;

(h) Contact, through the Secretariat, the executive bodies of conventions dealing with matters covered by this Convention with a view to establishing appropriate forms of cooperation with them; and

(i) Consider and undertake any additional action that may be required for the achievement of the purposes of this Convention in the light of experience gained in its operation.

5. The United Nations, its specialized agencies and the International Atomic Energy Agency, as well as any State not Party to this Convention, may be represented as observers at meetings of the Conference of the Parties. Any other body or agency, whether governmental or non-governmental, qualified in fields relating to conservation and sustainable use of biological diversity, which has informed the Secretariat of its wish to be represented as an observer at a meeting of the Conference of the Parties, may be admitted unless at least one third of the Parties present object. The admission and participation of observers shall be subject to the rules of procedure adopted by the Conference of the Parties.

Article 24 Secretariat

1. A secretariat is hereby established its functions shall be:

(a) To arrange for and service meetings of the Conference of the Parties provided for in Article 23;

(b) To perform the functions assigned to it by any protocol;

(c) To prepare reports on the execution of its functions under this Convention and present them to the Conference of the Parties;

(d) To coordinate with other relevant international bodies and, in particular to enter into such administrative and contractual arrangements as may be required for the effective discharge of its functions; and

(e) To perform such other functions as may be determined by the Conference of the Parties.

2. At its first ordinary meeting, the Conference of the Parties shall designate the secretariat from amongst those existing competent international organizations which have signified their willingness to carry out the secretariat functions under this Convention.

Article 25 Subsidiary body on scientific, technical and technological advice

1. A subsidiary body for the provision of scientific, technical and technological advice is hereby established to provide the Conference of the Parties and, as appropriate, its other subsidiary bodies with timely advice relating to the implementation of this Convention. This body shall be open to participation by all Parties and shall be multidisciplinary. It shall comprise government representatives competent in the relevant field of expertise. It shall report regularly to the Conference of the Parties on all aspects of its work.

2. Under the authority of and in accordance with guidelines laid down by the Conference of the Parties, and upon its request, this body shall:

(a) Provide scientific and technical assessments of the status of biological diversity;

(b) Prepare scientific and technical assessments of the effects of types of measures taken in accordance with the provisions of this Convention;

(c) Identify innovative, efficient and state-of-the-art technologies and know-how relating to the conservation and sustainable use of biological diversity and advise on the ways and means of promoting development and/or transferring such technologies;

(d) Provide advice on scientific programmes and international Cooperation in research and development related to conservation and sustainable use of biological diversity; and

(e) Respond to scientific technical, technological and methodological questions that the Conference of the Parties and its subsidiary bodies may put to the body.

3. The functions, terms of reference, organization and operation of this body may be further elaborated by the Conference of the Parties.

Article 26 Reports

Each Contracting Party shall, at intervals to be determined by the Conference of the Parties, present to the Conference of the Parties, reports on measures which it has taken for the implementation of the provisions of this Convention and their effectiveness in meeting the objectives of this Convention.

Article 27 Settlement of disputes

1. In the event of a dispute between Contracting Parties concerning the interpretation or application of this Convention, the parties concerned shall seek solution by negotiation.

2. If the parties concerned cannot reach agreement by negotiation, they may jointly seek the good offices of, or request mediation by, a third party.

3. When ratifying, accepting, approving or acceding to this Convention, or at any time thereafter, a State or regional economic integration organization may declare in writing to the Depositary that for a dispute not resolved in accordance with paragraph 1 or paragraph 2 above, it accepts one or both of the following means of dispute settlement as compulsory:

(a) Arbitration in accordance with the procedure laid down in Part 1 of Annex II;

(b) Submission of the dispute to the International Court of Justice.

4. If the parties to the dispute have not in accordance with paragraph 3 above, accepted the same or any procedure, the dispute shall be submitted to conciliation in accordance with Part 2 of Annex II unless the parties otherwise agree.

5. The provisions of this Article shall apply with respect to any protocol except as otherwise provided in the protocol concerned.

Article 28 Adoption of protocols

1. The Contracting Parties shall cooperate in the formulation and adoption of protocols to this Convention.

2. Protocols shall be adopted at a meeting of the Conference of the Parties.

3. The text of any proposed protocol shall be communicated to the Contracting Parties by the Secretariat at least six months before such a meeting.

Article 29 Amendment of the Convention or Protocols

1. Amendments to this Convention may be proposed by any Contracting Party. Amendments to any protocol may be proposed by any Party to that protocol.

2. Amendments to this Convention shall be adopted at a meeting of the Conference of the Parties. Amendments to any protocol shall be adopted at a meeting of the Parties to the Protocol in question. The text of any proposed amendment to this Convention or to any protocol, except as may otherwise be provided in such protocol, shall be communicated to the Parties to the instrument in question by the secretariat at least six months before the meeting at which it is proposed for adoption. The secretariat shall also communicate proposed amendments to the signatories to this Convention for information.

3. The Parties shall make every effort to reach agreement on any proposed amendment to this Convention or to any protocol by consensus. If all efforts at consensus have been exhausted, and no agreement reached, the amendment shall as a last resort be adopted by a two-third majority vote of the Parties to the instrument in question present and voting at the meeting, and shall be submitted by the Depositary to all Parties for ratification, acceptance or approval.

4. Ratification, acceptance or approval of amendments shall he notified to the Depositary in writing. Amendments adopted in accordance with paragraph 3 above shall enter into force among Parties having accepted them on the ninetieth day after the

deposit of instruments of ratification, acceptance or approval by at least two thirds of the Contracting Parties to this Convention or of the Parties to the protocol concerned, except as may otherwise be provided in such protocol. Thereafter the amendments shall enter into force for any other Party on the ninetieth day after that Party deposits its instrument of ratification, acceptance or approval of the amendments.

5. For the purposes of this Article. "Parties present and voting" means Parties present and casting an affirmative or negative vote.

Article 30 Adoption and amendment of annexes

1. The annexes to this Convention or to any protocol shall form an integral part of the Convention or of such protocol, as the case may be and, unless expressly provided otherwise, a reference to this Convention or its protocols constitutes at the same time a reference to any annexes thereto. Such annexes shall be restricted to procedural, scientific, technical and administrative matters.

2. Except as may be otherwise provided in any protocol with respect to its annexes, the following procedure shall apply to the proposal, adoption and entry into force of additional annexes to this Convention or of annexes to any protocol:

(a) Annexes to this Convention or to any protocol shall be proposed and adopted according to the procedure laid down in Article 29;

(b) Any Party that is unable to approve an additional annex to this Convention or an annex to any protocol to which it is Party shall so notify the Depositary, in writing, within one year from the date of the communication of the adoption by the Depositary. The Depositary shall without delay notify ail Parties of any such notification received. A Party may at any time withdraw a previous declaration of objection and the annexes shall thereupon enter into force for that Party subject to subparagraph (c) below;

(c) On the expiry of one year from the date of the communication of the adoption by the Depositary, the annex shall enter into force for all Parties to this Convention or to any protocol concerned which have not submitted a notification in accordance with the provisions of subparagraph (b) above.

3. The proposal, adoption and entry into force of amendments to annexes to this Convention or to any protocol shall be subject to the same procedure as for the proposal, adoption and entry into force of annexes to the Convention or annexes to any protocol.

4. If an additional annex or an amendment to an annex is related to an amendment to this Convention or to any protocol, the additional annex or amendment shall not enter into force until such time as the amendment to the Convention or to the protocol concerned enters into force.

Article 31 Right to vote

1. Except as provided for in paragraph 2 below, each Contracting Party to this

Convention or to any protocol shall have one vote.

2. Regional economic integration organizations, in matters within their competence, shall exercise their right to vote with a number of votes equal to the number of their member States which are Contracting Parties to this Convention or the relevant protocol. Such organizations shall not exercise their right to vote if their member States exercise theirs, and *vice versa*.

Article 32   Relationship between this Convention and Its Protocols

1. A State or a regional economic integration organization may not become a Party to a protocol unless it is, or becomes at the same time, a Contracting Party to this Convention.

2. Decisions under any protocol shall be taken only by the Parties to the protocol concerned. Any Contracting Party that has not ratified, accepted or approved a protocol may participate as an observer in any meeting of the parties to that protocol.

Article 33   Signature

This Convention shall be open for signature at Rio de Janeiro by ail States and any regional economic integration organization from 5 June 1992 until 14 June 1992, and at the United Nations Headquarters in New York from 15 June 1992 to 4 June 1993.

Article 34   Ratification, acceptance or approval

1. This Convention and any protocol shall be subject to ratification, acceptance or approval by States and by regional economic integration organizations. Instruments of ratification, acceptance or approval shall be deposited with the Depositary.

2. Any organization referred to in paragraph 1 above which becomes a Contracting Party to this Convention or any protocol without any of its member States being a Contracting Party shall be bound by all the obligations under the Convention or the protocol, as the case may be. In the case of such organizations, one or more of whose member States is a Contracting Party to this Convention or relevant protocol, the organization and its member States shall decide on their respective responsibilities for the performance of their obligations under the Convention or protocol, as the case may be. In such cases, the organization and the member States shall not be entitled to exercise rights under the Convention or relevant protocol concurrently.

3. In their instruments of ratification, acceptance or approval, the organizations referred to in paragraph 1 above shall declare the extent of their competence with respect to the matters governed by the Convention or the relevant protocol. These organizations shall also inform the Depositary of any relevant modification in the extent of their competence.

Article 35   Accession

1. This Convention and any protocol shall be open for accession by States and by

regional economic integration organizations from the date on which the Convention or the protocol concerned is closed for signature. The instruments of accession shall be deposited with the Depositary.

2. In their instruments of accession, the organizations referred to in paragraph 1 above shall declare the extent of their competence with respect to the matters governed by the Convention or the relevant protocol. These organizations shall also inform the Depositary of any relevant modification in the extent of their competence.

3. The provisions of Article 34, paragraph 2 shall apply to regional economic integration organizations which accede to this Convention or any protocol.

Article 36 Entry into force

1. This Convention shall enter into force on the ninetieth day after the date of deposit of the thirtieth instrument of ratification, acceptance, approval or accession.

2. Any protocol shall enter into force on the ninetieth day after the date of deposit of the number of instruments of ratification, acceptance, approval or accession, specified in that protocol, has been deposited.

3. For each Contracting Party which ratifies, accepts or approves this Convention or accedes thereto after the deposit of the thirtieth instrument of ratification, acceptance, approval or accession, it shall enter into force on the ninetieth day after the date of deposit by such Contracting Party of its instrument of ratification, acceptance, approval or accession.

4. Any protocol, except as otherwise provided in such protocol, shall enter into force for a Contracting Party that ratifies, accepts or approves that protocol or accedes thereto after its entry into force pursuant to paragraph 2 above, on the ninetieth day after the date on which that Contracting Party deposits its instrument of ratification, acceptance, approval or accession, or on the date on which this Convention enters into force for that Contracting Party, whichever shall be the later.

5. For the purposes of paragraphs 1 and 2 above, any instrument deposited by a regional economic integration organization shall not be counted as additional to those deposited by member States of such organization.

Article 37 Reservations

No reservations may be made to this Convention.

Article 38 Withdrawals

1. At any time after two years from the date on which this Convention has entered into force for a Contracting Party, that Contracting Party may withdraw from the Convention by giving written notification to the Depositary.

2. Any such withdrawal shall take place upon expiry of one year after the date of its receipt by the Depositary, or on such later date as may be specified in the notification of

the withdrawal.

3. Any Contracting Party which withdraws from this Convention shall be considered as also having withdrawn from any protocol to which it is party.

Article 39 Financial interim arrangements

Provided that it has been fully restructured in accordance with the requirements of Article 21, the Global Environment Facility of the United Nations Development Programme, the United Nations Environment Programme and the International Bank for Reconstruction and Development shall be the institutional structure referred to in Article 21 on an interim basis, for the period between the entry into force of this Convention and the first meeting of the Conference of the Parties or until the Conference of the Parties decides which institutional structure will be designated in accordance with Article 21.

Article 40 Secretariat interim arrangements

The secretariat to be provided by the Executive Director of the United Nations Environment Programme shall be the secretariat referred to in Article 24, paragraph 2, on an interim basis for the period between the entry into force of this Convention and the first meeting of the Conference of the Parties.

Article 41 Depositary

The Secretary-General of the United Nations shall assume the functions of Depositary of this Convention and any protocols.

Article 42 Authentic texts

The original of this Convention, of which the Arabic, Chinese, English, French, Russian and Spanish texts are equally authentic, shall be deposited with the Secretary-General of the United Nations.

IN WITNESS WHEREOF the undersigned, being duly authorized to that effect, have signed this Convention.

Done at Rio de Janeiro on this fifth day of June, one thousand nine hundred and ninety-two.

Annex I IDENTIFICATION AND MONITORING

1. Ecosystems and habitats: containing high diversity, large numbers of endemic or threatened species, or wilderness; required by migratory species; of social, economic, cultural or scientific importance: or, which are representative, unique or associated with key evolutionary or other biological processes;

2. Species and communities which are: threatened; wild relatives of domesticated or cultivated species; of medicinal, agricultural or other economic value; or social, scientific or cultural importance; or importance for research into the conservation and

sustainable use of biological diversity, such as indicator species; and

3. Described genomes and genes of social, scientific or economic importance.

Annex II

Part 1　Arbitration

Article 1

The claimant party shall notify the secretariat that the parties are referring a dispute to arbitration pursuant to Article 27. The notification shall state the subject-matter of arbitration and include, in particular, the articles of the Convention or the protocol, the interpretation or application of which are at issue. If the parties do not agree on the subject matter of the dispute before the President of the tribunal is designated, the arbitral tribunal shall determine the subject matter. The secretariat shall forward the information thus received to all Contracting Parties to this Convention or to the protocol concerned.

Article 2

1. In disputes between two parties, the arbitral tribunal shall consist of three members. Each of the parties to the dispute shall appoint an arbitrator and the two arbitrators so appointed shall designate by common agreement the third arbitrator who shall be the President of the tribunal. The latter shall not be a national of one of the parties to the dispute, nor have his or her usual place of residence in the territory of one of these parties, nor be employed by any of them, nor have dealt with the case in any other capacity.

2. In disputes between more than two parties, parties in the same interest shall appoint one arbitrator jointly by agreement.

3. Any vacancy shall be filled in the manner prescribed for the initial appointment.

Article 3

1. If the President of the arbitral tribunal has not been designated within two months of the appointment of the second arbitrator, the Secretary-General of the United Nations shall, at the request of a party, designate the President within a further two-month period.

2. If one of the parties to the dispute does not appoint an arbitrator within two months of receipt of the request, the other party may inform the Secretary-General who shall make the designation within a further two-month period.

Article 4

The arbitral tribunal shall render its decisions in accordance with the provisions of this Convention, any protocols concerned, and international law.

Article 5

Unless the parties to the dispute otherwise agree, the arbitral tribunal shall determine its own rules of procedure.

Article 6

The arbitral tribunal may, at the request of one of the parties, recommend essential interim measures of protection.

Article 7

The parties to the dispute shall facilitate the work of the arbitral tribunal and, in particular, using all means at their disposal, shall:

(a) Provide it with ail relevant documents, information and facilities; and

(b) Enable it, when necessary, to call witnesses or experts and receive their evidence.

Article 8

The parties and the arbitrators are under an obligation to protect the confidentiality of any information they receive in confidence during the proceedings of the arbitral tribunal.

Article 9

Unless the arbitral tribunal determines otherwise because of the particular circumstances of the case, the costs of the tribunal shall be borne by the parties to the dispute in equal shares. The tribunal shall keep a record of ail its costs, and shall furnish a final statement thereof to the parties.

Article 10

Any Contracting Party that has an interest of a legal nature in the subject-matter of the dispute which may be affected by the decision in the case, may intervene in the proceedings with the consent of the tribunal.

Article11

The tribunal may hear and determine counterclaims arising directly out of the subject-matter of the dispute.

Article 12

Decisions both on procedure and substance of the arbitral tribunal shall be taken by a majority vote of its members.

Article 13

If one of the parties to the dispute does not appear before the arbitral tribunal or fails to defend its case, the other party may request the tribunal to continue the proceedings and to make its award. Absence of a party or a failure of a party to defend its case shall not constitute a bar to the proceedings. Before rendering its final decision, the arbitral tribunal must satisfy itself that the claim is well founded in fact and law.

Article 14

The tribunal shall render its final decision within five months of the date on which it is fully constituted unless it finds it necessary to extend the time-limit for a period which should not exceed five more months.

Article 15

The final decision of the arbitral tribunal shall be confined to the subject-matter of the dispute and shall state the reasons on which it is based. It shall contain the names of the members who have participated and the date of the final decision. Any member of the tribunal may attach a separate or dissenting opinion to the final decision.

Article 16

The award shall be binding on the parties to the dispute. It shall be without appeal unless the parties to the dispute have agreed in advance to an appellate procedure.

Article 17

Any controversy which may arise between the parties to the dispute as regards the interpretation or manner of implementation of the final decision may be submitted by either party for decision to the arbitral tribunal which rendered it

Part 2   Conciliation

Article 1

A conciliation commission shall be created upon the request of one of the parties to the dispute. The commission shall, unless the parties otherwise agree, be composed of five members, two appointed by each Party concerned and a President chosen jointly by those members.

Article 2

In disputes between more than two parties, parties in the same interest shall appoint their members of the commission jointly by agreement. Where two or more parties have separate interests or there is a disagreement as to whether they are of the same interest, they shall appoint their members separately.

Article 3

If any appointments by the parties are not made within two months of the date of the request to create a conciliation commission, the Secretary-General of the United Nations shall, if asked to do so by the party that made the request, make those appointments within a further two-month period.

Article 4

If a President of the conciliation commission has not been chosen within two months of the last of the members of the commission being appointed, the Secretary-General of the united Nations shall, if asked to do so by a party, designate a President within a further two-month period.

Article 5

The conciliation commission shall take its decisions by majority vote of its members. It shall, unless the parties to the dispute otherwise agree, determine its own procedure. It shall render a proposal for resolution of the dispute, which the parties shall consider in good faith.

Article 6

A disagreement as to whether the conciliation commission has competence shall be decided by the commission.

(Source: https://moew.government.bg/static/media/ups/tiny/file/KVESMS/conventions_full/Convention_desertification_en.pdf)

三、注解(Notes)

International Bank for Reconstruction and Development

国际复兴开发银行(IBRD)，又称"世界银行"，是指根据1944年7月的《国际复兴开发银行协定》建立的国际金融机构。1945年12月27日成立，1946年6月营业，1947年11月成为联合国专门机构之一。宗旨是：向成员国政府或由政府担保的私营企业提供用于生产性投资的长期贷款和广泛的技术援助与合作，以促进成员国的经济发展和国际贸易与收支的平衡增长。资金来源的绝大部分为成员国认缴的股金份额，借款，向国际金融市场发行债券和银行营业收入等。到1989年，有成员国151个，高级工作人员3398人，认缴股本1156.68亿美元。中国是创始成员国之一，1980年恢复了在该行的合法席位。最高权力机构为理事会，由成员国委派正、副理事各一人，任期5年，每年举行一次会议。执行董事会是常务机构，由20人组成，其中5人由股金最多的5个成员国委派，其余的由选举产生。行长由董事会选出，可连任。设有经济发展学院和若干区域行政机构。总部设在美国华盛顿。同国际金融公司和国际开发协会一起组成世界银行集团。

(Source: https://baike.baidu.com/item/国际复兴开发银行)

四、相关词汇(Key Words and Phrases)

1. preamble   [priˈæmb(ə)l]   n.   序文；电报报头；先兆
2. derivative   [dɪˈrɪvətɪv]   n.   [化学]衍生物，派生物；导数

		adj.	派生的；引出
3. genome	[ˈdʒiːnəʊm]	n.	基因组；染色体组
4. biosphere	[ˈbaɪə(ʊ)sfɪə]	n.	生物圈
5. depositary	[dɪˈpɒzɪt(ə)rɪ]	n.	受托人
6. conservation	[kɒnsəˈveɪʃ(ə)n]	n.	保护
7. in-situ	[ɪnˈsaɪˌtu]	n.	原位，现场
8. remedial	[rɪˈmiːdɪəl/]	adj.	补救的，矫正的
9. indigenous	[ɪnˈdɪdʒɪnəs]	adj.	本土的；土著的；国产的；固有的
10. provision	[prəˈvɪʒ(ə)n]	n.	规定；条款；准备；[经]供应品
11. terrestrial	[təˈrestrɪəl]	adj.	地球的；陆地的，[生物]陆生的；人间的
		n.	陆地生物；地球上的人
12. domesticate	[dəˈmestɪkeɪt]	vt.	驯养；教化；引进
13. microbial	[maɪˈkrəʊbɪəl]	adj.	微生物的；由细菌引起的
14. alien	[ˈeɪlɪən]	adj.	外国的；相异的，性质不同的；不相容
15. propagation	[ˈprɒpəˈgeɪʃn]	n.	繁殖，增殖；传播，推广，普及
16. compatibility	[kəmˌpætɪˈbɪlɪtɪ]	n.	[计]兼容性
17. conciliation	[kənˌsɪlɪˈeɪʃn]	n.	调解；安抚；说服

五、长难句（Difficult Sentences）

1. States have, in accordance with the *Charter of the United Nations* and the principles of international law, the sovereign right to exploit their own resources pursuant to their own environmental policies, and the responsibility to ensure that activities within their jurisdiction or control do not cause damage to the environment of other States or of areas beyond the limits of national jurisdiction. (Article 3, Principle)

解释：句子的主干结构是"States have the sovereign right and the responsibility"。复合介词词组 in accordance with the Charter of the United Nations and the principles of international law 做句子的状语。动词不定式 to exploit 和 to ensure 分别做其前面名词的定语。

译文：依照《联合国宪章》和国际法原则，各国具有按照其环境政策开发其资源的主权权利，同时亦负有责任，确保在它管辖或控制范围内的活动，不致于对其他国家的环境或国家管辖范围以外地区的环境造成损害。

2. Promote national arrangements for emergency responses to activities or events, whether caused naturally or otherwise, which present a grave and imminent danger to biological diversity and encourage international cooperation to supplement such national

efforts and, where appropriate and agreed by the States or regional economic Integration organizations concerned, to establish joint contingency plans. (Article 14, 1e)

解释：whether caused naturally or otherwise 和 which present a grave and imminent danger to biological diversity 为定语，修饰 activities or events。encourage 和 Promote 是并列的关系。

译文：促进做出国家紧急应变安排，以处理大自然或其他原因引起即将严重危及生物多样性的活动或事件，鼓励旨在补充这种国家努力的国际合作，并酌情在有关国家或区域经济一体化组织同意的情况下制订联合应急计划。

3. The Parties shall consider the need for and modalities of a protocol setting out appropriate procedures, including, in particular, advance informed agreement, in the field of the safe transfer, handling and use of any living modified organism resulting from biotechnology that may have adverse effect on the conservation and sustainable use of biological diversity. (Article 19, 3)

解释：resulting from biotechnology 做定语修饰 organism。定语从句 that may have adverse effect on the conservation and sustainable use of biological diversity 修饰的先行词是 biotechnology。

译文：缔约国应考虑是否需要一项议定书，规定适当程序，特别包括事先知情协议，适用于可能对生物多样性的保护和持续利用产生不利影响的由生物技术改变的任何活生物体的安全转让、处理和使用，并考虑该议定书的形式。

4. Any protocol, except as otherwise provided in such protocol, shall enter into force for a Contracting Party that ratifies, accepts or approves that protocol or accedes thereto after its entry into force pursuant to paragraph 2 above, that Contracting Party deposits its instrument of ratification, acceptance, approval or accession, or on the date on which this Convention enters into force for that Contracting Party, whichever shall be the later. (Article 36, 4)

解释：that 引导的定语从句修饰名词词组 a Contracting Party。on the ninetieth day after the date on which…, or on the date on which…为并列的介词词组做时间状语，且 on which 引导定语从句修饰先行词 date。

译文：任何议定书，除非其中另有规定，对于该议定书依照以上第 2 款规定生效后批准、接受、核准或加入该议定书的缔约国，应于该缔约国的批准、接受、核准或加入书交存之日以后第 90 天生效，或于本公约对该缔约国生效之日生效，以两者中较后日期为准。

六、课后练习(Exercises)

1. Skimming and Scanning

Directions：Read the following passage excerpted from Convention on Biological Diversity. At the end of the passage, there are six statements. Each statement contains information given in one of the paragraphs of the passage. Identify the paragraph from which the information is derived. Each paragraph is marked with a letter. You may choose a paragraph more than once. Answer the questions by writing the corresponding letter in the bracket in front of each statement.

The Contracting Parties,

A. Conscious of the intrinsic value of biological diversity and of the ecological, genetic, social, economic, scientific, educational, cultural, recreational and aesthetic values of biological diversity and its components. Conscious also of the importance of biological diversity for evolution and for maintaining life sustaining systems of the biosphere, affirming that the conservation of biological diversity is a common concern of humankind. Reaffirming that States have sovereign rights over their own biological resources. Reaffirming also that States are responsible for conserving their biological diversity and for using their biological resources in a sustainable manner,

B. Concerned that biological diversity is being significantly reduced by certain human activities. aware of the general lack of information and knowledge regarding biological diversity and of the urgent need to develop scientific, technical and institutional capacities to provide the basic understanding upon which to plan and implement appropriate measures,

C. Noting that it is vital to anticipate, prevent and attack the causes of significant reduction or loss of biological diversity at source. Noting also that where there is a threat of significant reduction or loss of biological diversity, lack of full scientific certainty should not be used as a reason for postponing measures to avoid or minimize such a threat. Noting further that the fundamental requirement for the conservation of biological diversity is the in-situ conservation of ecosystems and natural habitats and the maintenance and recovery of viable populations of species in their natural surroundings. Noting further that ex-situ measures, preferably in the country of origin, also have an important role to play,

D. Recognizing the close and traditional dependence of many indigenous and local communities embodying traditional lifestyles on biological resources, and the desirability of sharing equitably benefits arising from the use of traditional knowledge, innovations and practices relevant to the conservation of biological diversity and the sustainable use of its components. Recognizing also the vital role that women play in the conservation and sustainable use of biological diversity and affirming the need for the full participation of women at all levels of policy-making and implementation for biological diversity conservation,

E. Stressing the importance of, and the need to promote, international, regional and global cooperation among States and intergovernmental organizations and the non-governmental sector for the conservation of biological diversity and the sustainable use of its components,

F. Acknowledging that the provision of new and additional financial resources and appropriate access to relevant technologies can be expected to make a substantial difference in the world's ability to address the loss of biological diversity. Acknowledging further that special provision is required to meet the needs of developing countries, including the provision of new and additional financial resources and appropriate access to relevant technologies. Noting in this regard the special conditions of the least developed countries and small island States. Acknowledging that substantial investments are required to conserve biological diversity and that there is the expectation of a broad range of environmental, economic and social benefits from those investments,

G. Recognizing that economic and social development and poverty eradication are the first and overriding priorities of developing countries. Aware that conservation and sustainable use of biological diversity is of critical importance for meeting the food, health and other needs of the growing world population, for which purpose access to and sharing of both genetic resources and technologies are essential,

H. Noting that, ultimately, the conservation and sustainable use of biological diversity will strengthen friendly relations among States and contribute to peace for humankind. Desiring to enhance and complement existing international arrangements for the conservation of biological diversity and sustainable use of its components, and determined to conserve and sustainably use biological diversity for the benefit of present and future generations.

(_____) (1) Females should play an important role in the protection and sustainable use of biological diversity.

(_____) (2) A great deal of money should be spent continuously in order to protect biological diversity and the corresponding benefits can be anticipated.

(_____) (3) Measures should be taken without delay to conserve the biological diversity without the doubts in the scientific field being the excuse.

(_____) (4) The conservation and sustainable use of biological diversity will ultimately enhance friendly relations among States and be beneficial to peace for humankind.

(_____) (5) Biological diversity is of significance for the process of gradual change that takes place over many generations.

(_____) (6) The economic and social development and poverty eradication are the first and overriding priorities of developing countries.

2. Reading Comprehension

Directions: Read **Article 10 Sustainable use of components of biological diversity** and **Article 21 Financial mechanism** from the United Nations Framework Convention on Climate Change Convention on Biological Diversity, and decide whether the following statements are True or False. Write T for True or F for False in the bracket in front of each statement.

A. Questions 1 to 3 are based on **Article 10 Sustainable use of components of biological diversity.**

(1) (_____) Governmental authorities should play a leading role in forming methods for sustainable use of biological resources.

(2) (_____) Traditional cultural practices can be in harmony with the protection and sustainable use of biological resources.

(3) (_____) Facing the choices, states should be determined to take the protection of biological resources into consideration in decision-making.

B. Questions 4 to 6 are based on **Article 21 Financial mechanism**

(4) (_____) Such institutional structure which the Conference of the Parties has made the decision to choose shall fulfill the operations of the financial mechanism during a series of meetings.

(5) (_____) The present available financial institutions are powerful to provide sufficient financial resources for the conservation and sustainable use of biological diversity.

(6) (_____) Standers, rules and instructions should be stipulated in detail at the first meeting, based upon which to make the judgement about whether the Conference of the Parties is qualified to have the power to use the financial resources with the regular check and assessment.

3. Extensive Reading

Directions: In this section, there is a passage with ten blanks. You are required to select one word for each blank from a list of choices given in a word bank following the passage. Read the passage through carefully before making your choices. Each choice in the bank is identified by a letter. You may not use any of the words in the bank more than once.

In the context of conservation science, the term "biodiversity", a (1) _____ of "biological diversity", is relatively young. "Biological diversity" in its current sense began to be used in the early 1980s, with interest in the concept elevated by publications such as "Limits to Growth", which discussed the (2) _____ of unrestricted population and economic growth on the environment. Use of the term has (3) _____ from a focus on species richness (number of different species in a location/sample) to greater emphasis on ecological and genetic diversity. The specific origin of the word "biodiversity" is often (4) _____ to W. G. Rosen in 1985 during planning for the "National Forum on Biodiversity" which took place in America later that year. The proceedings of the forum were published by E. O. Wilson in 1988 in a book entitled "Biodiversity", which is likely to have (5) _____ the widespread use of the word.

Initially the term biodiversity was used more in political forums than scientific ones, progressing over time to become a term used to (6) _____ the concept of the "richness of life on earth". Importantly, biodiversity does not exclusively refer to species richness. It also (7) _____ diversity at a wider scale meaning that differences in the genetic makeup of populations is important. Endemism has a key role to play in this context because endemic species are restricted to small areas and provide pockets of particularly high genetic diversity.

The concept of biodiversity continues to evolve and more (8) _____ it has been included in the idea of ecosystem services in that it is a form of 'natural capital' and thus underpins the functioning of ecosystems. Biodiversity itself is not generally considered an ecosystem service but rather supports environmental functions.

The increasing use of the term biodiversity is being driven by the fact that, in an ecological context, global biodiversity itself is being lost at a (an) (9) _____ rate. Although it has been shown that the significant global biodiversity loss that has occurred over the time frame of human existence has not stopped global human population increase, there is clear evidence that biodiversity loss can affect the wellbeing of society and have (10) _____ economic impacts.

A. initiated	B. attributed	C. contraction	D. passionate	E. transformation
F. ranged	G. encompasses	H. symbolize	I. negative	J. impacts
K. alarming	L. global	M. recently	N. implications	O. proceedings

4. Vocabulary Expanding

Directions: In this section, there are ten sentences from the United Nations Framework Convention on Climate Change. You are required to complete these sentences with the proper form of the words given in the brackets.

(1) Aware that conservation and sustainable use of biological diversity is of critical importance for meeting the food, health and other needs of the growing world population, for which purpose access to and sharing of both genetic resources and technologies are _____. (essence)

(2) Determined to conserve and _____ use biological diversity for the benefit of present and future generations. (sustain)

(3) States have, in accordance with the Charter of the United Nations and the principles of international law, the sovereign right to exploit their own resources pursuant to their own _____ policies, and the responsibility to ensure that activities within their jurisdiction or control do not cause damage to the environment of other States or of areas beyond the limits of national jurisdiction. (environment)

(4) Promote and encourage research which contributes to the conservation and sustainable use of biological diversity, particularly in developing countries, *inter alia*,

in accordance with decisions of the Conference of the Parties taken in consequence of _____ of the Subsidiary Body on Scientific, Technical and Technological Advice. (recommend)

(5) The Contracting Parties, recognizing that patents and other _____ property rights may have an influence on the implementation of this Convention, shall cooperate in this regard subject to national legislation and international law in order to ensure that such rights are supportive of and do not run counter to its objectives. (intellect)

(6) The Contracting Parties shall consider _____ existing financial institutions to provide financial resources for the conservation and sustainable use of biological diversity. (strength)

(7) If the parties to the dispute have not in accordance with paragraph 3 above, accepted the same or any procedure, the dispute shall be submitted to _____ in accordance with Part 2 of Annex II unless the parties otherwise agree. (conciliate)

(8) _____ economic integration organizations, in matters within their competence, shall exercise their right to vote with a number of votes equal to the number of their member States which are Contracting Parties to this Convention or the relevant protocol. (region)

(9) Ecosystems and habitats: containing high diversity, large numbers of endemic or threatened species, or wilderness; required by migratory species; of social, economic, cultural or scientific importance; or, which are representative, unique or associated with key _____ or other biological processes. (evolution)

(10) Any controversy which may arise between the parties to the dispute as regards the _____ or manner of implementation of the final decision may be submitted by either party for decision to the arbitral tribunal which rendered it. (interpret)

七、思考题(Questions for Discussion)

Directions: Work in groups and answer the following questions.

1. What are the origin and scope of the *Convention on Biological Diversity*?

2. What are the general measures for conservation and sustainable use of biological diversity?

3. As for the financial resources concerning the *Convention on Biological Diversity*, what are the different roles played by the developed country parties, developing country parties and the countries undergoing the process of transition to a market economy?

八、拓展学习(Further Studies)

Directions: Surf the Internet and find more information about the following topics before or after class. Present to the class some successful projects to illustrate the application of these concepts to practice.

1. Please give a summary of the meetings participated in by the contracting parties of the *Convention on Biological Diversity*.

2. Have you heard of any criticism targeting at the *Convention on Biological Diversity*?

九、模拟联合国大会(Model United Nations Simulations)

Directions: Work in teams and simulate the institutions and committees of the United Nations, featuring delegates of the UN members and the six committees of the General Assembly, negotiating issues of biodiversity in the world and working out resolutions. Students are suggested to focus on the following topics:

1. What is the real situation concerning the threat of significant reduction or loss of biological diversity?

2. What kind of financial support and incentives should each contracting party provide?

3. How to monitor the invasive species that lead to the decrease of biodiversity?

第六章

濒危野生动植物国际贸易公约

Convention on International Trade in Endangered Species of Wild Fauna and Flora

一、背景知识(Background)

《濒危野生动植物国际贸易公约》(Convention on International Trade in Endangered Species of Wild Fauna and Flora, CITES)签署于1973年3月3日,生效于1975年7月1日,修订于1979年6月22日。因为此公约在华盛顿签署,亦简称为《华盛顿公约》。CITES是管理濒危物种国际贸易的多边环境协议,属于国际法,其宗旨是为了预防濒危物种因国际贸易而遭到过度开发乃至灭绝。

该公约的成立始于国际保育社会有鉴于野生动植物国际贸易对部分野生动植物族群已造成直接或间接的威胁,为能永续使用此项资源,遂由世界最具规模与影响力的国际自然保护联盟(The International Union for Conservation of Nature and Natural Resources, IUCN)领衔,在1963年公开呼吁各国政府正视此一问题,着手野生动植物国际贸易管制的工作。历经十年的光景,终于催生出该公约。

依照我国《野生动物保护法》第四十条规定,CITES直接适用于我国。截至2020年7月,该公约有183个缔约方,包括主权国家和一些区域性政府组织。

(Source: http://trt.org.cn/cites.html; https://baike.baidu.com/item/华盛顿公约/909827)

二、公约原文(The Text of the Convention)

Convention on International Trade in Endangered Species of Wild Fauna and Flora

Prologue
The Contracting States,
Recognizing that wild fauna and flora in their many beautiful and varied forms are

an irreplaceable part of the natural systems of the earth which must be protected for this and the generations to come;

Conscious of the ever-growing value of wild fauna and flora from aesthetic, scientific, cultural, recreational and economic points of view;

Recognizing that peoples and States are and should be the best protectors of their own wild fauna and flora;

Recognizing, in addition, that international co-operation is essential for the protection of certain species of wild fauna and flora against over-exploitation through international trade;

Convinced of the urgency of taking appropriate measures to this end;

Have agreed as follows.

Article 1 Definitions

For the purpose of the present Convention, unless the context otherwise requires:

1. "Species" means any species, subspecies, or geographically separate population thereof;

2. "Specimen" means:

(a) any animal or plant, whether alive or dead;

(b) in the case of an animal: for species included in Appendices I and II, any readily recognizable part or derivative thereof; and for species included in Appendix III, any readily recognizable part or derivative thereof specified in Appendix III in relation to the species;

(c) and in the case of a plant: for species included in Appendix I, any readily recognizable part or derivative thereof; and for species included in Appendices II and III, any readily recognizable part or derivative thereof specified in Appendices II and III in relation to the species;

3. "Trade" means export, re-export, import and introduction from the sea;

4. "Re-export" means export of any specimen that has previously been imported;

5. "Introduction from the sea" means transportation into a State of specimens of any species which were taken in the marine environment not under the jurisdiction of any State;

6. "Scientific Authority" means a national scientific authority designated in accordance with Article 9;

7. "Management Authority" means a national management authority designated in accordance with Article 9;

8. "Party" means a State for which the present Convention has entered into force.

Article 2 Fundamental principles

1. Appendix I shall include all species threatened with extinction which are or may

be affected by trade. Trade in specimens of these species must be subject to particularly strict regulation in order not to endanger further their survival and must only be authorized in exceptional circumstances.

2. Appendix II shall include:

(a) all species which although not necessarily now threatened with extinction may become so unless trade in specimens of such species is subject to strict regulation in order to avoid utilization incompatible with their survival;

(b) and other species which must be subject to regulation in order that trade in specimens of certain species referred to in sub-paragraph (a) of this paragraph may be brought under effective control.

3. Appendix III shall include all species which any Party identifies as being subject to regulation within its jurisdiction for the purpose of preventing or restricting exploitation, and as needing the co-operation of other Parties in the control of trade.

4. The Parties shall not allow trade in specimens of species included in Appendices I, II and III except in accordance with the provisions of the present Convention.

Article 3 Regulation of trade in specimens of species included in Appendix I

1. All trade in specimens of species included in Appendix I shall be in accordance with the provisions of this Article.

2. The export of any specimen of a species included in Appendix I shall require the prior grant and presentation of an export permit. An export permit shall only be granted when the following conditions have been met:

(a) a Scientific Authority of the State of export has advised that such export will not be detrimental to the survival of that species;

(b) a Management Authority of the State of export is satisfied that the specimen was not obtained in contravention of the laws of that State for the protection of fauna and flora;

(c) a Management Authority of the State of export is satisfied that any living specimen will be so prepared and shipped as to minimize the risk of injury, damage to health or cruel treatment;

(d) and a Management Authority of the State of export is satisfied that an import permit has been granted for the specimen.

3. The import of any specimen of a species included in Appendix I shall require the prior grant and presentation of an import permit and either an export permit or a re-export certificate. An import permit shall only be granted when the following conditions have been met:

(a) a Scientific Authority of the State of import has advised that the import will be for purposes which are not detrimental to the survival of the species involved;

(b) a Scientific Authority of the State of import is satisfied that the proposed recipient of a living specimen is suitably equipped to house and care for it;

(c) and a Management Authority of the State of import is satisfied that the specimen is not to be used for primarily commercial purposes.

4. The re-export of any specimen of a species included in Appendix I shall require the prior grant and presentation of a re-export certificate. A re-export certificate shall only be granted when the following conditions have been met:

(a) a Management Authority of the State of re-export is satisfied that the specimen was imported into that State in accordance with the provisions of the present Convention;

(b) a Management Authority of the State of re-export is satisfied that any living specimen will be so prepared and shipped as to minimize the risk of injury, damage to health or cruel treatment;

(c) and a Management Authority of the State of re-export is satisfied that an import permit has been granted for any living specimen.

5. The introduction from the sea of any specimen of a species included in Appendix I shall require the prior grant of a certificate from a Management Authority of the State of introduction. A certificate shall only be granted when the following conditions have been met:

(a) a Scientific Authority of the State of introduction advises that the introduction will not be detrimental to the survival of the species involved;

(b) a Management Authority of the State of introduction is satisfied that the proposed recipient of a living specimen is suitably equipped to house and care for it;

(c) and a Management Authority of the State of introduction is satisfied that the specimen is not to be used for primarily commercial purposes.

Article 4 Regulation of trade in specimens of species included in Appendix II

1. All trade in specimens of species included in Appendix II shall be in accordance with the provisions of this Article.

2. The export of any specimen of a species included in Appendix II shall require the prior grant and presentation of an export permit. An export permit shall only be granted when the following conditions have been met:

(a) a Scientific Authority of the State of export has advised that such export will not be detrimental to the survival of that species;

(b) a Management Authority of the State of export is satisfied that the specimen was not obtained in contravention of the laws of that State for the protection of fauna and flora;

(c) and a Management Authority of the State of export is satisfied that any living specimen will be so prepared and shipped as to minimize the risk of injury, damage to health or cruel treatment.

3. A Scientific Authority in each Party shall monitor both the export permits granted by that State for specimens of species included in Appendix II and the actual exports of such specimens. Whenever a Scientific Authority determines that the export of

specimens of any such species should be limited in order to maintain that species throughout its range at a level consistent with its role in the ecosystems in which it occurs and well above the level at which that species might become eligible for inclusion in Appendix I, the Scientific Authority shall advise the appropriate Management Authority of suitable measures to be taken to limit the grant of export permits for specimens of that species.

4. The import of any specimen of a species included in Appendix II shall require the prior presentation of either an export permit or a re-export certificate.

5. The re-export of any specimen of a species included in Appendix II shall require the prior grant and presentation of a re-export certificate. A re-export certificate shall only be granted when the following conditions have been met:

(a) a Management Authority of the State of re-export is satisfied that the specimen was imported into that State in accordance with the provisions of the present Convention;

(b) and a Management Authority of the State of re-export is satisfied that any living specimen will be so prepared and shipped as to minimize the risk of injury, damage to health or cruel treatment.

6. The introduction from the sea of any specimen of a species included in Appendix II shall require the prior grant of a certificate from a Management Authority of the State of introduction. A certificate shall only be granted when the following conditions have been met:

(a) a Scientific Authority of the State of introduction advises that the introduction will not be detrimental to the survival of the species involved;

(b) and a Management Authority of the State of introduction is satisfied that any living specimen will be so handled as to minimize the risk of injury, damage to health or cruel treatment.

7. Certificates referred to in paragraph 6 of this Article may be granted on the advice of a Scientific Authority, in consultation with other national scientific authorities or, when appropriate, international scientific authorities, in respect of periods not exceeding one year for total numbers of specimens to be introduced in such periods.

Article 5　Regulation of trade in specimens of species included in Appendix III

1. All trade in specimens of species included in Appendix III shall be in accordance with the provisions of this Article.

2. The export of any specimen of a species included in Appendix III from any State which has included that species in Appendix III shall require the prior grant and presentation of an export permit. An export permit shall only be granted when the following conditions have been met:

(a) a Management Authority of the State of export is satisfied that the specimen was not obtained in contravention of the laws of that State for the protection of fauna and flora;

(b) and a Management Authority of the State of export is satisfied that any living specimen will be so prepared and shipped as to minimize the risk of injury, damage to health or cruel treatment.

3. The import of any specimen of a species included in Appendix III shall require, except in circumstances to which paragraph 4 of this Article applies, the prior presentation of a certificate of origin and, where the import is from a State which has included that species in Appendix III, an export permit.

4. In the case of re-export, a certificate granted by the Management Authority of the State of re-export that the specimen was processed in that State or is being re-exported shall be accepted by the State of import as evidence that the provisions of the present Convention have been complied with in respect of the specimen concerned.

Article 6　Permits and certificates

1. Permits and certificates granted under the provisions of Articles 3, 4, and 5 shall be in accordance with the provisions of this Article.

2. An export permit shall contain the information specified in the model set forth in Appendix IV, and may only be used for export within a period of six months from the date on which it was granted.

3. Each permit or certificate shall contain the title of the present Convention, the name and any identifying stamp of the Management Authority granting it and a control number assigned by the Management Authority.

4. Any copies of a permit or certificate issued by a Management Authority shall be clearly marked as copies only and no such copy may be used in place of the original, except to the extent endorsed thereon.

5. A separate permit or certificate shall be required for each consignment of specimens.

6. A Management Authority of the State of import of any specimen shall cancel and retain the export permit or re-export certificate and any corresponding import permit presented in respect of the import of that specimen.

7. Where appropriate and feasible a Management Authority may affix a mark upon any specimen to assist in identifying the specimen. For these purposes "mark" means any indelible imprint, lead seal or other suitable means of identifying a specimen, designed in such a way as to render its imitation by unauthorized persons as difficult as possible.

Article 7　Exemptions and other special provisions relating to trade

1. The provisions of Articles III, IV and V shall not apply to the transit or transhipment of specimens through or in the territory of a Party while the specimens remain in Customs control.

2. Where a Management Authority of the State of export or re-export is satisfied that a specimen was acquired before the provisions of the present Convention applied to that specimen, the provisions of Articles 3, 4 and 5 shall not apply to that specimen where the Management Authority issues a certificate to that effect.

3. The provisions of Articles 3, 4 and 5 shall not apply to specimens that are personal or household effects. This exemption shall not apply where:

(a) in the case of specimens of a species included in Appendix I, they were acquired by the owner outside his State of usual residence, and are being imported into that State;

(b) or in the case of specimens of species included in Appendix II:

i. they were acquired by the owner outside his State of usual residence and in a State where removal from the wild occurred;

ii. they are being imported into the owner's State of usual residence;

iii. and the State where removal from the wild occurred requires the prior grant of export permits before any export of such specimens; unless a Management Authority is satisfied that the specimens were acquired before the provisions of the present Convention applied to such specimens.

4. Specimens of an animal species included in Appendix I bred in captivity for commercial purposes, or of a plant species included in Appendix I artificially propagated for commercial purposes, shall be deemed to be specimens of species included in Appendix II.

5. Where a Management Authority of the State of export is satisfied that any specimen of an animal species was bred in captivity or any specimen of a plant species was artificially propagated, or is a part of such an animal or plant or was derived therefrom, a certificate by that Management Authority to that effect shall be accepted in lieu of any of the permits or certificates required under the provisions of Article 3, 4 or 5.

6. The provisions of Articles 3, 4 and 5 shall not apply to the non-commercial loan, donation or exchange between scientists or scientific institutions registered by a Management Authority of their State, of herbarium specimens, other preserved, dried or embedded museum specimens, and live plant materials which carry a label issued or approved by a Management Authority.

7. A Management Authority of any State may waive the requirements of Articles 3, 4 and 5 and allow the movement without permits or certificates of specimens which form part of a travelling zoo, circus, menagerie, plant exhibition or other travelling exhibition provided that:

(a) the exporter or importer registers full details of such specimens with that Management Authority;

(b) the specimens are in either of the categories specified in paragraph 2 or 5 of this Article;

(c) and the Management Authority is satisfied that any living specimen will be so transported and cared for as to minimize the risk of injury, damage to health or cruel treatment.

Article 8　Measures to be taken by the Parties

1. The Parties shall take appropriate measures to enforce the provisions of the present Convention and to prohibit trade in specimens in violation thereof. These shall include measures:

(a) to penalize trade in, or possession of, such specimens, or both;

(b) and to provide for the confiscation or return to the State of export of such specimens.

2. In addition to the measures taken under paragraph 1 of this Article, a Party may, when it deems it necessary, provide for any method of internal reimbursement for expenses incurred as a result of the confiscation of a specimen traded in violation of the measures taken in the application of the provisions of the present Convention.

3. As far as possible, the Parties shall ensure that specimens shall pass through any formalities required for trade with a minimum of delay. To facilitate such passage, a Party may designate ports of exit and ports of entry at which specimens must be presented for clearance. The Parties shall ensure further that all living specimens, during any period of transit, holding or shipment, are properly cared for so as to minimize the risk of injury, damage to health or cruel treatment.

4. Where a living specimen is confiscated as a result of measures referred to in paragraph 1 of this Article:

(a) the specimen shall be entrusted to a Management Authority of the State of confiscation;

(b) the Management Authority shall, after consultation with the State of export, return the specimen to that State at the expense of that State, or to a rescue centre or such other place as the Management Authority deems appropriate and consistent with the purposes of the present Convention;

(c) and the Management Authority may obtain the advice of a Scientific Authority, or may, whenever it considers it desirable, consult the Secretariat in order to facilitate the decision under sub-paragraph (b) of this paragraph, including the choice of a rescue centre or other place.

5. A rescue centre as referred to in paragraph 4 of this Article means an institution designated by a Management Authority to look after the welfare of living specimens, particularly those that have been confiscated.

6. Each Party shall maintain records of trade in specimens of species included in Appendices I, II and III which shall cover:

(a) the names and addresses of exporters and importers;

(b) and the number and type of permits and certificates granted; the States with which such trade occurred; the numbers or quantities and types of specimens, names of species as included in Appendices I, II and III and, where applicable, the size and sex of the specimens in question.

7. Each Party shall prepare periodic reports on its implementation of the present Convention and shall transmit to the Secretariat:

(a) an annual report containing a summary of the information specified in sub-paragraph (b) of paragraph 6 of this Article;

(b) and a biennial report on legislative, regulatory and administrative measures taken to enforce the provisions of the present Convention.

8. The information referred to in paragraph 7 of this Article shall be available to the public where this is not inconsistent with the law of the Party concerned.

Article 9　Management and scientific authorities

1. Each Party shall designate for the purposes of the present Convention:

(a) one or more Management Authorities competent to grant permits or certificates on behalf of that Party;

(b) and one or more Scientific Authorities.

2. A State depositing an instrument of ratification, acceptance, approval or accession shall at that time inform the Depositary Government of the name and address of the Management Authority authorized to communicate with other Parties and with the Secretariat.

3. Any changes in the designations or authorizations under the provisions of this Article shall be communicated by the Party concerned to the Secretariat for transmission to all other Parties.

4. Any Management Authority referred to in paragraph 2 of this Article shall, if so requested by the Secretariat or the Management Authority of another Party, communicate to it impression of stamps, seals or other devices used to authenticate permits or certificates.

Article 10　Trade with States not Parties to the Convention

Where export or re-export is to, or import is from, a State not a Party to the present Convention, comparable documentation issued by the competent authorities in that State which substantially conforms with the requirements of the present Convention for permits and certificates may be accepted in lieu thereof by any Party.

Article 11　Conference of the Parties

1. The Secretariat shall call a meeting of the Conference of the Parties not later than two years after the entry into force of the present Convention.

2. Thereafter the Secretariat shall convene regular meetings at least once every two years, unless the Conference decides otherwise, and extraordinary meetings at any time on the written request of at least one-third of the Parties.

3. At meetings, whether regular or extraordinary, the Parties shall review the implementation of the present Convention and may:

(a) make such provision as may be necessary to enable the Secretariat to carry out its duties, and adopt financial provisions;

(b) consider and adopt amendments to Appendices I and II in accordance with Article XV;

(c) review the progress made towards the restoration and conservation of the species included in Appendices I, II and III;

(d) receive and consider any reports presented by the Secretariat or by any Party;

(e) and where appropriate, make recommendations for improving the effectiveness of the present Convention.

4. At each regular meeting, the Parties may determine the time and venue of the next regular meeting to be held in accordance with the provisions of paragraph 2 of this Article.

5. At any meeting, the Parties may determine and adopt rules of procedure for the meeting.

6. The United Nations, its Specialized Agencies and the International Atomic Energy Agency, as well as any State not a Party to the present Convention, may be represented at meetings of the Conference by observers, who shall have the right to participate but not to vote.

7. Any body or agency technically qualified in protection, conservation or management of wild fauna and flora, in the following categories, which has informed the Secretariat of its desire to be represented at meetings of the Conference by observers, shall be admitted unless at least one-third of the Parties present object:

(a) international agencies or bodies, either governmental or non-governmental, and national governmental agencies and bodies;

(b) and national non-governmental agencies or bodies which have been approved for this purpose by the State in which they are located. Once admitted, these observers shall have the right to participate but not to vote.

Article 12　The Secretariat

1. Upon entry into force of the present Convention, a Secretariat shall be provided by the Executive Director of the United Nations Environment Programme. To the extent and in the manner he considers appropriate, he may be assisted by suitable inter-governmental or non-governmental international or national agencies and bodies technically qualified in protection, conservation and management of wild fauna and flora.

2. The functions of the Secretariat shall be:

(a) to arrange for and service meetings of the Parties;

(b) to perform the functions entrusted to it under the provisions of Articles 15 and 16 of the present Convention;

(c) to undertake scientific and technical studies in accordance with programmes authorized by the Conference of the Parties as will contribute to the implementation of the present Convention, including studies concerning standards for appropriate preparation and shipment of living specimens and the means of identifying specimens;

(d) to study the reports of Parties and to request from Parties such further information with respect thereto as it deems necessary to ensure implementation of the present Convention;

(e) to invite the attention of the Parties to any matter pertaining to the aims of the present Convention;

(f) to publish periodically and distribute to the Parties current editions of Appendices I, II and III together with any information which will facilitate identification of specimens of species included in those Appendices;

(g) to prepare annual reports to the Parties on its work and on the implementation of the present Convention and such other reports as meetings of the Parties may request;

(h) to make recommendations for the implementation of the aims and provisions of the present Convention, including the exchange of information of a scientific or technical nature;

(i) to perform any other function as may be entrusted to it by the Parties.

Article 13 International measures

1. When the Secretariat in the light of information received is satisfied that any species included in Appendix I or II is being affected adversely by trade in specimens of that species or that the provisions of the present Convention are not being effectively implemented, it shall communicate such information to the authorized Management Authority of the Party or Parties concerned.

2. When any Party receives a communication as indicated in paragraph 1 of this Article, it shall, as soon as possible, inform the Secretariat of any relevant facts insofar as its laws permit and, where appropriate, propose remedial action. Where the Party considers that an inquiry is desirable, such inquiry may be carried out by one or more persons expressly authorized by the Party.

3. The information provided by the Party or resulting from any inquiry as specified in paragraph 2 of this Article shall be reviewed by the next Conference of the Parties which may make whatever recommendations it deems appropriate.

Article 14 Effect on domestic legislation and international conventions

1. The provisions of the present Convention shall in no way affect the right of

Parties to adopt:

(a) stricter domestic measures regarding the conditions for trade, taking, possession or transport of specimens of species included in Appendices I, II and III, or the complete prohibition thereof;

(b) or domestic measures restricting or prohibiting trade, taking, possession or transport of species not included in Appendix I, II or III.

2. The provisions of the present Convention shall in no way affect the provisions of any domestic measures or the obligations of Parties deriving from any treaty, convention, or international agreement relating to other aspects of trade, taking, possession or transport of specimens which is in force or subsequently may enter into force for any Party including any measure pertaining to the Customs, public health, veterinary or plant quarantine fields.

3. The provisions of the present Convention shall in no way affect the provisions of, or the obligations deriving from, any treaty, convention or international agreement concluded or which may be concluded between States creating a union or regional trade agreement establishing or maintaining a common external Customs control and removing Customs control between the parties thereto insofar as they relate to trade among the States members of that union or agreement.

4. A State party to the present Convention, which is also a party to any other treaty, convention or international agreement which is in force at the time of the coming into force of the present Convention and under the provisions of which protection is afforded to marine species included in Appendix II, shall be relieved of the obligations imposed on it under the provisions of the present Convention with respect to trade in specimens of species included in Appendix II that are taken by ships registered in that State and in accordance with the provisions of such other treaty, convention or international agreement.

5. Notwithstanding the provisions of Articles 3, 4 and 5, any export of a specimen taken in accordance with paragraph 4 of this Article shall only require a certificate from a Management Authority of the State of introduction to the effect that the specimen was taken in accordance with the provisions of the other treaty, convention or international agreement in question.

6. Nothing in the present Convention shall prejudice the codification and development of the law of the sea by the United Nations Conference on the Law of the Sea convened pursuant to Resolution 2750 C (XXV) of the General Assembly of the United Nations nor the present or future claims and legal views of any State concerning the law of the sea and the nature and extent of coastal and flag State jurisdiction.

Article 15　Amendments to Appendices I and II

1. The following provisions shall apply in relation to amendments to Appendices I

and II at meetings of the Conference of the Parties:

(a) Any Party may propose an amendment to Appendix I or II for consideration at the next meeting. The text of the proposed amendment shall be communicated to the Secretariat at least 150 days before the meeting. The Secretariat shall consult the other Parties and interested bodies on the amendment in accordance with the provisions of sub-paragraphs (b) and (c) of paragraph 2 of this Article and shall communicate the response to all Parties not later than 30 days before the meeting.

(b) Amendments shall be adopted by a two-thirds majority of Parties present and voting. For these purposes "Parties present and voting" means Parties present and casting an affirmative or negative vote. Parties abstaining from voting shall not be counted among the two-thirds required for adopting an amendment.

(c) Amendments adopted at a meeting shall enter into force 90 days after that meeting for all Parties except those which make a reservation in accordance with paragraph 3 of this Article.

2. The following provisions shall apply in relation to amendments to Appendices I and II between meetings of the Conference of the Parties:

(a) Any Party may propose an amendment to Appendix I or II for consideration between meetings by the postal procedures set forth in this paragraph.

(b) For marine species, the Secretariat shall, upon receiving the text of the proposed amendment, immediately communicate it to the Parties. It shall also consult inter-governmental bodies having a function in relation to those species especially with a view to obtaining scientific data these bodies may be able to provide and to ensuring co-ordination with any conservation measures enforced by such bodies. The Secretariat shall communicate the views expressed and data provided by these bodies and its own findings and recommendations to the Parties as soon as possible.

(c) For species other than marine species, the Secretariat shall, upon receiving the text of the proposed amendment, immediately communicate it to the Parties, and, as soon as possible thereafter, its own recommendations.

(d) Any Party may, within 60 days of the date on which the Secretariat communicated its recommendations to the Parties under sub-paragraph (b) or (c) of this paragraph, transmit to the Secretariat any comments on the proposed amendment together with any relevant scientific data and information.

(e) The Secretariat shall communicate the replies received together with its own recommendations to the Parties as soon as possible.

(f) If no objection to the proposed amendment is received by the Secretariat within 30 days of the date the replies and recommendations were communicated under the provisions of sub-paragraph (e) of this paragraph, the amendment shall enter into force 90 days later for all Parties except those which make a reservation in accordance with paragraph 3 of this Article.

(g) If an objection by any Party is received by the Secretariat, the proposed amendment shall be submitted to a postal vote in accordance with the provisions of sub-paragraphs (h), (i) and (j) of this paragraph.

(h) The Secretariat shall notify the Parties that notification of objection has been received.

(i) Unless the Secretariat receives the votes for, against or in abstention from at least one-half of the Parties within 60 days of the date of notification under sub-paragraph (h) of this paragraph, the proposed amendment shall be referred to the next meeting of the Conference for further consideration.

(j) Provided that votes are received from one-half of the Parties, the amendment shall be adopted by a two-thirds majority of Parties casting an affirmative or negative vote.

(k) The Secretariat shall notify all Parties of the result of the vote.

(l) If the proposed amendment is adopted it shall enter into force 90 days after the date of the notification by the Secretariat of its acceptance for all Parties except those which make a reservation in accordance with paragraph 3 of this Article.

3. During the period of 90 days provided for by sub-paragraph (c) of paragraph 1 or sub-paragraph (l) of paragraph 2 of this Article any Party may by notification in writing to the Depositary Government make a reservation with respect to the amendment. Until such reservation is withdrawn the Party shall be treated as a State not a Party to the present Convention with respect to trade in the species concerned.

Article 16　Appendix III and amendments thereto

1. Any Party may at any time submit to the Secretariat a list of species which it identifies as being subject to regulation within its jurisdiction for the purpose mentioned in paragraph 3 of Article 2. Appendix III shall include the names of the Parties submitting the species for inclusion therein, the scientific names of the species so submitted, and any parts or derivatives of the animals or plants concerned that are specified in relation to the species for the purposes of sub-paragraph (b) of Article 1.

2. Each list submitted under the provisions of paragraph 1 of this Article shall be communicated to the Parties by the Secretariat as soon as possible after receiving it. The list shall take effect as part of Appendix III 90 days after the date of such communication. At any time after the communication of such list, any Party may by notification in writing to the Depositary Government enter a reservation with respect to any species or any parts or derivatives, and until such reservation is withdrawn, the State shall be treated as a State not a Party to the present Convention with respect to trade in the species or part or derivative concerned.

3. A Party which has submitted a species for inclusion in Appendix III may

withdraw it at any time by notification to the Secretariat which shall communicate the withdrawal to all Parties. The withdrawal shall take effect 30 days after the date of such communication.

4. Any Party submitting a list under the provisions of paragraph 1 of this Article shall submit to the Secretariat a copy of all domestic laws and regulations applicable to the protection of such species, together with any interpretations which the Party may deem appropriate or the Secretariat may request. The Party shall, for as long as the species in question is included in Appendix III, submit any amendments of such laws and regulations or any interpretations as they are adopted.

Article 17　Amendment of the Convention

1. An extraordinary meeting of the Conference of the Parties shall be convened by the Secretariat on the written request of at least one-third of the Parties to consider and adopt amendments to the present Convention. Such amendments shall be adopted by a two-thirds majority of Parties present and voting. For these purposes "Parties present and voting" means Parties present and casting an affirmative or negative vote. Parties abstaining from voting shall not be counted among the two-thirds required for adopting an amendment.

2. The text of any proposed amendment shall be communicated by the Secretariat to all Parties at least 90 days before the meeting.

3. An amendment shall enter into force for the Parties which have accepted it 60 days after two-thirds of the Parties have deposited an instrument of acceptance of the amendment with the Depositary Government. Thereafter, the amendment shall enter into force for any other Party 60 days after that Party deposits its instrument of acceptance of the amendment.

Article 18　Resolution of disputes

1. Any dispute which may arise between two or more Parties with respect to the interpretation or application of the provisions of the present Convention shall be subject to negotiation between the Parties involved in the dispute.

2. If the dispute can not be resolved in accordance with paragraph 1 of this Article, the Parties may, by mutual consent, submit the dispute to arbitration, in particular that of the Permanent Court of Arbitration at The Hague, and the Parties submitting the dispute shall be bound by the arbitral decision.

Article 19　Signature

The present Convention shall be open for signature at Washington until 30th April 1973 and thereafter at Berne until 31st December 1974.

Article 20　Ratification, acceptance, approval

The present Convention shall be subject to ratification, acceptance or approval. Instruments of ratification, acceptance or approval shall be deposited with the Government of the Swiss Confederation which shall be the Depositary Government.

Article 21   Accession

The present Convention shall be open indefinitely for accession. Instruments of accession shall be deposited with the Depositary Government.

Article 22   Entry into force

1. The present Convention shall enter into force 90 days after the date of deposit of the tenth instrument of ratification, acceptance, approval or accession, with the Depositary Government.

2. For each State which ratifies, accepts or approves the present Convention or accedes thereto after the deposit of the tenth instrument of ratification, acceptance, approval or accession, the present Convention shall enter into force 90 days after the deposit by such State of its instrument of ratification, acceptance, approval or accession.

Article 23   Reservations

1. The provisions of the present Convention shall not be subject to general reservations. Specific reservations may be entered in accordance with the provisions of this Article and Articles 15 and 16.

2. Any State may, on depositing its instrument of ratification, acceptance, approval or accession, enter a specific reservation with regard to:

(a) any species included in Appendix I, II or III;

(b) or any parts or derivatives specified in relation to a species included in Appendix III.

3. Until a Party withdraws its reservation entered under the provisions of this Article, it shall be treated as a State not a Party to the present Convention with respect to trade in the particular species or parts or derivatives specified in such reservation.

Article 24   Denunciation

Any Party may denounce the present Convention by written notification to the Depositary Government at any time. The denunciation shall take effect twelve months after the Depositary Government has received the notification.

Article 25   Depositary

1. The original of the present Convention, in the Chinese, English, French, Russian and Spanish languages, each version being equally authentic, shall be deposited with the Depositary Government, which shall transmit certified copies thereof to all States that have signed it or deposited instruments of accession to it.

2. The Depositary Government shall inform all signatory and acceding States and the Secretariat of signatures, deposit of instruments of ratification, acceptance, approval or accession, entry into force of the present Convention, amendments thereto, entry and

withdrawal of reservations and notifications of denunciation.

3. As soon as the present Convention enters into force, a certified copy thereof shall be transmitted by the Depositary Government to the Secretariat of the United Nations for registration and publication in accordance with Article 102 of the *Charter of the United Nations*.

4. In witness whereof the undersigned Plenipotentiaries, being duly authorized to that effect, have signed the present Convention.

Done at Washington this third day of March, One Thousand Nine Hundred and Seventy-three.

(Source: https://www.cites.org/eng/disc/text.php)

三、注解(Notes)

The United Nations Conference on the Law of the Sea

联合国海洋法会议。联合国为讨论制定海洋法而召开的一系列会议。第一次会议于1958年2~4月在日内瓦举行。有八十多个国家参加。会议通过有利于少数海洋大国的《领海及毗连区公约》《公海公约》《大陆架公约》和《公海渔业和生物资源保护公约》。第二次会议于1960年3~4月在日内瓦举行，专门讨论各国领海宽度和渔区范围问题。由于各方意见不一，会议未达成协议。第三次会议自1973年12月召开，150多个国家参加，至1982年12月结束，共举行11期会议。1982年4月30日，会议通过《联合国海洋法公约》。该公约自1982年12月10日至1984年12月10日在牙买加和联合国总部开放签字。至签字截止日止，在该公约上签字的国家达159个(包括中国)。该公约于1994年11月16日生效。

四、相关词汇(Key Words and Phrases)

1.	aesthetic	[iːsˈθetɪk]	adj.	美的；美学的；审美的，具有审美趣味的
2.	endorse	/ɪnˈdɔrs/	vt.	支持，赞同；批注(文件，公文等)
3.	affix	[əˈfɪks]	vt. n.	粘上；署名；将罪责加之于 [语]词缀；附加物
4.	captivity	[kæpˈtɪvɪtɪ]	n.	囚禁；被关
5.	embed	[ɪmˈbed]	vt. & vi. adj.	嵌入 嵌入的；植入的；内含的
6.	waive	[weɪv]	vt.	放弃；搁置
7.	formality	[fɔːˈmælətɪ]	n.	礼节；拘谨；仪式；正式手续

8. implementation	[ˌɪmplɪmenˈteɪʃ(ə)n]	n.	[计]实现；履行；安装启用
9. legislative	[ˈledʒɪslətɪv]	n.	立法权；立法机构
		adj.	立法的；有立法权的
10. convene	[kənˈviːn]	vt. & vi.	召集，集合；传唤
11. insofar	[ˌɪnsə(ʊ)ˈfɑː]	adv.	在…的范围；在…情况下
12. notwithstanding	[ˌnɒtwɪðˈstændɪŋ；-wɪθ-]	conj.	虽然 prep. 尽管，虽然
		adv.	尽管，仍然
13. codification	[ˌkɑdəfəˈkeʃən]	n.	编纂，整理；法典编纂；法律汇编
14. negotiation	[nɪˌɡəʊʃɪˈeɪʃ(ə)n]	n.	谈判；转让；顺利的通过
15. plenipotentiary	/ˌplenɪpəˈtenʃəri/	adj.	全权代表的；有全权的
		n.	全权代表；全权大使
16. be subject to			受支配，从属于；常遭受；有倾向的
17. be detrimental to			有害于；对不利
18. in contravention of			违反
19. in lieu of			代，代替
20. be relieved of			被解除；被消除
21. mutual consent			双方同意
22. abstain from			放弃，戒除
23. in respect of			关于

五、长难句(Difficult Sentences)

1. Recognizing that wild fauna and flora in their many beautiful and varied forms are an irreplaceable part of the natural systems of the earth which must be protected for this and the generations to come. (Prologue)

解析：此句中 that 引导宾语从句，in their many beautiful and varied forms 是 wild fauna and flora 的后置定语，which must be protected for this and the generations to come 为一定语从句，which 指代 wild fauna and flora，为了我们这一代的今后世世代代，必须加以保护。

译文：缔约各国认识到，许多美丽的、种类繁多的野生动物和植物是地球自然系统中不可代替的一部分，为了我们这一代和今后世世代代，必须加以保护。

2. All species which although not necessarily now threatened with extinction may become so unless trade in specimens of such species is subject to strict regulation in order to avoid utilization incompatible with their survival. (Article 2, 2a)

解析：此句中 which 引导了一个定语从句，which 指代前面的 species，although not necessarily now threatened with extinction 做状语，become so 意指前面

的 threatened with extinction。unless 引导一个条件状语从句，表"除非……"。in order to 引导的是目的状语从句，utilization 意为"利用，使用"，incompatible 意为不相容的矛盾的，表达了"为了防止对其生存不利的利用"的意思。

译文：所有那些目前虽未濒临灭绝，但如对其贸易不严加管理，以防止不利其生存的利用，就可能变成有灭绝危险的物种。

3. Whenever a Scientific Authority determines that the export of specimens of any such species should be limited in order to maintain that species throughout its range at a level consistent with its role in the ecosystems in which it occurs and well above the level at which that species might become eligible for inclusion in Appendix I, the Scientific Authority shall advise the appropriate Management Authority of suitable measures to be taken to limit the grant of export permits for specimens of that species.（Article 4，3）

解析：此句中 whenever 引导时间状语从句，that 引导宾语从句，做 determine 的宾语，consistent with 意为"符合，与……一致"，ecosystem 意为"生态系统"，in which 在定语从句中做地点状语，eligible for 意为"合格，够资格"。

译文：当科学机构确定，此类物种标本的出口应受到限制，以便保持该物种在其分布区内的生态系中与它应有作用相一致的地位，或者大大超出该物种够格成为附录一所属范畴的标准时，该科学机构就应建议主管的管理机构采取适当措施，限制发给该物种标本出口许可证。

4. The import of any specimen of a species included in Appendix III shall require, except in circumstances to which paragraph 4 of this Article applies, the prior presentation of a certificate of origin and, where the import is from a State which has included that species in Appendix III, an export permit.（Article 5，3）

解析：此句的主句为" the import of any specimen of a species included in Appendix III shall require the prior presentation of a certificate of origin and an export permit"，" except in circumstances to which paragraph 4 of this Article applies"和" where the import is from a State which has included that species in Appendix III"为插入语，且前一句中 to which 的 which 引导一定语从句，在句中 to which 做 apply 的宾语，to 由 apply to 固定表达而来，apply to 意为"适用于，与……有关"。

译文：除本条第 4 款涉及的情况外，附录三所列物种的任何标本的进口，应事先交验原产地证明书。如该出口国已将该物种列入附录三，则应交验该国所发给的出口许可证。

5. For these purposes "mark" means any indelible imprint, lead seal or other suitable means of identifying a specimen, designed in such a way as to render its imitation by unauthorized persons as difficult as possible.（Article 6，7）

解析：此句中，designed 作为前面提到的 imprint, lead seal 和 other suitable means 的后置定语，indelible 意为"难忘的，擦不掉的"，in such a way 后面的句子修饰 way，as to 表示"至于，关于"，render 有"着色"之意。

译文：此类"标记"系指任何难以除去导读的印记、铅封或识别该标本的其他合适的办法，尽量防止无权发证者进行伪造。

6. In addition to the measures taken under paragraph 1 of this Article, a Party may, when it deems it necessary, provide for any method of internal reimbursement for expenses incurred as a result of the confiscation of a specimen traded in violation of the measures taken in the application of the provisions of the present Convention. (Article 8, 2)

解析：in addition to 意为"除……之外"，"taken under paragraph 1 of this Article"修饰前面的 measures，"when it deems it necessary"作插入语，as a result of 意为"作为……的结果"，the confiscation of a specimen traded in violation of the measures taken in the application of the provisions of the present Convention 在 of 后面，作为一个整体，是 of 后面的宾语。

译文：除本条第1款所规定的措施外，违反本公约规定措施的贸易标本，予以没收所用的费用，如成员国认为必要，可采取任何办法内部补偿。

六、课后练习(Exercises)

1. Skimming and Scanning

Directions：Read the following passage excerpted from Convention on International Trade in Endangered Species of Wild Fauna and Flora. At the end of the passage, there are six statements. Each statement contains information given in one of the paragraphs of the passage. Identify the paragraph from which the information is derived. Each paragraph is marked with a letter. You may choose a paragraph more than once. Answer the questions by writing the corresponding letter in the bracket in front of each statement.

Article 4 Regulation of trade in specimens of species included in Appendix II

1. All trade in specimens of species included in Appendix II shall be in accordance with the provisions of this Article.

2. The export of any specimen of a species included in Appendix II shall require the prior grant and presentation of an export permit. An export permit shall only be granted when the following conditions have been met:

(a) a Scientific Authority of the State of export has advised that such export will not be detrimental to the survival of that species;

(b) a Management Authority of the State of export is satisfied that the specimen was not obtained in contravention of the laws of that State for the protection of fauna and flora;

(c) and a Management Authority of the State of export is satisfied that any living specimen will be so prepared and shipped as to minimize the risk of injury, damage to health or cruel treatment.

3. A Scientific Authority in each Party shall monitor both the export permits granted

by that State for specimens of species included in Appendix II and the actual exports of such specimens. Whenever a Scientific Authority determines that the export of specimens of any such species should be limited in order to maintain that species throughout its range at a level consistent with its role in the ecosystems in which it occurs and well above the level at which that species might become eligible for inclusion in Appendix I, the Scientific Authority shall advise the appropriate Management Authority of suitable measures to be taken to limit the grant of export permits for specimens of that species.

4. The import of any specimen of a species included in Appendix II shall require the prior presentation of either an export permit or a re-export certificate.

5. The re-export of any specimen of a species included in Appendix II shall require the prior grant and presentation of a re-export certificate. A re-export certificate shall only be granted when the following conditions have been met:

(a) a Management Authority of the State of re-export is satisfied that the specimen was imported into that State in accordance with the provisions of the present Convention;

(b) and a Management Authority of the State of re-export is satisfied that any living specimen will be so prepared and shipped as to minimize the risk of injury, damage to health or cruel treatment.

6. The introduction from the sea of any specimen of a species included in Appendix II shall require the prior grant of a certificate from a Management Authority of the State of introduction. A certificate shall only be granted when the following conditions have been met:

(a) a Scientific Authority of the State of introduction advises that the introduction will not be detrimental to the survival of the species involved;

(b) and a Management Authority of the State of introduction is satisfied that any living specimen will be so handled as to minimize the risk of injury, damage to health or cruel treatment.

7. Certificates referred to in paragraph 6 of this Article may be granted on the advice of a Scientific Authority, in consultation with other national scientific authorities or, when appropriate, international scientific authorities, in respect of periods not exceeding one year for total numbers of specimens to be introduced in such periods.

Article 5　Regulation of trade in specimens of species included in Appendix III

8. All trade in specimens of species included in Appendix III shall be in accordance with the provisions of this Article.

9. The export of any specimen of a species included in Appendix III from any State which has included that species in Appendix III shall require the prior grant and presentation of an export permit. An export permit shall only be granted when the following conditions have been met: a Management Authority of the State of export is satisfied that the specimen was not obtained in contravention of the laws of that State for the protection of fauna and flora; and a Management Authority of the State of export is

satisfied that any living specimen will be so prepared and shipped as to minimize the risk of injury, damage to health or cruel treatment.

10. The import of any specimen of a species included in Appendix III shall require, except in circumstances to which paragraph 4 of this Article applies, the prior presentation of a certificate of origin and, where the import is from a State which has included that species in Appendix III, an export permit.

11. In the case of re-export, a certificate granted by the Management Authority of the State of re-export that the specimen was processed in that State or is being re-exported shall be accepted by the State of import as evidence that the provisions of the present Convention have been complied with in respect of the specimen concerned.

(_____)(1) Good preparation must be made to safeguard the health of any living specimen and reduce the maltreatment to the lowest possible level as for specimens of species included in Appendix III.

(_____)(2) The export permits and the actual exports shall be checked by a Scientific Authority in each party.

(_____)(3) Without presenting an export permit or re-export certificate any specimen of a species in Appendix II will not be allowed to import.

(_____)(4) The introduction from the sea of any specimen of a species included in Appendix II will not be harmful to the survival of the species concerned.

(_____)(5) Only the specimen of a species that cannot do harm to the survival of that species will get export permit.

(_____)(6) Certificates referred to in paragraph 6 of this Article expire in the period of less than one year.

2. Reading Comprehension

Directions: Read **Article 8 Measures to be taken by the Parties 4** and **Article 12 The Secretariat 2** from Convention on International Trade in Endangered Species of Wild Fauna and Flora, and decide whether the following statements are True or False. Write T for True or F for False in the bracket in front of each statement.

A. Questions 1-3 are based on **Article 8 Measures to be taken by the Parties 4.**

(1)(_____) The state of confiscation, together with the parallel Management Authority, shall be responsible for the living specimen confiscated.

(2)(_____) The State of Export should cover part of the cost concerning a living specimen confiscated.

(3)(_____) The Management Authority may turn to the help of a Scientific Authority or Secretariat concerning how to deal with a living specimen confiscated.

B. Questions 4-6 are based on **Article 12 The Secretariat 2.**

(4)(_____) The Secretariat shall be to arouse the attention of the parties to any matter contradictory to the purposes of the present convention

(5) (_____) The Secretariat shall be responsible for planning and organizing the meetings of the parties.

(6) (_____) The Secretariat shall be to promise the conduct of the scientific and economic researches according to the programs permitted officially by the concerned parties.

3. Extensive Reading

Directions: In this section, there is a passage with ten blanks. You are required to select one word for each blank from a list of choices given in a word bank following the passage. Read the passage through carefully before making your choices. Each choice in the bank is identified by a letter. You may not use any of the words in the bank more than once.

Ecological Risk Assessment Process under the Endangered Species Act

This document provides an overview of the Environmental Protection Agency's (EPA) ecological risk assessment process for the (1) _____ of potential risk to endangered and threatened (listed) species from (2) _____ to pesticides. The assessments described in this document are conducted by the Office of Pesticide Programs (OPP).

Organized into eight sections and two appendices, this document begins with a description of the purpose and organization of the document (Section I).

It continues with a brief overview of the statutory (3) _____ under which OPP operates (Section II), followed by a discussion of OPP's mission and organizational structure, and basic information about OPP's regulatory processes (Section III). Section III also (4) _____ the importance of evaluating regulatory actions for their potential impact to listed species and briefly describes the steps being taken to (5) _____ that listed species concerns are addressed. Section IV provides an overview of the Environmental Fate and Effects Division (EFED), which conducts most of the (6) _____ screening-level assessments to evaluate the potential impact of pesticides on non-target species, including listed species. This section addresses EFED's procedures, data requirements, and processes to support the development of ecological assessments based on sound science. Section V provides a (7) _____ review of EFED's screening-level assessment process, which is based on risk assessment procedures outlined in (8) _____, documents and standard evaluation procedures.

If a pesticide is determined to potentially impact listed species, a species-specific assessment is conducted, which is described in Section VI. Sections V and VI summarize the screening-level and species-specific assessments that are generally conducted in OPP. It should be noted, however, that the ecological risk assessment process within OPP may, on a case-by-case basis, (9) _____ additional methodologies, models, and lines of evidence that are technically appropriate for risk management objectives. Examples of additional information and methodologies include monitoring the incident data and evaluation of routes of exposure not (10) _____ considered, but suggested by other lines of evidence.

Finally, the document concludes with a list of support documents (Section VII), references (Section VIII), and appendices.

A. exposure	B. comprehensive	C. incorporate	D. assessment	E. initial
F. impact	G. framework	H. additional	I. acknowledges	J. guidance
K. prescribes	L. routinely	M. impulsive	N. evaluation	O. ensure

4. Vocabulary Expanding

Directions: In this section, there are ten sentences from the Convention on International Trade in Endangered Species of Wild Fauna and Flora. You are required to complete these sentences with the proper form of the words given in the brackets.

(1) Recognizing, in addition, that international co-operation is essential for the protection of certain species of wild fauna and flora against over- _____ through international trade. (exploit)

(2) All species which although not necessarily now threatened with extinction may become so unless trade in specimens of such species is subject to strict regulation in order to avoid utilization _____ with their survival. (compatible)

(3) A Scientific Authority of the State of import is satisfied that the proposed _____ of a living specimen is equipped to house and care for it. (receive)

(4) A Management Authority of the State of introduction is satisfied that the specimen is not to be used for primarily _____ purposes. (commerce)

(5) In the case of re-export, a certificate granted by the Management Authority of the State of re-export that the specimen was processed in that State or is being re-exported shall be accepted by the State of import as evidence that the _____ of the present Convention have been complied with in respect of the specimen concerned. (provide)

(6) The Management Authority is satisfied that any living specimen will be so transported and cared for as to _____ the risk of injury, damage to health or cruel treatment. (minimum)

(7) A State depositing an instrument of ratification, acceptance, approval or _____ shall at that time inform the Depositary Government of the name and address of the Management Authority authorized to communicate with other Parties and with the Secretariat. (access)

(8) Where the Party considers that an inquiry is _____, such inquiry may be carried out by one or more persons expressly authorized by the Party. (desire)

(9) If the proposed amendment is adopted it shall enter into force 90 days after the date of the notification by the Secretariat of its acceptance for all Parties except those which make a _____ in accordance with paragraph 3 of this Article. (reserve)

(10) An _____ shall enter into force for the Parties which have accepted it 60 days after two-thirds of the Parties have deposited an instrument of acceptance of the amendment with the Depositary Government. (amend)

七、思考题(Questions for Discussion)

Directions: Work in groups and answer the following questions.

1. What are the export quotas of Convention on International Trade in Endangered Species of Wild Fauna and Flora?

2. What are the permanent committees established by The Conference of the Parties of Convention on International Trade in Endangered Species of Wild Fauna and Flora?

3. What is the structure of CITES Secretariat?

八、拓展学习(Further Studies)

Directions: Surf the Internet and find more information about the following topics before or after class. Present to the class some successful projects to illustrate the application of these concepts to practice.

1. Please give some details about the animal and plant species subject to different degrees of regulation listed in the Appendices of Convention on International Trade in Endangered Species of Wild Fauna and Flora.

2. What are the exemptions from the marking provisions and the use of alternative marking methods?

九、模拟联合国大会(Model United Nations Simulations)

Directions: Work in teams and simulate the institutions and committees of the United Nations, featuring delegates of the UN members and the six committees of the General Assembly, negotiating issues of global wildlife trafficking and working out resolutions. Students are suggested to focus on the following topics:

1. What is the situation of global wildlife trafficking?
2. How to enhance the global cooperation concerning this issue?
3. How to prevent the global wildlife trafficking effectively?

第七章

国际植物新品种保护公约

International Convention for the Protection of New Varieties of Plants

一、背景知识(Background)

《国际植物新品种保护公约》(UPOV)制定于1961年12月2日,1972年11月10日、1978年10月23日、1991年3月19日在日内瓦修订,1981年11月8日生效。《国际植物新品种保护公约》是保护育种者权益的重要国际协定,通过协调各成员国之间在植物新品种保护方面的政策、法律和技术,确保各成员国授予符合新颖性、特异性、一致性和稳定性要求的植物新品种的育种者保护权或专利权。公约旨在保护植物多样性,鼓励新物种的研发,造福社会。该公约于1968年8月10日开始生效,总部设在日内瓦。1997年3月20日,国务院发布了《中华人民共和国植物新品种保护条例》,1999年4月23日,我国加入了《国际植物新品种保护公约》1978年文本,成为国际植物新品种保护联盟(Union for the Protection of New Varieties of Plants, UPOV)第39个成员国。我国植物新品种保护工作是由国家林草局和农业部两个部门管理。保护范围包括粮食、蔬菜、林木、竹、木质藤本、观赏植物、果树及木本油料、饮料、调料、木本药材、藻类等。

(Source:https://baike.baidu.com/item/)

二、公约原文(The Text of the Convention)

International Convention for the Protection of New Varieties of Plants

of December 2, 1961
as Revised at Geneva on November 10, 1972,
on October 23, 1978, and on March 19, 1991

CHAPTER I DEFINITIONS

Article 1 Definitions

For the purposes of this Act:

(1) "this Convention" means the present (1991) Act of the International Convention for the Protection of New Varieties of Plants;

(2) "Act of 1961/1972" means the International Convention for the Protection of New Varieties of Plants of December 2, 1961, as amended by the Additional Act of November 10, 1972;

(3) "Act of 1978" means the Act of October 23, 1978, of the International Convention for the Protection of New Varieties of Plants;

(4) "breeder" means

(a) the person who bred, or discovered and developed, a variety,

(b) the person who is the employer of the aforementioned person or who has commissioned the latter's work, where the laws of the relevant Contracting Party so provide, or

(c) the successor in title of the first or second aforementioned person, as the case may be;

(5) "breeder's right" means the right of the breeder provided for in this Convention;

(6) "variety" means a plant grouping within a single botanical taxon of the lowest known rank, which grouping, irrespective of whether the conditions for the grant of a breeder's right are fully met, can be

(a) defined by the expression of the characteristics resulting from a given genotype or combination of genotypes,

(b) distinguished from any other plant grouping by the expression of at least one of the said characteristics and

(c) considered as a unit with regard to its suitability for being propagated unchanged;

(7) "Contracting Party" means a State or an intergovernmental organization party to this Convention;

(8) "territory", in relation to a Contracting Party, means, where the Contracting Party is a State, the territory of that State and, where the Contracting Party is an intergovernmental organization, the territory in which the constituting treaty of that intergovernmental organization applies;

(9) "authority" means the authority referred to in Article 30(1)(ii);

(10) "Union" means the Union for the Protection of New Varieties of Plants founded by the Act of 1961 and further mentioned in the Act of 1972, the Act of 1978 and in this Convention;

(11) "member of the Union" means a State party to the Act of 1961/1972 or the Act of 1978, or a Contracting Party.

CHAPTER II GENERAL OBLIGATIONS OF THE CONTRACTING PARTIES

Article 2 Basic obligation of the Contracting Parties

Each Contracting Party shall grant and protect breeders' rights.

Article 3 Genera and species to be protected

(1) [*States already members of the Union*] Each Contracting Party which is bound by the Act of 1961/1972 or the Act of 1978 shall apply the provisions of this Conven-tion,

(a) at the date on which it becomes bound by this Convention, to all plant genera and species to which it applies, on the said date, the provisions of the Act of 1961/1972 or the Act of 1978 and,

(b) at the latest by the expiration of a period of five years after the said date, to all plant genera and species.

(2) [*New members of the Union*] Each Contracting Party which is not bound by the Act of 1961/1972 or the Act of 1978 shall apply the provisions of this Convention,

(a) at the date on which it becomes bound by this Convention, to at least 15 plant genera or species and,

(b) at the latest by the expiration of a period of 10 years from the said date, to all plant genera and species.

Article 4 National Treatment

(1) [*Treatment*] Without prejudice to the rights specified in this Convention, nationals of a Contracting Party as well as natural persons resident and legal entities having their registered offices within the territory of a Contracting Party shall, insofar as the grant and protection of breeders' rights are concerned, enjoy within the territory of each other Contracting Party the same treatment as is accorded or may hereafter be accorded by the laws of each such other Contracting Party to its own nationals, provided that the said nationals, natural persons or legal entities comply with the conditions and formalities imposed on the nationals of the said other Contracting Party.

(2) [*"Nationals"*] For the purposes of the preceding paragraph, "nationals" means, where the Contracting Party is a State, the nationals of that State and, where the Contracting Party is an intergovernmental organization, the nationals of the States which are members of that organization.

CHAPTER III CONDITIONS FOR THE GRANT OF THE BREEDER'S RIGHT

Article 5 Conditions of Protection

(1) [*Criteria to be satisfied*] The breeder's right shall be granted where the variety is

(a) new,

(b) distinct,

(c) uniform and

(d) stable.

(2) [*Other conditions*] The grant of the breeder's right shall not be subject to any further or different conditions, provided that the variety is designated by a denomination in accordance with the provisions of Article 20, that the applicant complies with the formalities provided for by the law of the Contracting Party with whose authority the application has been filed and that he pays the required fees.

Article 6 Novelty

(1) [*Criteria*] The variety shall be deemed to be new if, at the date of filing of the application for a breeder's right, propagating or harvested material of the variety has not been sold or otherwise disposed of to others, by or with the consent of the breeder, for purposes of exploitation of the variety

(a) in the territory of the Contracting Party in which the application has been filed earlier than one year before that date and

(b) in a territory other than that of the Contracting Party in which the appli-cation has been filed earlier than four years or, in the case of trees or of vines, earlier than six years before the said date.

(2) [*Varieties of recent creation*] Where a Contracting Party applies this Convention to a plant genus or species to which it did not previously apply this Convention or an earlier Act, it may consider a variety of recent creation existing at the date of such extension of protection to satisfy the condition of novelty defined in paragraph (1) even where the sale or disposal to others described in that paragraph took place earlier than the time limits defined in that paragraph.

(3) ["*Territory*" *in certain cases*] For the purposes of paragraph (1), all the Contracting Parties which are member States of one and the same intergovernmental organization may act jointly, where the regulations of that organization so require, to assimilate acts done on the territories of the States members of that organization to acts done on their own territories and, should they do so, shall notify the Secretary-General accordingly.

Article 7 Distinctness

The variety shall be deemed to be distinct if it is clearly distinguishable from any other variety whose existence is a matter of common knowledge at the time of the filing of the application. In particular, the filing of an application for the granting of a breeder's right or for the entering of another variety in an official register of varieties, in any country, shall be deemed to render that other variety a matter of common knowledge from the date of the application, provided that the application leads to the granting of a breeder's right or to the entering of the said other variety in the official register of varieties, as the case may be.

Article 8　Uniformity

The variety shall be deemed to be uniform if, subject to the variation that may be expected from the particular features of its propagation, it is sufficiently uniform in its relevant characteristics.

Article 9　Stability

The variety shall be deemed to be stable if its relevant characteristics remain unchanged after repeated propagation or, in the case of a particular cycle of propagation, at the end of each such cycle.

CHAPTER IV　APPLICATION FOR THE GRANT OF THE BREEDER'S RIGHT

Article 10　Filing of applications

(1) [*Place of first application*] The breeder may choose the Contracting Party with whose authority he wishes to file his first application for a breeder's right.

(2) [*Time of subsequent applications*] The breeder may apply to the authorities of other Contracting Parties for the grant of breeders' rights without waiting for the grant to him of a breeder's right by the authority of the Contracting Party with which the first application was filed.

(3) [*Independence of protection*] No Contracting Party shall refuse to grant a breeder's right or limit its duration on the ground that protection for the same variety has not been applied for, has been refused or has expired in any other State or intergovernmental organization.

Article 11　Right of priority

(1) [*The right; its period*] Any breeder who has duly filed an application for the protection of a variety in one of the Contracting Parties (the "first application") shall, for the purpose of filing an application for the grant of a breeder's right for the same variety with the authority of any other Contracting Party (the "subsequent application"), enjoy a right of priority for a period of 12 months. This period shall be computed from the date of filing of the first application. The day of filing shall not be included in the latter period.

(2) [*Claiming the right*] In order to benefit from the right of priority, the breeder shall, in the subsequent application, claim the priority of the first application. The authority with which the subsequent application has been filed may require the breeder to furnish, within a period of not less than three months from the filing date of the

subsequent application, a copy of the documents which constitute the first application, certified to be a true copy by the authority with which that application was filed, and samples or other evidence that the variety which is the subject matter of both applications is the same.

(3) [*Documents and material*] The breeder shall be allowed a period of two years after the expiration of the period of priority or, where the first application is rejected or withdrawn, an appropriate time after such rejection or withdrawal, in which to furnish, to the authority of the Contracting Party with which he has filed the subsequent application, any necessary information, document or material required for the purpose of the examination under Article 12, as required by the laws of that Contracting Party.

(4) [*Events occurring during the period*] Events occurring within the period provided for in paragraph (1), such as the filing of another application or the publication or use of the variety that is the subject of the first application, shall not constitute a ground for rejecting the subsequent application. Such events shall also not give rise to any third-party right.

Article 12 Examination of the Application

Any decision to grant a breeder's right shall require an examination for compliance with the conditions under Articles 5 to 9. In the course of the examination, the authority may grow the variety or carry out other necessary tests, cause the growing of the variety or the carrying out of other necessary tests, or take into account the results of growing tests or other trials which have already been carried out. For the purposes of examination, the authority may require the breeder to furnish all the necessary information, documents or material.

Article 13 Provisional Protection

Each Contracting Party shall provide measures designed to safeguard the interests of the breeder during the period between the filing or the publication of the application for the grant of a breeder's right and the grant of that right. Such measures shall have the effect that the holder of a breeder's right shall at least be entitled to equitable remuneration from any person who, during the said period, has carried out acts which, once the right is granted, require the breeder's authorization as provided in Article 14. A Contracting Party may provide that the said measures shall only take effect in relation to persons whom the breeder has notified of the filing of the application.

CHAPTER V THE RIGHTS OF THE BREEDER

Article 14 Scope of the breeder's right

(1) [*Acts in respect of the propagating material*]

(a) Subject to Articles 15 and 16, the following acts in respect of the propagating material of the protected variety shall require the authorization of the breeder:

(i) production or reproduction (multiplication),

(ii) conditioning for the purpose of propagation,

(iii) offering for sale,

(iv) selling or other marketing,

(v) exporting,

(vi) importing,

(vii) stocking for any of the purposes mentioned in (i) to (vi), above.

(b) The breeder may make his authorization subject to conditions and limitations.

(2) [*Acts in respect of the harvested material*] Subject to Articles 15 and 16, the acts referred to in items (i) to (vii) of paragraph (1)(a) in respect of harvested material, including entire plants and parts of plants, obtained through the unauthorized use of propagating material of the protected variety shall require the authorization of the breeder, unless the breeder has had reasonable opportunity to exercise his right in relation to the said propagating material.

(3) [*Acts in respect of certain products*] Each Contracting Party may provide that, subject to Articles 15 and 16, the acts referred to in items (i) to (vii) of paragraph (1)(a) in respect of products made directly from harvested material of the protected variety falling within the provisions of paragraph (2) through the unauthorized use of the said harvested material shall require the authorization of the breeder, unless the breeder has had reasonable opportunity to exercise his right in relation to the said harvested material.

(4) [*Possible additional acts*] Each Contracting Party may provide that, subject to Articles 15 and 16, acts other than those referred to in items (i) to (vii) of paragraph (1)(a) shall also require the authorization of the breeder.

(5) [*Essentially derived and certain other varieties*]

(a) The provisions of paragraphs (1) to (4) shall also apply in relation to

(i) varieties which are essentially derived from the protected variety, where the protected variety is not itself an essentially derived variety,

(ii) varieties which are not clearly distinguishable in accordance with Article 7 from the protected variety and

(iii) varieties whose production requires the repeated use of the protected variety.

(b) For the purposes of subparagraph (a)(i), a variety shall be deemed to be essentially derived from another variety ("the initial variety") when

(i) it is predominantly derived from the initial variety, or from a variety that is itself predominantly derived from the initial variety, while retaining the expression of the essential characteristics that result from the genotype or combination of genotypes of the initial variety,

(ii) it is clearly distinguishable from the initial variety and

(iii) except for the differences which result from the act of derivation, it conforms to the initial variety in the expression of the essential characteristics that result from the genotype or combination of genotypes of the initial variety.

(c) Essentially derived varieties may be obtained for example by the selection of a natural or induced mutant, or of a somaclonal variant, the selection of a variant individual from plants of the initial variety, backcrossing, or transformation by genetic engineering.

Article 15　Exceptions to the breeder's right

(1) [*Compulsory exceptions*] The breeder's right shall not extend to

(a) acts done privately and for non-commercial purposes,

(b) acts done for experimental purposes and

(c) acts done for the purpose of breeding other varieties, and, except where the provisions of Article 14(5) apply, acts referred to in Article 14(1) to (4) in respect of such other varieties.

(2) [*Optional exception*] Notwithstanding Article 14, each Contracting Party may, within reasonable limits and subject to the safeguarding of the legitimate interests of the breeder, restrict the breeder's right in relation to any variety in order to permit farmers to use for propagating purposes, on their own holdings, the product of the harvest which they have obtained by planting, on their own holdings, the protected variety or a variety covered by Article 14(5)(a)(i) or (ii).

Article 16　Exhaustion of the breeder's right

(1) [*Exhaustion of right*] The breeder's right shall not extend to acts concerning any material of the protected variety, or of a variety covered by the provisions of Article 14(5), which has been sold or otherwise marketed by the breeder or with his consent in the territory of the Contracting Party concerned, or any material derived from the said material, unless such acts

(i) involve further propagation of the variety in question or

(ii) involve an export of material of the variety, which enables the propagation of the variety, into a country which does not protect varieties of the plant genus or species to which the variety belongs, except where the exported material is for final consumption purposes.

(2) [*Meaning of "material"*] For the purposes of paragraph (1), "material" means, in relation to a variety,

(i) propagating material of any kind,

(ii) harvested material, including entire plants and parts of plants, and

(iii) any product made directly from the harvested material.

(3) [*"Territory" in certain cases*] For the purposes of paragraph (1), all the Contracting Parties which are member States of one and the same intergovernmental organization may act jointly, where the regulations of that organization so require, to assimilate acts done on the territories of the States members of that organization to acts done on their own territories and, should they do so, shall notify the Secretary-General accordingly.

Article 17　Restrictions on the exercise of the breeder's right

(1) [*Public interest*] Except where expressly provided in this Convention, no Contracting Party may restrict the free exercise of a breeder's right for reasons other than of public interest.

(2) [*Equitable remuneration*] When any such restriction has the effect of authorizing a third party to perform any act for which the breeder's authorization is required, the Contracting Party concerned shall take all measures necessary to ensure that the breeder receives equitable remuneration.

Article 18　Measures regulating commerce

The breeder's right shall be independent of any measure taken by a Contracting Party to regulate within its territory the production, certification and marketing of material of varieties or the importing or exporting of such material. In any case, such measures shall not affect the application of the provisions of this Convention.

Article 19　Duration of the breeder's right

(1) [*Period of protection*] The breeder's right shall be granted for a fixed period.

(2) [*Minimum period*] The said period shall not be shorter than 20 years from the date of the grant of the breeder's right. For trees and vines, the said period shall not be shorter than 25 years from the said date.

CHAPTER VI　VARIETY DENOMINATION

Article 20　Variety denomination

(1) [*Designation of varieties by denominations; use of the denomination*]

(a) The variety shall be designated by a denomination which will be its generic designation.

(b) Each Contracting Party shall ensure that, subject to paragraph (4), no rights in the designation registered as the denomination of the variety shall hamper the free use of the denomination in connection with the variety, even after the expiration of the breeder's right.

(2) [*Characteristics of the denomination*] The denomination must enable the variety to be identified. It may not consist solely of figures except where this is an established practice for designating varieties. It must not be liable to mislead or to cause confusion concerning the characteristics, value or identity of the variety or the identity of the

breeder. In particular, it must be different from every denomination which designates, in the territory of any Contracting Party, an existing variety of the same plant species or of a closely related species.

(3) [*Registration of the denomination*] The denomination of the variety shall be submitted by the breeder to the authority. If it is found that the denomination does not satisfy the requirements of paragraph (2), the authority shall refuse to register it and shall require the breeder to propose another denomination within a prescribed period. The denomination shall be registered by the authority at the same time as the breeder's right is granted.

(4) [*Prior rights of third persons*] Prior rights of third persons shall not be affected. If, by reason of a prior right, the use of the denomination of a variety is forbidden to a person who, in accordance with the provisions of paragraph (7), is obliged to use it, the authority shall require the breeder to submit another denomination for the variety.

(5) [*Same denomination in all Contracting Parties*] A variety must be submitted to all Contracting Parties under the same denomination. The authority of each Contracting Party shall register the denomination so submitted, unless it considers the denomination unsuitable within its territory. In the latter case, it shall require the breeder to submit another denomination.

(6) [*Information among the authorities of Contracting Parties*] The authority of a Contracting Party shall ensure that the authorities of all the other Contracting Parties are informed of matters concerning variety denominations, in particular the submission, registration and cancellation of denominations. Any authority may address its observations, if any, on the registration of a denomination to the authority which communicated that denomination.

(7) [*Obligation to use the denomination*] Any person who, within the territory of one of the Contracting Parties, offers for sale or markets propagating material of a variety protected within the said territory shall be obliged to use the denomination of that variety, even after the expiration of the breeder's right in that variety, except where, in accordance with the provisions of paragraph (4), prior rights prevent such use.

(8) [*Indications used in association with denominations*] When a variety is offered for sale or marketed, it shall be permitted to associate a trademark, trade name or other similar indication with a registered variety denomination. If such an indication is so associated, the denomination must nevertheless be easily recognizable.

CHAPTER VII NULLITY AND CANCELLATION OF THE BREEDER'S RIGHT

Article 21 Nullity of the breeder's right

(1) [*Reasons of nullity*] Each Contracting Party shall declare a breeder's right

granted by it null and void when it is established

(i) that the conditions laid down in Articles 6 or 7 were not complied with at the time of the grant of the breeder's right,

(ii) that, where the grant of the breeder's right has been essentially based upon information and documents furnished by the breeder, the conditions laid down in Articles 8 or 9 were not complied with at the time of the grant of the breeder's right, or

(iii) that the breeder's right has been granted to a person who is not entitled to it, unless it is transferred to the person who is so entitled.

(2) [*Exclusion of other reasons*] No breeder's right shall be declared null and void for reasons other than those referred to in paragraph (1).

Article 22　Cancellation of the breeder's right

(1) [*Reasons for cancellation*]

(a) Each Contracting Party may cancel a breeder's right granted by it if it is established that the conditions laid down in Articles 8 or 9 are no longer fulfilled.

(b) Furthermore, each Contracting Party may cancel a breeder's right granted by it if, after being requested to do so and within a prescribed period,

(i) the breeder does not provide the authority with the information, documents or material deemed necessary for verifying the maintenance of the variety,

(ii) the breeder fails to pay such fees as may be payable to keep his right in force, or

(iii) the breeder does not propose, where the denomination of the variety is cancelled after the grant of the right, another suitable denomination.

(2) [*Exclusion of other reasons*] No breeder's right shall be cancelled for reasons other than those referred to in paragraph (1).

CHAPTER VIII　THE UNION

Article 23　Members

The Contracting Parties shall be members of the Union.

Article 24　Legal status and seat

(1) [*Legal personality*] The Union has legal personality.

(2) [*Legal capacity*] The Union enjoys on the territory of each Contracting Party, in conformity with the laws applicable in the said territory, such legal capacity as may be necessary for the fulfillment of the objectives of the Union and for the exercise of its functions.

(3) [*Seat*] The seat of the Union and its permanent organs are at Geneva.

(4) [*Headquarters agreement*] The Union has a headquarters agreement with the

Swiss Confederation.

Article 25　Organs

The permanent organs of the Union are the Council and the Office of the Union.

Article 26　The Council

(1)[*Composition*] The Council shall consist of the representatives of the members of the Union. Each member of the Union shall appoint one representative to the Council and one alternate. Representatives or alternates may be accompanied by assistants or advisers.

(2)[*Officers*] The Council shall elect a President and a first Vice-President from among its members. It may elect other Vice-Presidents. The first Vice-President shall take the place of the President if the latter is unable to officiate. The President shall hold office for three years.

(3)[*Sessions*] The Council shall meet upon convocation by its President. An ordinary session of the Council shall be held annually. In addition, the President may convene the Council at his discretion; he shall convene it, within a period of three months, if one-third of the members of the Union so request.

(4)[*Observers*] States not members of the Union may be invited as observers to meetings of the Council. Other observers, as well as experts, may also be invited to such meetings.

(5)[*Tasks*] The tasks of the Council shall be to:

(a) study appropriate measures to safeguard the interests and to encourage the development of the Union;

(b) establish its rules of procedure;

(c) appoint the Secretary-General and, if it finds it necessary, a Vice Secretary-General and determine the terms of appointment of each;

(d) examine an annual report on the activities of the Union and lay down the program for its future work;

(e) give to the Secretary-General all necessary directions for the accomplishment of the tasks of the Union;

(f) establish the administrative and financial regulations of the Union;

(g) examine and approve the budget of the Union and fix the contribution of each member of the Union;

(h) examine and approve the accounts presented by the Secretary-General;

(i) fix the date and place of the conferences referred to in Article 38 and take the measures necessary for their preparation; and

(j) in general, take all necessary decisions to ensure the efficient functioning of the Union.

(6)[*Votes*]

(a) Each member of the Union that is a State shall have one vote in the Council.

(b) Any Contracting Party that is an intergovernmental organization may, in matters within its competence, exercise the rights to vote of its member States that are members of the Union. Such an intergovernmental organization shall not exercise the rights to vote of its member States if its member States exercise their right to vote, and vice versa.

(7)[*Majorities*] Any decision of the Council shall require a simple majority of the votes cast, provided that any decision of the Council under paragraphs (5)(b), (d) and (g), and under Articles 28(3), 29(5)(b) and 38(1) shall require three-fourths of the votes cast. Abstentions shall not be considered as votes.

Article 27　The Office of the union

(1)[*Tasks and direction of the Office*] The Office of the Union shall carry out all the duties and tasks entrusted to it by the Council. It shall be under the direction of the Secretary-General.

(2)[*Duties of the Secretary-General*] The Secretary-General shall be responsible to the Council; he shall be responsible for carrying out the decisions of the Council. He shall submit the budget of the Union for the approval of the Council and shall be responsible for its implementation. He shall make reports to the Council on his administration and the activities and financial position of the Union.

(3)[*Staff*] Subject to the provisions of Article 26(5)(c), the conditions of appointment and employment of the staff necessary for the efficient performance of the tasks of the Office of the Union shall be fixed in the administrative and financial regulations.

Article 28　Languages

(1)[*Languages of the Office*] The English, French, German and Spanish languages shall be used by the Office of the Union in carrying out its duties.

(2)[*Languages in certain meetings*] Meetings of the Council and of revision conferences shall be held in the four languages.

(3)[*Further languages*] The Council may decide that further languages shall be used.

Article 29　Finances

(1)[*Income*] The expenses of the Union shall be met from

(a) the annual contributions of the States members of the Union,

(b) payments received for services rendered,

(c) miscellaneous receipts.

(2)[*Contributions: units*]

(a) The share of each State member of the Union in the total amount of the annual contributions shall be determined by reference to the total expenditure to be met from the contributions of the States members of the Union and to the number of contribution units applicable to it under paragraph (3). The said share shall be computed according to paragraph (4).

(b) The number of contribution units shall be expressed in whole numbers or fractions thereof, provided that no fraction shall be smaller than one-fifth.

(3) [*Contributions: share of each member*]

(a) The number of contribution units applicable to any member of the Union which is party to the Act of 1961/1972 or the Act of 1978 on the date on which it becomes bound by this Convention shall be the same as the number applicable to it immediately before the said date.

(b) Any other State member of the Union shall, on joining the Union, indicate, in a declaration addressed to the Secretary-General, the number of contribution units applicable to it.

(c) Any State member of the Union may, at any time, indicate, in a declaration addressed to the Secretary-General, a number of contribution units different from the number applicable to it under subparagraph (a) or (b). Such declaration, if made during the first six months of a calendar year, shall take effect from the beginning of the subsequent calendar year; otherwise, it shall take effect from the beginning of the second calendar year which follows the year in which the declaration was made.

(4) [*Contributions: computation of shares*]

(a) For each budgetary period, the amount corresponding to one contribution unit shall be obtained by dividing the total amount of the expenditure to be met in that period from the contributions of the States members of the Union by the total number of units applicable to those States members of the Union.

(b) The amount of the contribution of each State member of the Union shall be obtained by multiplying the amount corresponding to one contribution unit by the number of contribution units applicable to that State member of the Union.

(5) [*Arrears in contributions*]

(a) A State member of the Union which is in arrears in the payment of its contributions may not, subject to subparagraph (b), exercise its right to vote in the Council if the amount of its arrears equals or exceeds the amount of the contribution due from it for the preceding full year. The suspension of the right to vote shall not relieve such State member of the Union of its obligations under this Convention and shall not deprive it of any other rights thereunder.

(b) The Council may allow the said State member of the Union to continue to exercise its right to vote if, and as long as, the Council is satisfied that the delay in payment is due to exceptional and unavoidable circumstances.

(6) [*Auditing of the accounts*] The auditing of the accounts of the Union shall be effected by a State member of the Union as provided in the administrative and financial regulations. Such State member of the Union shall be designated, with its agreement, by the Council.

(7) [*Contributions of intergovernmental organizations*] Any Contracting Party which is an intergovernmental organization shall not be obliged to pay contributions. If, nevertheless, it chooses to pay contributions, the provisions of paragraphs (1) to (4) shall be applied accordingly.

CHAPTER IX IMPLEMENTATION OF THE CONVENTION; OTHER AGREEMENTS

Article 30 Implementation of the Convention

(1) [*Measures of implementation*] Each Contracting Party shall adopt all measures necessary for the implementation of this Convention; in particular, it shall:

(a) provide for appropriate legal remedies for the effective enforcement of breeders' rights;

(b) maintain an authority entrusted with the task of granting breeders' rights or entrust the said task to an authority maintained by another Contracting Party;

(c) ensure that the public is informed through the regular publication of information concerning

(i) applications for and grants of breeders' rights, and

(ii) proposed and approved denominations.

(2) [*Conformity of laws*] It shall be understood that, on depositing its instrument of ratification, acceptance, approval or accession, as the case may be, each State or intergovernmental organization must be in a position, under its laws, to give effect to the provisions of this Convention.

Article 31 Relations between contracting parties and states bound by earlier acts

(1) [*Relations between States bound by this Convention*] Between States members of the Union which are bound both by this Convention and any earlier Act of the Convention, only this Convention shall apply.

(2) [*Possible relations with States not bound by this Convention*] Any State member of the Union not bound by this Convention may declare, in a notification addressed to the Secretary-General, that, in its relations with each member of the Union bound only by this Convention, it will apply the latest Act by which it is bound. As from the expiration of one month after the date of such notification and until the State member of the Union making the declaration becomes bound by this Convention, the said member

of the Union shall apply the latest Act by which it is bound in its relations with each of the members of the Union bound only by this Convention, whereas the latter shall apply this Convention in respect of the former.

Article 32　Special Agreements

Members of the Union reserve the right to conclude among themselves special agreements for the protection of varieties, insofar as such agreements do not contravene the provisions of this Convention.

CHAPTER X　FINAL PROVISIONS

Article 33　Signature

This Convention shall be open for signature by any State which is a member of the Union at the date of its adoption. It shall remain open for signature until March 31, 1992.

Article 34　Ratification, acceptance or approval; accession

(1) [*States and certain intergovernmental organizations*]

(a) Any State may, as provided in this Article, become party to this Convention.

(b) Any intergovernmental organization may, as provided in this Article, become party to this Convention if it

(i) has competence in respect of matters governed by this Convention,

(ii) has its own legislation providing for the grant and protection of breeders' rights binding on all its member States and

(iii) has been duly authorized, in accordance with its internal procedures, to accede to this Convention.

(2) [*Instrument of adherence*] Any State which has signed this Convention shall become party to this Convention by depositing an instrument of ratification, acceptance or approval of this Convention. Any State which has not signed this Convention and any intergovernmental organization shall become party to this Convention by depositing an instrument of accession to this Convention. Instruments of ratification, acceptance, approval or accession shall be deposited with the Secretary-General.

(3) [*Advice of the Council*] Any State which is not a member of the Union and any intergovernmental organization shall, before depositing its instrument of accession, ask the Council to advise it in respect of the conformity of its laws with the provisions of this Convention. If the decision embodying the advice is positive, the instrument of accession may be deposited.

Article 35　Reservations

(1) [*Principle*] Subject to paragraph (2), no reservations to this Convention are permitted.

(2) [*Possible exception*]

(a) Notwithstanding the provisions of Article 3(1), any State which, at the time of becoming party to this Convention, is a party to the Act of 1978 and which, as far as varieties reproduced asexually are concerned, provides for protection by an industrial property title other than a breeder's right shall have the right to continue to do so without applying this Convention to those varieties.

(b) Any State making use of the said right shall, at the time of depositing its instr-ument of ratification, acceptance, approval or accession, as the case may be, notify the Secretary-General accordingly. The same State may, at any time, withdraw the said notification.

Article 36 Communications concerning legislation and the genera and species protected; information to be published

(1) [*Initial notification*] When depositing its instrument of ratification, acceptance or approval of or accession to this Convention, as the case may be, any State or intergovernmental organization shall notify the Secretary-General of

(a) its legislation governing breeder's rights and

(b) the list of plant genera and species to which, on the date on which it will become bound by this Convention, it will apply the provisions of this Convention.

(2) [*Notification of changes*] Each Contracting Party shall promptly notify the Secretary-General of

(a) any changes in its legislation governing breeders' rights and

(b) any extension of the application of this Convention to additional plant genera and species.

(3) [*Publication of the information*] The Secretary-General shall, on the basis of communications received from each Contracting Party concerned, publish information on

(a) the legislation governing breeders' rights and any changes in that legislation, and

(b) the list of plant genera and species referred to in paragraph (1)(a) and any extension referred to in paragraph (2)(b).

Article 37 Entry into force; closing of earlier acts

(1) [*Initial entry into force*] This Convention shall enter into force one month after five States have deposited their instruments of ratification, acceptance, approval or accession, as the case may be, provided that at least three of the said instruments have been deposited by States party to the Act of 1961/1972 or the Act of 1978.

(2) [*Subsequent entry into force*] Any State not covered by paragraph (1) or any intergovernmental organization shall become bound by this Convention one month after the date on which it has deposited its instrument of ratification, acceptance, approval or accession, as the case may be.

(3) [*Closing of the* 1978 *Act*] No instrument of accession to the Act of 1978 may

be deposited after the entry into force of this Convention according to paragraph (1), except that any State that, in conformity with the established practice of the General Assembly of the United Nations, is regarded as a developing country may deposit such an instrument until December 31, 1995, and that any other State may deposit such an instrument until December 31, 1993, even if this Convention enters into force before that date.

Article 38　Revision of the Convention

(1)[*Conference*] This Convention may be revised by a conference of the members of the Union. The convocation of such conference shall be decided by the Council.

(2)[*Quorum and majority*] The proceedings of a conference shall be effective only if at least half of the States members of the Union are represented at it. A majority of three-quarters of the States members of the Union present and voting at the conference shall be required for the adoption of any revision.

Article 39　Denunciation

(1) [*Notifications*] Any Contracting Party may denounce this Convention by notification addressed to the Secretary-General. The Secretary-General shall promptly notify all members of the Union of the receipt of that notification.

(2)[*Earlier Acts*] Notification of the denunciation of this Convention shall be deemed also to constitute notification of the denunciation of any earlier Act by which the Contracting Party denouncing this Convention is bound.

(3)[*Effective date*] The denunciation shall take effect at the end of the calendar year following the year in which the notification was received by the Secretary-General.

(4)[*Acquired rights*] The denunciation shall not affect any rights acquired in a variety by reason of this Convention or any earlier Act prior to the date on which the denunciation becomes effective.

Article 40　Preservation of Existing Rights

This Convention shall not limit existing breeders' rights under the laws of Contracting Parties or by reason of any earlier Act or any agreement other than this Convention concluded between members of the Union.

Article 41　Original and Official Texts of the Convention

(1)[*Original*] This Convention shall be signed in a single original in the English, French and German languages, the French text prevailing in case of any discrepancy among the various texts. The original shall be deposited with the Secretary-General.

(2)[*Official texts*] The Secretary-General shall, after consultation with the interested Governments, establish official texts of this Convention in the Arabic, Dutch, Italian, Japanese and Spanish languages and such other languages as the Council may designate.

Article 42　Depositary Functions

(1) [*Transmittal of copies*] The Secretary-General shall transmit certified copies of this Convention to all States and intergovernmental organizations which were represented in the Diplomatic Conference that adopted this Convention and, on request, to any other State or intergovernmental organization.

(2) [*Registration*] The Secretary-General shall register this Convention with the Secretariat of the United Nations.

Resolution on Article 14(5)

The Diplomatic Conference for the Revision of the International Convention for the Protection of New Varieties of Plants held from March 4 to 19, 1991, requests the Secretary-General of UPOV to start work immediately after the Conference on the establishment of draft standard guidelines, for adoption by the Council of UPOV, on essentially derived varieties.

Recommendation Relating to Article 15(2)

The Diplomatic Conference recommends that the provisions laid down in Article 15 (2) of the International Convention for the Protection of New Varieties of Plants of December 2, 1961, as Revised at Geneva on November 10, 1972, on October 23, 1978, and on March 19, 1991, should not be read so as to be intended to open the possibility of extending the practice commonly called "farmer's privilege" to sectors of agricultural or horticultural production in which such a privilege is not a common practice on the territory of the Contracting Party concerned.

Common statement relating to Article 34

The Diplomatic Conference noted and accepted a declaration by the Delegation of Denmark and a declaration by the Delegation of the Netherlands according to which the Convention adopted by the Diplomatic Conference will not, upon its ratification, acceptance, approval or accession by Denmark or the Netherlands, be automatically applicable, in the case of Denmark, in Greenland and the Faroe Islands and, in the case of the Netherlands, in Aruba and the Netherlands Antilles. The said Convention will only apply in the said territories if and when Denmark or the Netherlands, as the case may be, expressly so notifies the Secretary-General.

(Source：https：//www.wipo.int/edocs/lexdocs/treaties/en/upov/trt_upov_3.pdf)

三、注解(Notes)

1. International Union for the Protection of New Varieties of Plants (UPOV)

国际植物新品种保护联盟(UPOV)是根据《保护植物新品种国际公约》成立的政府间国际组织，总部设在瑞士日内瓦。截至2015年，UPOV成员已达到75个。

UPOV 现任秘书长是弗朗西斯·古里。国际植物新品种保护联盟的职责是以造福社会，鼓励植物新品种的开发为目的，建立发展一个有效的植物品种保护系统。该联盟在协调和促进成员国之间在行政和技术领域的合作，特别是在制定基本的法律和技术准则、交流信息、促进国际合作等方面发挥着重大作用。

（Source：http：//baike. sm. cn/item）

2. International Day for Biological Diversity

国际生物多样性日为每年5月22日。联合国环境署于1988年11月召开生物多样性特设专家工作组会议，探讨一项生物多样性国际公约的必要性。1989年5月，建立了技术和法律特设专家工作组，拟定一个保护和可持续利用生物多样性的国际法律文书。1992年5月22日，内罗毕会议最后通过了《生物多样性公约》协议。公约于1993年12月29日生效。联合国大会于2000年12月20日，通过第55、201号决议，决定将每年5月22日定为"国际生物多样性日"。1992年，我国成为世界上首先批准《生物多样性公约》的6个国家之一，并成立了生物多样性保护委员会，制订了《中国生物多样性保护行动计划》。

（Source：http：//mip-shufadashi-com. sm-tc. cn）

四、相关词汇（Key Words and Phrases）

1.	variety	[vəˈraɪətɪ]	n.	品种；种类；多样化；变化
2.	botanical	[bəˈtænɪkl]	adj.	植物学的
3.	taxon	[ˈtæksɒn]	n.	分类；（复数）taxa
4.	genotype	[ˈdʒenətaɪp]	n.	基因型；属型
5.	propagate	[ˈprɒpəgeɪt]	v.	繁殖；繁衍；使遗传；扩散
6.	authority	[ɔːˈθɒrɪtɪ]	n.	主管机关；权威；学术权威
7.	genera	[ˈdʒenərə]	n.	属；类
8.	species	[ˈspiːʃiːz]	n.	生物（物）种
9.	expiration	[ˌekspɪˈreɪʃ(ə)n]	n.	到期；截止；呼气
10.	novelty	[ˈnɒv(ə)ltɪ]	n.	新颖性；新奇
11.	denunciation	[dɪˌnʌnsɪˈeɪʃ(ə)n]	n.	退约；指责；弹劾；控诉
12.	mutant	[ˈmjuːt(ə)nt]	n.	变种生物；变异体；突变异种
13.	contravene	[ˌkɒntrəˈviːn]	v.	抵触；违背；与……不相容
14.	backcross	[ˈbækkrɒs]	v.	回交
			n.	回交杂种
15.	remuneration	[rɪˌmjuːnəˈreɪʃ(ə)n]	n.	薪酬；工资；偿还
16.	denomination	[dɪˌnɒmɪˈneɪʃ(ə)n]	n.	名称；宗教；教派
17.	legal personality		n.	法人
18.	miscellaneous receipts		n.	杂项收入
19.	provisional protection			临时性保护
20.	permanent organ			常设机构

五、长难句(Difficult Sentences)

1. Without prejudice to the rights specified in this Convention, nationals of a Contracting Party as well as natural persons resident and legal entities having their registered offices within the territory of a Contracting Party shall, insofar as the grant and protection of breeders' rights are concerned, enjoy within the territory of each other Contracting Party the same treatment as is accorded or may hereafter be accorded by the laws of each such other Contracting Party to its own nationals, provided that the said nationals, natural persons or legal entities comply with the conditions and formalities imposed on the nationals of the said other Contracting Party. (Article 4, 1)

解析：本句的真正的主语是 nationals, natural persons resident and legal entities；having their registered office 等同于从句 who have their registered office。shall enjoy 是谓语动词，insofar as the grant and protection of breeders' rights are concerned 也可以看作是一个插入语。宾语是 the same treatment。Provided 在本句话相当于 on condition that…。

译文：在不损害本公约规定的权利的前提下，缔约方的国民以及自然人居民和在缔约方的领土内有其注册办事处的法人，就育种者权利的授予和保护而言，在缔约方各自的领土内，相互享有另一缔约方根据其法律所给予或将给予其自己的国民同等的待遇，只要上述国民、自然人或是法人遵守上述另一缔约方对国民的规定条件和手续。

2. The grant of the breeder's right shall not be subject to any further or different conditions, provided that the variety is designated by a denomination in accordance with the provisions of Article 20, that the applicant complies with the formalities provided for by the law of the Contracting Party with whose authority the application has been filed and that he pays the required fees. (Article 5, 2)

解析：provided 后面跟有三个并列的 that 引导的句子：(1) that the variety is designated by a denomination；(2) that the applicant complies with the formalities；(3) that he pays the required fees。动词词组 comply with 的词义是 to obey a rule, an order, etc. 遵守；遵从；服从。例如，It is the fundamental codes of conduct that every citizen should comply with. 这是每一个公民都应该遵守的基本行为准则。

译文：凡育种者育出的品种是按照第20条规定的名称命名的，申请者履行缔约方法律规定的手续，向主管机关提出申请，交纳必要的手续费，则对育种者权利的授予就不应附带任何其他的条件。

3. For the purposes of paragraph (1), all the Contracting Parties which are member States of one and the same intergovernmental organization may act jointly, where the regulations of that organization so require, to assimilate acts done on the territories of the States members of that organization to acts done on their own territories and, should they do so, shall notify the Secretary-General accordingly. (Article 6, 13)

解析：… and should they do so, shall notify the Secretary-General accordingly 是条件从句倒装句，省略了 if。完整的句子是 If they should do so, they shall notify the Secretary-General accordingly。

译文：[某些情况下所指的"领土"] 为(1)款之目的，属一个和同一政府间组织成员国的所有缔约方，可按其组织章程采取统一行动，使该组织成员国领土范围内的行动与各国领土上的行动协调一致，如果这样做，应就此通报秘书长。

六、课后练习(Exercises)

1. Skimming and Scanning

Directions: Reading **Chapter Ⅲ and Chapter Ⅳ** from International Convention for the Protection of New Varieties of Plants and six statements attached to it. Each statement contains information given in one of the paragraphs. Identify the paragraph from which the information is derived. Each paragraph is marked with a letter. You may choose a paragraph more than once. Answer the questions by writing the corresponding letter in the bracket in front of each statement.

A. The breeder's right shall be granted where the variety is new, distinct, uniform and stable. The grant of the breeder's right shall not be subject to any further or different conditions, provided that the variety is designated by a denomination in accordance with the provisions of Article 20, that the applicant complies with the formalities provided for by the law of the Contracting Party with whose authority the application has been filed and that he pays the required fees.

B. The variety shall be deemed to be new if, at the date of filing of the application for a breeder's right, propagating or harvested material of the variety has not been sold or otherwise disposed of to others, by or with the consent of the breeder, for purposes of exploitation of the variety in the territory of the Contracting Party in which the application has been filed earlier than one year before that date and in a territory other than that of the Contracting Party in which the application has been filed earlier than four years or, in the case of trees or of vines, earlier than six years before the said date.

C. Where a Contracting Party applies this Convention to a plant genus or species to which it did not previously apply this Convention or an earlier Act, it may consider a variety of recent creation existing at the date of such extension of protection to satisfy the condition of novelty defined in paragraph (1) even where the sale or disposal to others described in that paragraph took place earlier than the time limits defined in that paragraph.

D. For the purposes of paragraph (1), all the Contracting Parties which are member States of one and the same intergovernmental organization may act jointly, where the regulations of that organization so require, to assimilate acts done on the territories of the States members of that organization to acts done on their own territories and, should they do so, shall notify the Secretary-Genral accordingly.

E. The variety shall be deemed to be distinct if it is clearly distinguishable from any other variety whose existence is a matter of common knowledge at the time of the filing of the application. In particular, the filing of an application for the granting of a breeder's right or for the entering of another variety in an official register of varieties, in any country, shall be deemed to render that other variety a matter of common knowledge from the date of the application, provided that the application leads to the granting of a breeder's right or to the entering of the said other variety in the official register of varieties, as the case may be.

F. The variety shall be deemed to be uniform if, subject to the variation that may be expected from the particular features of its propagation, it is sufficiently uniform in its relevant characteristics.

G. The variety shall be deemed to be stable if its relevant characteristics remain unchanged after repeated propagation or, in the case of a particular cycle of propagation, at the end of each such cycle.

H. The breeder may choose the Contracting Party with whose authority he wishes to file his first application for a breeder's right.

I. The breeder may apply to the authorities of other Contracting Parties for the grant of breeders' rights without waiting for the grant to him of a breeder's right by the authority of the Contracting Party with which the first application was filed.

J. No Contracting Party shall refuse to grant a breeder's right or limit its duration on the ground that protection for the same variety has not been applied for, has been refused or has expired in any other State or intergovernmental organization.

K. Any breeder who has duly filed an application for the protection of a variety in one of the Contracting Parties (the "first application") shall, for the purpose of filing an application for the grant of a breeder's right for the same variety with the authority of any other Contracting Party (the "subsequent application"), enjoy a right of priority for a period of 12 months. This period shall be computed from the date of filing of the first application. The day of filing shall not be included in the latter period.

L. In order to benefit from the right of priority, the breeder shall, in the subsequent application, claim the priority of the first application. The authority with which the subsequent application has been filed may require the breeder to furnish, within a period of not less than three months from the filing date of the subsequent application, a copy of the documents which constitute the first application, certified to be a true copy by the authority with which that application was filed, and samples or other evidence that the variety which is the subject matter of both applications is the same.

M. The breeder shall be allowed a period of two years after the expiration of the period of priority or, where the first application is rejected or withdrawn, an appropriate time after such rejection or withdrawal, in which to furnish, to the authority of the Contracting Party with which he has filed the subsequent application, any necessary information, document or material required for the purpose of the examination under Article 12, as required by the laws of that Contracting Party.

N. Events occurring within the period provided for in paragraph (1), such as the filing of another application or the publication or use of the variety that is the subject of the first application, shall not constitute a ground for rejecting the subsequent application. Such events shall also not give rise to any third-party right.

(_____)(1) The breeder may choose any Contracting Party to file his first application for a breeder's right of his own accord.

(_____)(2) If the applicant has denominated the variety in accordance with the law and he has been filed and has paid the required fees, the contracting Party should grant his right without further conditions.

(_____)(3) The breeder who filed his first application for the protection of a variety in any Contract Party may file an application to any other Contracting Party but he enjoys a priority of 12 months.

(_____)(4) The variety is stable provided it keeps its relevant characteristics unchanged even after repeated propagation.

(_____)(5) All Contracting Parties grant the breeder's right where the variety is new, distinct, uniform and stable.

(_____)(6) If the variety is clearly different from other existing variety at the time of application, it can be regarded as being distinct.

2. Reading Comprehension

Directions: Read **Article 14 Scopes of the Breeder's Right** and **Article 20 Variety Denomination** from International Convention for The Protection of New Varieties of Plants and decide whether the following statements are True or False. Write T for True or F for False in the bracket in front of each statement.

A. Questions 1-3 are based on **Article 14 Scope of the Breeder's Right.**

(1) (_____) Farmers who plan to reproduce the protected variety have to require the authorization of the breeder.

(2) (_____) The export of the varieties derived from the protected variety where the protected variety is not a derived variety need not require the authorization of the breeder.

(3) (_____) A variety transformed by genetic engineering or backcrossing would not be regarded as one derived from the initial variety.

B. Questions 4-6 are based on **Article 20 Variety Denomination.**

(4) (_____) Solely figures cannot be used as the denomination of a variety even

if this is an established practice.

(5) (_____) Unless the authority of the Contracting Party considers the denomination unsuitable within its territory, all the Contracting Parties should use the same denomination.

(6) (_____) After the expiration of the breeder's right, the Contracting Parties have right to use different denominations to the variety for sale or for markets propagating material.

3. Extensive Reading

Directions: In this section, there is a passage with ten blanks. You are required to select one word for each blank from a list of choices given in a word bank following the passage. Read the passage through carefully before making your choices. Each choice in the bank is identified by a letter. You may not use any of the words in the bank more than once.

New varieties of plants with improved yields, higher quality or better resistance to pests and diseases increase quality and productivity in agriculture, horticulture and forestry, while minimizing the pressure on the environment. The tremendous progress in agricultural productivity in various parts of the world is largely based on improved plant varieties. More so, plant breeding has benefits that (1) _____ beyond increasing food production.

The development of new improved varieties with, for example, higher quality, increases the value and marketability of crops. In addition, breeding programs for ornamental plants can be of substantial economic importance for an exporting country. The breeding and (2) _____ of new varieties is a decisive factor in improving rural income and overall economic development. Furthermore, the development of breeding programs for certain (3) _____ species can remove the threat to their survival out in nature, as in the case of medicinal plants. While the process of plant breeding requires (4) _____ investments in terms of money and time, once released, a new plant variety can be easily reproduced in a way that would (5) _____ its breeder of the opportunity to be rewarded for his investment. Clearly, few breeders are willing to spend years making substantial economic investment in developing a new variety of plants if there were no means of protecting and rewarding their (6) _____. Therefore, an effective system for the protection of plant variety is essential to encourage breeders to invest in plant breeding and (7) _____ to the development of agriculture, horticulture and forestry and for the benefit of society as a whole.

Plant variety protection, also called a "plant breeder's right" (PBR), is a form of intellectual property right (8) _____ to the breeder of a new plant variety. According to this right, certain acts concerning the exploitation of the protected variety require the prior authorization of the breeder. Any person who creates, or discovers and develops, a plant variety may apply for PBR. Once the PBR has been granted to the breeder, it means in practice that the title holder is the owner of the variety and anyone else who wants to (9) _____ that protected variety requires the authorization of the holder of the PBR. This authorization is (10) _____ in the form of a license agreement between the title holder and those who sell the variety.

A. commercialize	B. stretched	C. decisive	D. awarded	E. endangered
F. normally	G. substantial	H. deprive	I. attribute	J. regularly
K. contribute	L. commitment	M. granted	N. exploitation	O. extend

4. Vocabulary Expanding

(1) Each Contracting Party which is bound by the Act of 1961 or the Act of 1978 shall apply the provisions of this Convention, at the latest by the _____ of a period of five years after the said date, to all plant genera and species. (expire)

(2) All the Contracting Parties may act _____, where the regulations of that organization so require, to assimilate acts done on the territories of the States members of that organization to acts done on their own territories. (joint)

(3) The variety shall be deemed to be distinct if it is clearly distinguishable from any other variety whose existence is a matter of common knowledge at the time of filing of the _____. (apply)

(4) The variety shall be deemed to be uniform, if subject to the variation that may be expected from the particular features of its propagation, it is _____ uniform in its relevant characteristics. (sufficient)

(5) Harvested material obtained through the unauthorized use of propagating material of the protected variety shall require the authorization of the breeder, unless the breeder has had _____ opportunity to exercise his right in relation to the said propagating material. (reason)

(6) It must not be liable to _____ or to cause confusion concerning the characteristics, value or identity of the variety or the identity of the breeder. (lead)

(7) The authority of a Contracting Party shall ensure that the authorities of all the other Contracting Parties are informed of matters concerning variety denomination, in particular the submission, registration and _____ of denomination. (cancel)

(8) The council shall consist of the representatives of the members of the Union and each member of the Union shall appoint one representative to the Council and one _____. (alter)

(9) The authority of a Contracting Party shall register the denomination so submitted, unless it considers the denomination _____ within its territory. (suit)

(10) The Union should perform the task of examining and approving the budget of the Union and fix the _____ of each member of the Union. (contribute)

七、思考题(Questions for Discussion)

Directions: Work in groups and answer the following questions.
1. What is the definition of "breeders"?
2. What is a plant breeder's right?
3. What are the exceptions to the breeder's right?
4. What are the conditions for obtaining protection?

八、拓展学习(Further Studies)

Directions: Surf the Internet and find more information about the following topics before or after class. Present to the class some successful projects to illustrate the application of these concepts to practice.
1. What are the benefits of plant variety protection?
2. What's the impact of plant variety protection in China?
3. What are genetically modified (GM) organisms and GM foods?

九、模拟联合国大会(Model United Nations Practice)

Directions: Work in teams and simulate the institutions and committees of the United Nations, featuring delegates of the UN members and the six committees of the General Assembly, negotiating issues of plant variety protection in the world and working out resolutions. Students are suggested to focus on the following topics:
1. Plant variety protection and food security;
2. Plant variety protection and environmental protection;
3. Plant variety protection and global food issue.

第八章

国际森林文书

Non-legally Binding Instrument on All Types of Forests

一、背景知识（Background）

《国际森林文书》的全称是《关于所有类型森林的无法律约束力文书》，是国际森林问题谈判所取得的成果。国际森林问题谈判启动于1992年联合国环境与发展大会，先后经历了政府间森林问题工作组（Intergovernmental Panel on Forests，IPF）、政府间森林论坛（Intergovernmental Panel on Forests，IFF）和联合国森林论坛（United Nations Forum on Forests，UNFF）15年的艰苦谈判，于2007年举行的联合国森林论坛第7次会议上形成了《国际森林文书》，并经同年12月第62届联合国大会正式审议通过。《国际森林文书》把森林可持续经营问题和全球粮食危机、气候变化放在了同等高度，具有历史性里程碑意义。

《国际森林文书》共设立了4个全球目标：一是通过可持续森林经营，包括保护、恢复、植树造林和再造林，扭转世界各地森林覆盖不断缩减的趋势，更加努力地防止森林退化；二是增强森林的经济、社会和环境效益，方法包括改善依靠以森林为生者的生计；三是大幅增加世界各地保护森林和其他可持续经营森林的面积以及可持续经营森林产品所占比例；四是扭转在森林可持续经营方面官方援助减少的趋势，从各种来源大幅增加新的和额外的金融资源，用于实行可持续森林经营。为实现上述目标，《国际森林文书》提出了通过国家行动和国际合作方式履约。其中国家行动涉及政策、法规、造林、资源管理、生物多样性保护、教育、能力建设等方面的25项条款，以及推动相关领域国际合作的18项条款。

2016年联合国对该文书进行了修订，命名为《联合国森林文书》（United Nations Forest Instrument）。2017年4月27日，第71届联合国大会审议通过了

《联合国森林战略规划(2017—2030)》,(United Nations Strategic Plan for Forests 2017-2030),首次以联合国名义对全球森林发展做出了战略规划,我国已印发给相关单位遵照执行。

(Source: http://www.gov.cn/govweb/gzdt/2009-04-16/content_1287373.htm)

二、公约原文(The Text of the Convention)

Non-legally Binding Instrument on All Types of Forests

Member States,

Recognizing that forests and trees outside forests provide multiple economic, social and environmental benefits, and emphasizing that sustainable forest management contributes significantly to sustainable development and poverty eradication,

Recalling the *Non-legally Binding Authoritative Statement of Principles for a Global Consensus on Management, Conservation and Sustainable Development of All Types of Forests (Forest Principles)*;[①] chapter 11 of *Agenda 21*;[②] the proposals for action of the Intergovernmental Panel on Forests/Intergovernmental Forum on Forests; resolutions and decisions of the United Nations Forum on Forests; the *Johannesburg Declaration on Sustainable Development and the Plan of Implementation of the World Summit on Sustainable Development*;[③] the *Monterrey Consensus of the International Conference on Financing for Development*;[④] the internationally agreed development goals, including the Millennium Development Goals; the 2005 World Summit Outcome;[⑤] and existing international legally binding instruments relevant to forests,

Welcoming the accomplishments of the international arrangement on forests since its inception by the Economic and Social Council in its resolution 2000/35 of 18 October 2000, and recalling the decision of the Council, in its resolution 2006/49 of 28 July 2006, to strengthen the international arrangement on forests,

---

① *Report of the United Nations Conference on Environment and Development*, Rio de Janeiro, 3-14 June 1992, vol. I, *Resolutions Adopted by the Conference* (United Nations publication, Sales No. E. 93. I. 8 and corrigendum), resolution 1, annex III.

② Ibid., annex II.

③ *Report of the World Summit on Sustainable Development*, Johannesburg, South Africa, 26 August-4 September 2002 (United Nations publication, Sales No. E. 03. II. A. 1 and corrigendum), chap. I, resolution I, annex, and resolution 2, annex.

④ *Report of the International Conference on Financing for Development*, Monterrey, Mexico, 18-22 March 2002 (United Nations publication, Sales No. E. 02. II. A. 7), chap. I, resolution 1, annex.

⑤ See resolution 60/1.

Reaffirming their commitment to the *Rio Declaration on Environment and Development*,① including that States have, in accordance with the Charter of the United Nations and the principles of international law, the sovereign right to exploit their own resources pursuant to their own environmental and developmental policies and the responsibility to ensure that activities within their jurisdiction or control do not cause damage to the environment of other States or of areas beyond the limits of national jurisdiction, and to the common but differentiated responsibilities of countries, as set out in Principle 7 of the Rio Declaration,

Recognizing that sustainable forest management, as a dynamic and evolving concept, is intended to maintain and enhance the economic, social and environmental value of all types of forests, for the benefit of present and future generations,

Expressing their concern about continued deforestation and forest degradation, as well as the slow rate of afforestation and forest cover recovery and reforestation, and the resulting adverse impact on economies, the environment, including biological diversity, and the livelihoods of at least a billion people and their cultural heritage, and emphasizing the need for more effective implementation of sustainable forest management at all levels to address these critical challenges,

Recognizing the impact of climate change on forests and sustainable forest management, as well as the contribution of forests to addressing climate change,

Reaffirming the special needs and requirements of countries with fragile forest ecosystems, including those of low-forest-cover countries,

Stressing the need to strengthen political commitment and collective efforts at all levels, to include forests in national and international development agendas, to enhance national policy coordination and international cooperation and to promote intersectoral coordination at all levels for the effective implementation of sustainable management of all types of forests,

Emphasizing that effective implementation of sustainable forest management is critically dependent upon adequate resources, including financing, capacity development and the transfer of environmentally sound technologies, and recognizing in particular the need to mobilize increased financial resources, including from innovative sources, for developing countries, including least developed countries, landlocked developing countries and small island developing States, as well as countries with economies in transition,

Also emphasizing that implementation of sustainable forest management is also

---

① *Report of the United Nations Conference on Environment and Development*, Rio de Janeiro, 3–14 June 1992, vol. I, Resolutions Adopted by the Conference (United Nations publication, Sales No. E. 93. I. 8 and corrigendum), resolution 1, annex I.

critically dependent upon good governance at all levels,

Noting that the provisions of this instrument do not prejudice the rights and obligations of Member States under international law,

Have committed themselves as follows.

I. Purpose

1. The purpose of this instrument is:

(a) To strengthen political commitment and action at all levels to implement effectively sustainable management of all types of forests and to achieve the shared global objectives on forests;

(b) To enhance the contribution of forests to the achievement of the internationally agreed development goals, including the Millennium Development Goals, in particular with respect to poverty eradication and environmental sustainability;

(c) To provide a framework for national action and international cooperation.

II. Principles

2. Member States should respect the following principles, which build upon the *Rio Declaration on Environment and Development* and the *Rio Forest Principles*:³

(a) The instrument is voluntary and non-legally binding;

(b) Each State is responsible for the sustainable management of its forests and for the enforcement of its forest-related laws;

(c) Major groups as identified in *Agenda 21*,① local communities, forest owners and other relevant stakeholders contribute to achieving sustainable forest management and should be involved in a transparent and participatory way in forest decision-making processes that affect them, as well as in implementing sustainable forest management, in accordance with national legislation;

(d) Achieving sustainable forest management, in particular in developing countries as well as in countries with economies in transition, depends on significantly increased, new and additional financial resources from all sources;

(e) Achieving sustainable forest management also depends on good governance at all levels;

(f) International cooperation, including financial support, technology transfer, capacity-building and education, plays a crucial catalytic role in supporting the efforts of all countries, particularly developing countries as well as countries with economies in transition, to achieve sustainable forest management.

---

① The major groups identified in *Agenda* 21 are women, children and youth, indigenous people and their communities, non-governmental organizations, local authorities, workers and trade unions, business and industry, scientific and technological communities, and farmers.

III. Scope

3. The present instrument applies to all types of forests.

4. Sustainable forest management, as a dynamic and evolving concept, aims to maintain and enhance the economic, social and environmental values of all types of forests, for the benefit of present and future generations.

IV. Global objectives on forests

5. Member States reaffirm the following shared global objectives on forests and their commitment to work globally, regionally and nationally to achieve progress towards their achievement by 2015:

Global objective 1

Reverse the loss of forest cover worldwide through sustainable forest management, including protection, restoration, afforestation and reforestation, and increase efforts to prevent forest degradation;

Global objective 2

Enhance forest-based economic, social and environmental benefits, including by improving the livelihoods of forest-dependent people;

Global objective 3

Increase significantly the area of protected forests worldwide and other areas of sustainably managed forests, as well as the proportion of forest products from sustainably managed forests;

Global objective 4

Reverse the decline in official development assistance for sustainable forest management and mobilize significantly increased, new and additional financial resources from all sources for the implementation of sustainable forest management.

V. National policies and measures

6. To achieve the purpose of the present instrument, and taking into account national policies, priorities, conditions and available resources, Member States should:

(a) Develop, implement, publish and, as necessary, update national forest programmes or other strategies for sustainable forest management which identify actions needed and contain measures, policies or specific goals, taking into account the relevant proposals for action of the Intergovernmental Panel on Forests/Intergovernmental Forum on Forests and resolutions of the United Nations Forum on Forests;

(b) Consider the seven thematic elements of sustainable forest management,[①] which are drawn from the criteria identified by existing criteria and indicators processes,

---

① The elements are (i) extent of forest resources; (ii) forest biological diversity; (iii) forest health and vitality; (iv) productive functions of forest resources; (v) protective functions of forest resources; (vi) socio-economic functions of forests; and (vii) legal, policy and institutional framework.

as a reference framework for sustainable forest management and, in this context, identify, as appropriate, specific environmental and other forest-related aspects within those elements for consideration as criteria and indicators for sustainable forest management;

(c) Promote the use of management tools to assess the impact on the environment of projects that may significantly affect forests, and promote good environmental practices for such projects;

(d) Develop and implement policies that encourage the sustainable management of forests to provide a wide range of goods and services and that also contribute to poverty reduction and the development of rural communities;

(e) Promote efficient production and processing of forest products, with a view, *inter alia*, to reducing waste and enhancing recycling;

(f) Support the protection and use of traditional forest-related knowledge and practices in sustainable forest management with the approval and involvement of the holders of such knowledge, and promote fair and equitable sharing of benefits from their utilization, in accordance with national legislation and relevant international agreements;

(g) Further develop and implement criteria and indicators for sustainable forest management that are consistent with national priorities and conditions;

(h) Create enabling environments to encourage private-sector investment, as well as investment by and involvement of local and indigenous communities, other forest users and forest owners and other relevant stakeholders, in sustainable forest management, through a framework of policies, incentives and regulations;

(i) Develop financing strategies that outline the short-, medium- and long-term financial planning for achieving sustainable forest management, taking into account domestic, private-sector and foreign funding sources;

(j) Encourage recognition of the range of values derived from goods and services provided by all types of forests and trees outside forests, as well as ways to reflect such values in the marketplace, consistent with relevant national legislation and policies;

(k) Identify and implement measures to enhance cooperation and cross-sectoral policy and programme coordination among sectors affecting and affected by forest policies and management, with a view to integrating the forest sector into national decision-making processes and promoting sustainable forest management, including by addressing the underlying causes of deforestation and forest degradation, and by promoting forest conservation;

(l) Integrate national forest programmes, or other strategies for sustainable forest management, as referred to in paragraph 6 (a) above, into national strategies for sustainable development, relevant national action plans and poverty-reduction strategies;

(m) Establish or strengthen partnerships, including public-private partnerships, and joint programmes with stakeholders to advance the implementation of sustainable forest management;

(n) Review and, as needed, improve forest-related legislation, strengthen forest law enforcement and promote good governance at all levels in order to support sustainable forest management, to create an enabling environment for forest investment and to combat and eradicate illegal practices, in accordance with national legislation, in the forest and other related sectors;

(o) Analyse the causes of, and address solutions to, threats to forest health and vitality from natural disasters and human activities, including threats from fire, pollution, pests, disease and invasive alien species;

(p) Create, develop or expand, and maintain networks of protected forest areas, taking into account the importance of conserving representative forests, by means of a range of conservation mechanisms, applied within and outside protected forest areas;

(q) Assess the conditions and management effectiveness of existing protected forest areas with a view to identifying improvements needed;

(r) Strengthen the contribution of science and research in advancing sustainable forest management by incorporating scientific expertise into forest policies and programmes;

(s) Promote the development and application of scientific and technological innovations, including those that can be used by forest owners and local and indigenous communities to advance sustainable forest management;

(t) Promote and strengthen public understanding of the importance of and the benefits provided by forests and sustainable forest management, including through public awareness programmes and education;

(u) Promote and encourage access to formal and informal education, extension and training programmes on the implementation of sustainable forest management;

(v) Support education, training and extension programmes involving local and indigenous communities, forest workers and forest owners, in order to develop resource management approaches that will reduce the pressure on forests, particularly fragile ecosystems;

(w) Promote active and effective participation by major groups, local communities, forest owners and other relevant stakeholders in the development, implementation and assessment of forest-related national policies, measures and programmes;

(x) Encourage the private sector, civil society organizations and forest owners to develop, promote and implement in a transparent manner voluntary instruments, such as voluntary certification systems or other appropriate mechanisms, to develop and promote forest products from sustainably managed forests harvested in accordance with domestic legislation, and to improve market transparency;

(y) Enhance access by households, small-scale forest owners, forest-dependent local and indigenous communities, living in and outside forest areas, to forest resources and relevant markets in order to support livelihoods and income diversification from forest management, consistent with sustainable forest management.

VI. International cooperation and means of implementation

7. To achieve the purpose of the present instrument, Member States should:

(a) Make concerted efforts to secure a sustained high-level political commitment to strengthen the means of implementation of sustainable forest management, including financial resources, to provide support, in particular for developing countries and countries with economies in transition, as well as to mobilize and provide significantly increased, new and additional financial resources from private, public, domestic and international sources to and within developing countries, as well as countries with economies in transition;

(b) Reverse the decline in official development assistance for sustainable forest management and mobilize significantly increased, new and additional financial resources from all sources for the implementation of sustainable forest management;

(c) Take action to raise the priority of sustainable forest management in national development plans and other plans, including poverty-reduction strategies, in order to facilitate increased allocation of official development assistance and financial resources from other sources for sustainable forest management;

(d) Develop and establish positive incentives, in particular for developing countries as well as countries with economies in transition, to reduce the loss of forests, to promote reforestation, afforestation and rehabilitation of degraded forests, to implement sustainable forest management and to increase the area of protected forests;

(e) Support the efforts of countries, particularly developing countries as well as countries with economies in transition, to develop and implement economically, socially and environmentally sound measures that act as incentives for the sustainable management of forests;

(f) Strengthen the capacity of countries, in particular developing countries, to significantly increase the production of forest products from sustainably managed forests;

(g) Enhance bilateral, regional and international cooperation with a view to promoting international trade in forest products from sustainably managed forests harvested according to domestic legislation;

(h) Enhance bilateral, regional and international cooperation to address illicit international trafficking in forest products through the promotion of forest law enforcement and good governance at all levels;

(i) Strengthen, through enhanced bilateral, regional and international cooperation, the capacity of countries to combat effectively illicit international trafficking in forest products, including timber, wildlife and other forest biological resources;

(j) Strengthen the capacity of countries to address forest-related illegal practices, including wildlife poaching, in accordance with domestic legislation, through enhanced public awareness, education, institutional capacity-building, technological transfer and technical cooperation, law enforcement and information networks;

(k) Enhance and facilitate access to and transfer of appropriate, environmentally sound and innovative technologies and corresponding know-how relevant to sustainable forest management and to efficient value-added processing of forest products, in particular to developing countries, for the benefit of local and indigenous communities;

(l) Strengthen mechanisms that enhance sharing among countries and the use of best practices in sustainable forest management, including through freeware-based information and communications technology;

(m) Strengthen national and local capacity in keeping with their conditions for the development and adaptation of forest-related technologies, including technologies for the use of fuelwood;

(n) Promote international technical and scientific cooperation, including South-South cooperation and triangular cooperation, in the field of sustainable forest management, through the appropriate international, regional and national institutions and processes;

(o) Enhance the research and scientific forest-related capacities of developing countries and countries with economies in transition, particularly the capacity of research organizations to generate and have access to forest-related data and information, and promote and support integrated and interdisciplinary research on forest-related issues, and disseminate research results;

(p) Strengthen forestry research and development in all regions, particularly in developing countries and countries with economies in transition, through relevant organizations, institutions and centres of excellence, as well as through global, regional and subregional networks;

(q) Strengthen cooperation and partnerships at the regional and subregional levels to promote sustainable forest management;

(r) As members of the governing bodies of the organizations that form the Collaborative Partnership on Forests, help ensure that the forest-related priorities and programmes of members of the Partnership are integrated and mutually supportive, consistent with their mandates, taking into account relevant policy recommendations of the United Nations Forum on Forests;

(s) Support the efforts of the Collaborative Partnership on Forests to develop and implement joint initiatives.

VII. Monitoring, assessment and reporting

8. Member States should monitor and assess progress towards achieving the purpose of the present instrument.

9. Member States should submit, on a voluntary basis, taking into account the

availability of resources and the requirements and conditions for the preparation of reports for other bodies or instruments, national progress reports as part of their regular reporting to the Forum.

VIII. Working modalities

10. The Forum should address, within the context of its multi-year programme of work, the implementation of the present instrument.

三、注解(Notes)

1. The *Non-legally Binding Authoritative Statement of Principles for a Global Consensus on Management, Conservation and Sustainable Development of All Types of Forests* (Forest Principles)

《关于所有类型森林的管理、保存和可持续开发的无法律约束力的全球协商一致意见权威性原则声明》，简称《有关森林问题的原则声明》，由联合国环境与发展大会于1992年6月14日在里约热内卢通过。1992年6月3日至14日，在巴西里约热内卢召开了联合国环境与发展会议。《有关森林问题的原则声明》是本届环境与发展大会通过的一个重要文件。

2. *Agenda 21*

《21世纪议程》，这是1992年6月3日至14日在巴西里约热内卢召开的联合国环境与发展大会通过的重要文件之一。这是一项"世界范围内可持续发展行动计划"，关于政府、政府间组织和非政府组织所应采取行动的广泛计划，是旨在鼓励在发展的同时保护环境的全球可持续发展计划的行动蓝图。

3. The *Johannesburg Declaration on Sustainable Development and the Plan of Implementation of the World Summit on Sustainable Development*

《约翰内斯堡可持续发展承诺》和《执行计划》，是2002年9月在南非首都约翰内斯堡举行的可持续发展世界首脑会议上通过的两个文件。这次会议是1992年里约地球峰会的后续，会议召开之时，正值世界范围内贫富分化更趋严重，人类在健康、生物多样性、农业生产、水和能源五大领域面临严峻挑战，全球可持续发展状况有恶化的趋势。因而，在作为会议政治宣言的《约翰内斯堡可持续发展承诺》中，各国承诺将不遗余力地执行可持续发展战略，把世界建成一个以人为本、人类与自然协调发展的美好社会。《执行计划》则指出，当今世界面临的最严峻的全球性挑战是贫困，消除贫困是全球可持续发展必不可少的条件。把消除贫困纳入可持续发展理念之中、并作为这次峰会的主旋律之一，标志着人类可持续发展理念提高到了一个新的层次。

4. The *Monterrey Consensus of the International Conference on Financing for Development*

《发展筹资问题国际会议蒙特雷共识》，简称《蒙特雷共识》。2002年3月，为期5天的联合国发展筹资国际会议于3月22日在墨西哥北部工业城市蒙特雷落下帷幕。各国家元首或政府首脑就国际发展筹资达成共识,即《蒙特雷共识》。《蒙特雷共识》主要包括调动国内经济资源、增加私人国际投资、开放市场和确保公平的贸易体制、增加官方发展援助、解决发展中国家的债务困难和改善全球和区域金融结构、发展中国家在国际决策中的公正代表性六方面内容。《蒙特雷共识》指出:发达国家和发展中国家应该建立一种新的伙伴关系,全面落实《联合国千年宣言》中提出的旨在实现消除贫困、改善社会状况、提高生活水平和保护环境等各项可持续发展目标。

四、相关词汇(Key Words and Phrases)

1. binding [ˈbaɪndɪŋ] n. 装订;捆绑;粘合物
   adj. 有约束力的;捆绑的
2. inception [ɪnˈsepʃ(ə)n] n. 开始;开端
3. resolution [rezəˈluːʃ(ə)n] n. 决议;解决;决心
4. exploit [ˈeksplɔɪt; ɪkˈsplɔɪt] vt. 开发,开拓;剥削;开采
5. dynamic [daɪˈnæmɪk] adj. 动态的;动力的;有活力的
6. livelihood [ˈlaɪvlɪhʊd] n. 生计
7. fragile [ˈfrædʒaɪl] adj. 易碎的;易损的;不牢固的;脆弱的
8. landlocked [ˈlændlɒkt] adj. (尤指国家)无海岸线或海港的;陆围的;内陆的
9. mobilize [ˈməʊbəlaɪz] vt. & vi. 动员,调动;集合,组织;使……流通;使……松动
10. catalytic [ˌkætəˈlɪtɪk] adj. 接触反应的;起催化作用的;
    n. 催化剂;刺激因素
11. reverse [rɪˈvɜːs] vt. & vi. 颠倒;撤销;反转;交换;倒车;
    adj. 相反的;背面的;颠倒的
12. utilization [ˌjuːtɪlaɪˈzeɪʃən] n. 利用,使用
13. incentive [ɪnˈsentɪv] n. 激励;奖励;诱因;奖励措施
14. expertise [ˌekspɜːˈtiːz] n. 专门知识;专门技术;专家的意见
15. allocation [æləˈkeɪʃ(ə)n] n. 分配,配置;安置
16. illicit [ɪˈlɪsɪt] adj. 违法的;不正当的
17. trafficking [ˈtræfɪkɪŋ] n. 非法交易(尤指毒品买卖)

五、长难句(Difficult Sentences)

1. Reaffirming their commitment to the *Rio Declaration on Environment and Development*, including that States have, in accordance with the *Charter of the United Nations* and the principles of international law, the sovereign right to exploit their own

resources pursuant to their own environmental and developmental policies and the responsibility to ensure that activities within their jurisdiction or control do not cause damage to the environment of other States or of areas beyond the limits of national jurisdiction, and to the common but differentiated responsibilities of countries, as set out in *Principle of the Rio Declaration*. (Preamble, Para. 4)

解析：commitment 后有两个介词 to，一个是 to the *Rio Declaration on Environment and Development*；另一个是 to the common but differentiated responsibilities of countries。including that 引导的宾语从句主谓语是 States have，宾语是 the sovereign right to exploit…and the responsibility to ensure that…

译文：重申其对《关于环境与发展的里约宣言》的承诺，包括根据《联合国宪章》和国际法原则，各国拥有按照本国环境与发展政策开发本国资源的主权权利，并有责任确保在本国管辖或控制下的活动不致损害其他国家或本国管辖范围以外地区的环境，以及对《关于环境与发展的里约宣言》原则所述各国共同承担但又有差别的责任的承诺。

2. Develop, implement, publish and, as necessary, update national forest programmes or other strategies for sustainable forest management which identify actions needed and contain measures, policies or specific goals, taking into account the relevant proposals for action of the Intergovernmental Panel on Forests/Intergovernmental Forum on Forests and resolutions of the United Nations Forum on Forests. (Article 6, a)

解析：句中 which identify actions needed and contain measures, policies or specific goals 是定语从句。taking into account the relevant proposals for action of…分词短语做状语。

译文：制定、执行、公布并视需要更新国家森林方案或其他可持续森林管理战略，其中查明所需行动并列出各项措施、政策或具体目标，同时考虑到政府间森林小组/政府间森林论坛相关的行动建议以及联合国森林论坛的决议。

3. Identify and implement measures to enhance cooperation and cross-sectoral policy and programme coordination among sectors affecting and affected by forest policies and management, with a view to integrating the forest sector into national decision-making processes and promoting sustainable forest management, including by addressing the underlying causes of deforestation and forest degradation, and by promoting forest conservation. (Article 6, k)

解析：with a view to 是目的状语。including 后接两个 by 表示手段。

译文：为了将森林部门纳入国家决策过程、促进可持续性森林管理，解决造成森林砍伐和森林退化的根本原因，从而促进森林保护，应该确定和执行各种措施，以加强影响森林政策制定和管理模式以及受其影响的部门之间的合作，加强各部门之间的政策和计划协调。

4. Make concerted efforts to secure a sustained high-level political commitment to strengthen the means of implementation of sustainable forest management, including

financial resources, to provide support, in particular for developing countries and countries with economies in transition, as well as to mobilize and provide significantly increased, new and additional financial resources from private, public, domestic and international sources to and within developing countries, as well as countries with economies in transition. (Article 7, a)

解析：句中 efforts 后接三个 to 做后置定语：to secure a sustained high-level political commitment, to provide support…和 as well as to mobilize and provide。

译文：齐心合力确保做出持久的高级别政治承诺，加强实施包括财政资源在内的可持续森林管理手段，尤其是为发展中国家和经济转型国家提供支持；动员私人，公共，国内和国际资源为发展中国家和经济转型国家提供大量新增和额外的财政资助。

六、课后练习(Exercises)

1. Skimming and scanning

Directions: Read the following passage excerpted from the Non-legally Binding Instrument on All Types of Forests. At the end of the passage, there are six statements. Each statement contains information given in one of the paragraphs of the passage. Identify the paragraph from which the information is derived. Each paragraph is marked with a letter. You may choose a paragraph more than once. Answer the questions by writing the corresponding letter in the bracket in front of each statement.

To achieve the purpose of the present instrument, and taking into account national policies, priorities, conditions and available resources, Member States should:

A. Develop, implement, publish and, as necessary, update national forest programmes or other strategies for sustainable forest management which identify actions needed and contain measures, policies or specific goals, taking into account the relevant proposals for action of the Intergovernmental Panel on Forests/Intergovernmental Forum on Forests and resolutions of the United Nations Forum on Forests;

B. Consider the seven thematic elements of sustainable forest management, which are drawn from the criteria identified by existing criteria and indicators processes, as a reference framework for sustainable forest management and, in this context, identify, as appropriate, specific environmental and other forest-related aspects within those elements for consideration as criteria and indicators for sustainable forest management;

C. Support the protection and use of traditional forest-related knowledge and practices in sustainable forest management with the approval and involvement of the holders of such knowledge, and promote fair and equitable sharing of benefits from their utilization, in accordance with national legislation and relevant international agreements;

D. Identify and implement measures to enhance cooperation and cross-sectoral policy and programme coordination among sectors affecting and affected by forest policies and management, with a view to integrating the forest sector into national decision-making processes and promoting sustainable forest management, including by addressing the underlying causes of deforestation and forest degradation, and by promoting forest conservation;

E. Review and, as needed, improve forest-related legislation, strengthen forest law enforcement and promote good governance at all levels in order to support sustainable forest management, to create an enabling environment for forest investment and to combat and eradicate illegal practices, in accordance with national legislation, in the forest and other related sectors;

F. Create, develop or expand, and maintain networks of protected forest areas, taking into account the importance of conserving representative forests, by means of a range of conservation mechanisms, applied within and outside protected forest areas;

G. Support education, training and extension programmes involving local and indigenous communities, forest workers and forest owners, in order to develop resource management approaches that will reduce the pressure on forests, particularly fragile ecosystems;

H. Encourage the private sector, civil society organizations and forest owners to develop, promote and implement in a transparent manner voluntary instruments, such as voluntary certification systems or other appropriate mechanisms, to develop and promote forest products from sustainably managed forests harvested in accordance with domestic legislation, and to improve market transparency;

I. Enhance access by households, small-scale forest owners, forest-dependent local and indigenous communities, living in and outside forest areas, to forest resources and relevant markets in order to support livelihoods and income diversification from forest management, consistent with sustainable forest management.

(_____) (1) Traditional forest-related knowledge and practices in sustainable forest management will be protected and used with the approval and involvement of the holders of such knowledge.

(_____) (2) An enabling environment shall be created for forest investment to combat and eradicate illegal practices in the forest and other related sectors.

(_____) (3) National forest programmes shall be developed, implemented, published and necessarily updated to achieve the purpose of the present instrument.

(_____) (4) To develop and promote forest products, voluntary certification systems or other appropriate mechanisms shall be developed, promoted and implemented in a transparent manner.

(_____) (5) The forest sector shall be integrated into national decision-making processes to promote sustainable forest management by addressing the underlying causes of deforestation and forest degradation.

(_____) (6) From the criteria identified by existing criteria and indicators processes, seven thematic elements of sustainable forest management are drawn as a reference framework for sustainable forest management.

2. Reading Comprehension

Directions: Read the Non-legally Binding Instrument on All Types of Forests, and decide whether the following statements are True or False. Write T for True or F for False in the bracket in front of each statement.

(1)(_____) The Member States have the sovereign right to exploit their own resources pursuant to their own environmental and developmental policies with the responsibility to ensure that activities within their jurisdiction or control do not cause damage to the environment of other States.

(2)(_____) Thanks to the international concern over deforestation and forest degradation, the world is witnessing a higher rate of afforestation, forest cover recovery and reforestation.

(3)(_____) It needs to mobilize increased financial resources for developed countries to enable effective implementation of sustainable forest management.

(4)(_____) The Non-legally Binding Instrument on All Types of Forests is voluntary and non-legally binding.

(5)(_____) Traditional forest-related knowledge and practices should be replaced by modern approaches to sustainable forest management.

(6)(_____) Bilateral, regional and international cooperation must be enhanced to address illicit international trafficking in forest products through the promotion of forest law enforcement and good governance at all levels.

3. Extensive Reading

Directions: In this section, there is a passage with ten blanks. You are required to select one word for each blank from a list of choices given in a word bank following the passage. Read the passage through carefully before making your choices. Each choice in the bank is identified by a letter. You may not use any of the words in the bank more than once.

In May 2007, the United Nations Forum on Forests (UNFF) adopted a non-legally binding instrument on all types of forests (NLBI), also commonly known as the "Forest Instrument". This significant international consensus was reached to (1) _____ sustainable forest management (SFM), and thus to maintain and enhance the economic, social and environmental values of all types of forests, for the (2) _____ of present and future generations.

Implementation of the Forest Instrument will help reduce deforestation and forest degradation, which are major (3) _____ of greenhouse gas emissions. It will therefore (4) _____ to mitigating the effects of climate change and to implementing the United Nations Framework Convention on Climate Change. Countries' efforts to combat deforestation and forest degradation, and to achieve sustainable forest management require a strong policy and (5) _____ capacity. The Forest Instrument provides a framework for this.

In 2008 Ghana became the first country to (6) _____ implement the Forest Instrument, with technical support from the United Nations Food and Agriculture Organization (FAO) and the German Agency for Technical Cooperation (GTZ) and funding from the German Federal Ministry for Economic Cooperation and Development (BMZ).

The 24 policies and measures agreed in the Forest Instrument that are to be implemented at national level represent a wide range of actions the forest sector of a given country should undertake to achieve sustainable forest management. Most countries are already implementing at least some of these policies and measures at various levels and with (7) _____ degrees of success. However, most forestry stakeholders are unaware of the existence of the Forest Instrument and of the (8) _____ contributions of their ongoing activities to its implementation.

In view of this, it was considered important to raise the (9) _____ of stakeholders in Ghana about the Forest Instrument and its significance for their country and to carry out an assessment of the current situation of Ghana vis-à-vis（关于）its implementation. Using the national and regional multi-stakeholder fora（forum 的复数）(10) _____ through Ghana's national forest programme as a basis, three regional workshops and one national workshop were conducted with the participation of a wide range of stakeholders. (349 words)

A. awareness	B. benefit	C. boost	D. contribute	E. decrease
F. established	G. institutional	H. objective	I. partially	J. potential
K. sources	L. systematically	M. technical	N. varying	O. yearning

4. Vocabulary Expanding

Directions: In this section, there are ten sentences from the Non-legally Binding Instrument on All Types of Forests. You are required to complete these sentences with the proper form of the words given in the brackets.

(1) Major groups should be involved in a transparent and _____ way in forest decision-making processes that affect them. (participate)

(2) To achieve the purpose of the present instrument, Member States should consider the seven thematic elements of sustainable forest management, which are drawn from the criteria identified by existing criteria and indicators processes. (theme)

(3) Member states should further develop and implement criteria and _____ for sustainable forest management that are consistent with national priorities and conditions. (indicate)

(4) Member states should encourage _____ of the range of values derived from goods and services provided by all types of forests and trees outside forests. (recognize)

(5) Review and, as needed, improve forest-related legislation, strengthen forest law enforcement and promote good _____ at all levels in order to support sustainable forest management. (govern)

(6) Enhance access by households, small-scale forest owners, forest-dependent local and indigenous communities, living in and outside forest areas, to forest resources and relevant markets in order to support livelihoods and income _____ from forest management. (diverse)

(7) Reverse the decline in official development assistance for sustainable forest management and _____ significantly increased, new and additional financial resources from all sources for the implementation of sustainable forest management. (mobile)

(8) Strengthen the capacity of countries to combat effectively illicit international trafficking in forest products, including timber, wildlife and other forest biological resources. (biology)

(9) Promote international technical and scientific cooperation, including South-South cooperation and _____ cooperation, in the field of sustainable forest management. (triangle)

(10) As members of the governing bodies of the organizations that form the Collaborative Partnership on Forests, help ensure that the forest-related priorities and programmes of members of the Partnership are integrated and _____ supportive. (mutual)

七、思考题(Questions for Discussion)

Directions: Work in groups and answer the following questions.

1. What is the purpose of the *Non-legally Binding Instrument on All Types of Forests*?
2. What are the global objectives of the *Non-legally Binding Instrument on All Types of Forests*?
3. What are more concerned in the *Non-legally Binding Instrument on All Types of Forests*?

八、拓展学习(Further Studies)

Directions: Surf the Internet and find more information about the following topics before or after class. Present to the class some successful projects to illustrate the application of these concepts to practice.

1. The background and significance of the *Non-legally Binding Instrument on All*

Types of Forests.

2. China's efforts in implementing the *Non-legally Binding Instrument on All Types of Forests*.

九、模拟联合国大会(Model United Nations Practice)

Directions: Work in teams and simulate the institutions and committees of the United Nations, featuring delegates of the UN members and the six committees of the General Assembly, negotiating issues of forest in the world and working out resolutions. Students are suggested to focus on the following topics:

1. What is the present situation of forest worldwide?

2. How should a country manage and protect its forest resources?

3. What cooperation can be achieved between nations to deal with deforestation issues?